By Liz Smith

DISHING
NATURAL BLONDE
THE MOTHER BOOK

for Jim

DISHING

Great Dish—and Dishes—from America's
Most Beloved Gossip Columnist

LIZ SMITH

Love

Simon & Schuster

New York London Toronto Sydney

Liz Smith

SIMON & SCHUSTER
Rockefeller Center
1230 Avenue of the Americas
New York, NY 10020

SIMON & SCHUSTER and colophon are registered trademarks
of Simon & Schuster, Inc.

For information about special discounts for bulk purchases,
please contact Simon & Schuster Special Sales at
1-800-456-6798 or business@simonandschuster.com

Designed by C. Linda Dingler

Photography consultant: Kevin Kwan

Manufactured in the United States of America

1   3   5   7   9   10   8   6   4   2

Library of Congress Cataloging-in-Publication Data

Smith, Liz, 1923–
Dishing : great dish—and dishes—from America's most beloved gossip columnist /
Liz Smith.
p.   cm.
1. Gastronomy.   I. Title.

TX631.S63   2005
641'.01'3—dc22   2004066279

ISBN 0-7432-5156-3

Dedicated to those alive and dead who have fed, taught, and inspired me with food and its adventures.

M. F. K. Fisher, Elizabeth David, Craig Claiborne, James Beard, Julia Child, Ruth Reichl

and to
Lee Bailey, Nora Ephron, Gael Greene,
Diane Judge, Rachel Clark, Julia Reed, Jason Epstein,
Sean Driscoll, Billy Norwich

and, of course, to
Henri Soulé and Sirio Maccioni

The publisher gratefully acknowledges the following:

HarperCollins Publishers Inc., for permission to reprint "The Eggplant Epithalamion" from *Becoming Light: Poems New and Selected* by Erica Jong, copyright © 1961, 1962, 1971, 1973, 1975, 1977, 1979, 1981, 1983, 1987, 1991 by Erica Mann Jong. Reprinted by permission of Harper-Collins Publishers Inc.

Hyperion, for permission to reprint the chapter "Unbind My Asparagus" from *Natural Blonde* by Liz Smith, © 2000 Liz Smith.

Grove/Atlantic, Inc., for permission to reprint the bouillabaisse recipe from *Frankie's Place* by Jim Sterba, copyright © 2003 by Jim Sterba. Used by permission of Grove/Atlantic, Inc.

Little, Brown and Company, for permission to reprint Jessie Duncan's Steak Three Inches Thick from *James Beard's American Cookery* by James Beard, copyright © 1972 by James A. Beard (text); copyright © 1972 by Little, Brown and Company (illustrations). By permission of Little, Brown and Company.

Harry Abrams Inc., Stewart Tabori & Chang division, for permission to reprint the recipe for Tuscan Fried Potatoes from *Maccioni Family Cookbook* by Egi Maccioni, copyright © 2003 by Egdiana Maccioni and Peter Kaminsky.

Chronicle Books, for permission to reprint Rick Rodgers's frying technique from *Fried & True: Crispy and Delicious Dishes from Appetizers to Desserts* by Rick Rodgers; photographs by Christopher Hirscheimer. Text copyright © 1999 by Rick Rodgers; photographs copyright © 1999 by Christopher Hirscheimer.

Artisan, for permission to reprint the recipe for Watermelon Granita from *Granita Magic*, copyright © 2003 by Nadia Roden. Used by permission of Artisan, a division of Workman Publishing Co., Inc., New York. All Rights Reserved.

Beautiful America Publishing Company, for permission to reprint the recipe for Deep-fried Turkey from *Entertaining with Betsy Bloomingdale*, copyright © 1994 by Beautiful America Publishing Company.

André Deutsch Limited, Carlton Publishing Group, for permission to reprint the poem entitled "The Strange Case of Mr. Palliser's Palate" from *Candy Is Dandy: The Best of Ogden Nash* by Ogden Nash with an Introduction by Anthony Burgess, first published by André Deutsch in Great Britain in 1994.

Random House, Inc., for permission to reprint the recipe for Lee's Heat-Resistant Biscuits from *Lee Bailey's Country Weekends* by Lee Bailey. Copyright © 1983 by Lee Bailey and Joshua Green. Used by permission of Clarkson Potter/Publishers, a division of Random House, Inc.

Nora Ephron, for permission to reprint her recipe for Lee's Baked Lima Beans and Pears, which appeared in her novel *Heartburn*.

Random House, Inc., for permission to reprint the recipes for Chicken-Fried Steak, a.k.a. Elvis's Ugly Steak and for Elvis Fried Potato Sandwich from *The Life and Cuisine of Elvis Presley* by David Adler. Copyright © 1993 by David Adler. Used by Permission of Crown Publishers, a division of Random House, Inc.

Random House, Inc., for permission to reprint the recipes for Lobster Rolls and for Savory Watermelon Salad from *The Lobster Roll* by Jodi Della Femina and Andrea Terry. Copyright © 2003 by Jodi della Femina and Andrea Terry. Photographs copyright © 2003 by Ben Fink. Used by permission of Clarkson Potter/Publishers, a division of Random House, Inc.

Texas Monthly, for permission to reprint the recipe for Chicken-fried Steak. Reprinted with permission from *Texas Monthly*.

CONTENTS

CONTENTS

INTRODUCTION

You do know the definition of eternity—two people and a ham. I suppose Ogden Nash could have made a poem out of that idea, but—never mind—one of his best ones about food is the following. Read this out loud and practice your French.

THE

STRANGE CASE

OF MR. PALLISER'S PALATE

by Ogden Nash

Once there was a man named Mr. Palliser and he asked his wife, May I be a
gourmet?
>And she said, You sure may,
>But she also said, If my kitchen is going to produce a Cordon Blue,
>It won't be me, it will be you.
>And he said, You mean Cordon Bleu?
>And she said to never mind the pronunciation so long as it was him
and not heu.
>But he wasn't discouraged; he bought a white hat and The Cordon
Bleu Cook Book and said, How about some Huîtres en Robe de Chambre?
>And she sniffed and said, Are you reading a cookbook or Forever
Ambre?
>And he said, Well, if you prefer something more Anglo-Saxon,
>Why suppose I whip up some tasty Filets de Sole Jackson,
>And she pretended not to hear, so he raised his voice and said, Could

I please you with Paupiettes de Veau à la Grecque *or* Cornets de Jambon Lucullus *or perhaps some nice* Moules à la Bordelaise?

And she said, Kindly lower your voice or the neighbors will think we are drunk and disordelaise, *And she said, Furthermore the whole idea of your cooking anything fit to eat is a farce. So what did Mr. Palliser do then?*

Well, he offered her Oeufs Farcis Maison *and* Homard Farci Saint-Jacques *and* Tomate Farcie à la Bayonne *and* Aubergines Farcies Provençales, *as well as* Aubergines Farcies Italiennes,

And she said, Edward, kindly accompany me as usual to Hamburger Heaven and stop playing the fool,

And he looked in the book for one last suggestion and it suggested Croques Madame, *so he did, and now he dines every evening on* Crème de Comcombres Glacée, Côtelettes de Volaille Vicomtesse *and* Artichauds à la Barigoule.

CHAPTER 1

FOOD,

GLORIOUS

FOOD!

(As They Sang in the Musical Oliver!)

"Nearly everyone wants at least one outstanding meal a day,"

—Duncan Hines

On the other hand, I am taken with former restaurateur Dan Ho's sardonic, "I've always found it funny that we've all decided cooking and feeding are high art. Art lasts; you know what food becomes!" *

Why do we want to glorify food? Food makes us fat, and in these times, being fat is not a good thing. We aren't out there anymore as field hands, warriors on horseback, or hunters and gatherers just trying to keep

---

* Dan Ho has written one of the best books about lifestyle in existence. Titled *Rescue from House Gorgeous*, it is a manual for escaping from the pressing needs for "house, food & garden perfection."

body and soul together with enough nourishment to sustain ourselves day-to-day. We are actively working to avoid food, with its attendant evils—fat, high cholesterol, high blood pressure, heart problems, obesity weighing down our bones and muscles, and so on. As someone has pointed out, instead of being hunters and gatherers, these days we are shoppers and consumers.

But Thackeray said, "Next to eating good dinners, a healthy man with a benevolent turn of mind must like, I think, to read about them." Ah, reading about food. Now, that's another matter. Setting tables in our minds can be quite a lot of fun. And Clifton Fadiman noted that we are all food writers in our way, "every man . . . having in him an autobiographical novel. . . . This would consist of an account of ourselves as eaters, recording the development of our palates, telling over like the beads of a rosary the memories of the best meals of our lives." He added that writing about food belongs to "the literature of power, linking brain to stomach, etherealizing the euphoria of feeding with the finer essence of reflection."

Ford Madox Ford said that Anglo-Saxons don't really talk about food any more than they talk about love and heaven. But he certainly found food a fit subject as he deplored other forms of popular passion: "The tantrums of cloth-headed celluloid idols are deemed fit for grown-up conversation, while silence settles over such a truly important matter as food."

Well, I personally have had a lifetime of talking, writing, and lecturing about "cloth-headed celluloid idols" over fifty years in the gossip and show biz vineyard. So it has been a relief to abandon celebrity culture, infotainment, sex-drugs-rock 'n' roll and think about food. My philosophy is that you *can* serve people fattening food. In their hearts they'll love you for it and maybe even forgive you for it. The answer to the problem lies in not doing it too often nor to excess, and the answer also lies in the self-discipline of eaters when it comes to proportion. The great and attractive cooking of France and Italy seems rich and fattening to the diet-conscious, but it's funny, no one I know ever gains weight on vacations in those countries. You'd have to be a real pig. If one never serves anything forbidden or delicious, then it seems to me you are forcing a kind of unilateral "it's good for you" regime on your guests. We need to do unusual, wonderful things for special occasions. People must diet on their own terms and at their own times. The great New York hostesses I know always offer fabulous menus and assume their guests have common sense.

Dieting is probably the most unpleasant word in our current lexicon. It can make us awfully unhappy even as we embrace its necessity. It is noted that before he was executed in 1984, one Ronald O'Bryan ordered his last meal—a T-bone steak, french fries, salad, and iced tea. With the tea he took an artificial sweetener, not sugar. A reporter observed, "He was going for the healthy option."

Even cookbook authors get the overkill blues. Reporter Chris Howes points to disgust as "the strongest emotion seeping out of the late Elizabeth David's Christmas book. She loathed December 25 and said, " 'My Christmas day eating and drinking would consist of an omelette and cold ham and a nice bottle of wine at lunchtime and a smoked salmon sandwich with a glass of champagne on a tray in bed in the evening.' "

As the old saw goes, "Everything I like is either illegal, immoral, or fattening," and some people do associate eating as a surrogate for illicit sex—wickedly tempting, licentious, or guilt inducing. So reading about food is the next best thing to eating it. People want to eat and not gain weight just as they like to have sex without getting pregnant, but the only comparable contraceptive would be to read a book rather than eat everything or even anything described in it. Mr. Howes adds, "For consumers of food porn, cookery books are not manuals but fantasy reading—if it can be called reading."

People seek companionship, comfort, reassurance, a sense of warmth and well-being from food. Maybe they can get some of that from this book.

CHAPTER 2

YOU CAN PUT YOUR BOOTS IN THE OVEN BUT THAT DON'T MAKE 'EM BISCUITS!

—OLD TEXAS SAYING

"EATING! WHAT A CONCEPT!" exclaims my actress-friend Holland Taylor as we prepare to order in a restaurant. This Emmy winner is not a cook and neither am I. But we always approach food as an adventure. What I love about Holland's inevitable jokey remark is the philosophical wisdom in her observation of the human condition.

We living things are all food-processing machines, manufacturing energy and sometimes pleasure in sheer necessity. But more than necessity is the socializing motive behind eating together, sitting down *à deux*, coming together for meals, entertaining ourselves at lunch and dinner, or "taking" a breakfast meeting, solidifying our families, our friendships, our business connections, and our social values by our need to keep company and put delicious things in our mouths at the same time.

In fact, although I now and then look forward to being alone and "left alone"* to eat a bowl of Campbell's tomato soup or gorge on a bag of

* It was Greta Garbo's supposed remark "I vant to be alone" that symbolized the screen idol's retiring narcissism. But what she actually said was, "I vant to be left alone!" Big difference.

Lay's potato chips and a delicious apple, I find I feel rather self-conscious when eating alone. The food takes on too much importance. I like diminishing what's on the table by whose fanny is on the chair nearby. Or, as W. S. Gilbert wrote, "It isn't so much what's on the table that matters, as what's on the chairs."

All the mechanisms of sharing, enjoying, gossiping, relaxing, and accomplishing something blend into a sensual meld when we eat with others. Some of this is unconscious. Some is ritual, like the rearranging of silverware, which I know is considered rude but is a mania of mine. Some is gustatory anticipation or the quelling of immediate hunger. But conversation should pile on top of food. It can be quick, fast, and greedy or drawn out, cadenced with courses, and fulfilled by intent. (Such as, "I'll wait for dessert and coffee to spill the beans, to make my declaration, to ask for a divorce, to throw down the gauntlet!")

Back in the ravishingly extravagant eighties and nineties it was being said that restaurants were the new theater in New York. Some of that feeling still remains. Restaurants in the twenty-first century can be grand indeed, reservations difficult to come by with astronomical checks at dinner's end. But these places usually are faddish and may not last. It is the very act of eating—high or low—that offers one of life's few and true instant gratifications and serves a generally healthy (or perhaps unhealthy) purpose, keeping us intimate and together. We can always hope to leave the debris of the uncleared table with a sense of satisfaction, pleasure, accomplishment, and, yes, ducking any responsibility for the mess. Of course, often we do have the cleanup detail, but oh the joy of having help or eating out where we can stroll off in satiated satisfaction, picking our teeth. As Nora Ephron says, "What my mother believed about cooking is that if you worked hard and prospered, someone else would do it for you."

I HAVE HAD SOME GREAT COOKS "do it for me" and I own many photographs from a long life spent in the public eye, interviewing celebrities over necessary meals or relaxing intervals of drinks and dining. Some of these show great dinners, exotic trappings, famous chefs, dressy occasions. But my favorite is a black-and-white snapshot from the fifties of my family's dining-room table in Gonzales, Texas, population 5,000. My mother is at the head of the table and my two brothers are on the side. I must have taken the picture. Obviously, the time was summer. An electric fan is caught in flight, whirring on the table. A loaf of what is called "light bread" down South is in its waxed wrapper on the table. There is a milk carton next to a platter of what looks like fried meat. (What else?) I see a bowl of fluffy mashed potatoes.

And looking at it sentimentally, as I often do because in my family only my younger brother is also still alive, I realize this is one of those famous Smith family five o'clock pickup suppers. ("What time is dinner?" they ask in Texas. "Five o'clock—four-thirty if it's ready!" goes the ravenous answer. You can read a little later Elizabeth Taylor's version of this philosophy.)

Studying the picture, it's obvious that my demanding father is not there. He would never have tolerated a milk carton on the table, nor the loaf of commercially wrapped bread. He wouldn't have cared a whit if the blowing fan dried out the bread slices; it just wouldn't do. Bread went in a basket, to be covered by a napkin. He had an oddly fastidious instinct and wanted everything "decanted"* into saucers and bowls and crystal jelly dishes. He detested condiment bottles. Whatever it was—jam, jelly, pickles, olives, even ketchup—"Make it look nice!" was his upwardly aspiring motto.

Sloan Smith never heard of the "Miss Manners" column. He'd have enjoyed Judith Martin's wit and wisdom. "It happens that while putting a milk carton or ketchup bottle on the table is a high etiquette crime, disguising the wine bottle is considered excessively genteel. Go figure."

He surely would have agreed with Judith Martin, who believes the dinner table to be the centerpiece for the teaching and practicing not just of manners but of conversation, consideration, tolerance, family feeling, "and just about all the other accomplishments of polite society except the minuet."

Had Daddy been at home, he'd have been the first to his seat, his silver Gorham dinner knife at the ready to whack any elbow that strayed on the table. (I still have the dents.) The setting would have been much

* My favorite story in this regard has nothing to do with food, but I'll tell it anyway. The elegant Dede Ryan was a working girl in thrall to the late *Harper's Bazaar*/*Vogue* legend Diana Vreeland. Then she married well and became increasingly "grand." One day a society PR type asked her to sign some letters for a charity event. She examined the ink on his desk and said she couldn't sign as he had only red, green, and blue ink. "Letters must be signed in black ink," said Dede. "Oh, dear! I have just lots of black ink at home but can't bring it here. It's all been decanted."

nicer—damask napkins, candles, the good china and flatware, a pretty cloth covering the table.

My mother, who hated to cook but loved to "keep house," knew it was important to keep the peace and do it her husband's way when he was around. So she did. But I love this old Gonzales snapshot because it shows two traditions—the absolute gathering at table of whatever family was in residence, plus Smithlike subliminal rebellion in action. "Hand over the ketchup bottle," Bobby is probably saying to James. "Daddy is in some West Texas diner wondering why they don't have mint jelly and paper leggings on the lamb chops." James is grinning. "Yeah, but they never heard of lamb chops in the first place. That's cattle country; they only know from burned steak. You know, he'll be lucky to get some beans wrapped in a tortilla!"

My mother actually loved it when Sloan was long gone on the road, buying cotton as a broker. Then this great lady, my Mississippi belle of a mother, could slam together a meal in any manner she pleased. She could satisfy my bottom-feeding brothers without bothering to add the niceties. She used paper napkins and kept food in its original cartons and always said, "Let's get it over and done with." She was actually anti-food, seriously not interested.

Speaking of informality, Frank Sinatra was once berated by his tempestuous, controlling mother, Dolly, for standing in the open door of the refrigerator drinking milk direct from the carton. My mother would have ignored such boorish boyish behavior, simply saying, "You're letting all the cold air out!" My father would have joined Dolly Sinatra in an etiquette lesson, reading the riot act about behaving "like poor white trash," causing the culprit to slink away in shame.

When Sloan was home, he did exhibit a sense of fun when it came to snacking late at night after the dinner hour was long past. He never went to bed without reciting this rhyme: "To bed, to bed, said Sleepy Head. Wait awhile, said Slow. Put on the pot, said Greedy Gut, we'll have a bite before we go." And we kids would troop with him into the kitchen for cereal, ice cream, or leftovers. My mother thought this was just ridiculous. To her, this only meant dirty dishes in the morning. "If you ate properly at dinner, you would not need a snack!" she'd say.

Sometimes we'd exalt: "But, Mother—Daddy is going to make chocolate fudge from scratch." She would gasp and sigh: "Oh, my lord, then that will be all over the walls, the sink, the stove, the ceiling—and think of the dirty pots and pans. We'll probably have to repaint the kitchen." Well, it was true that Sloan had the splashy creative impulses of most male chefs and he considered wife and "chillun" as kitchen slaves. We were his willing sous chefs, though we'd never heard the description. We knew it would be unmanly for Daddy to wash a dish.

More than the group photos in graduation gowns, or the Christmas get-togethers before the tree, or the family reunion pictures where there are always two or three people you can't remember to save your soul, this worn, torn, unreprintable little summer snapshot says it all for me. It's a big part of the story of family at table, together in informality, relaxing from my martinet father, yet still just an ordinary assemblage, which we all were ex-pected to join. Dinner or supper or whatever it was—together at five, or six, or seven.

Hungry families are all alike, as Tolstoy might have said!

CHAPTER 3

DISHING

IT

UP

Dining is and always was a great artistic opportunity.

—FRANK LLOYD WRIGHT

I GUESS *DISHING*, a book about food, cooking, and eating seems like a funny idea coming from someone who has been contemplating turning her apartment kitchen into a closet. About all I do in my kitchen is use the saucepan for soup, hit the buttons on the microwave, and make coffee.* But as you'll see from the names that have influenced my dedication, eating and food have played quite a role in my life.

But writing a book? Never intended to. And so here's how this work

---

* Frederick the Great made his own coffee. Unlike old Fred, I don't use Champagne instead of water. He also added a pinch of powdered mustard.

came about. There once was a charming little boy named Jacob who I used to see when I'd visit his famous mother.* Jacob would invariably show me his copy of L. Frank Baum's *The Wonderful Wizard of Oz* and he'd go through the illustrations, telling me about Dorothy, Toto, the Tin Woodman, the Scarecrow, the Cowardly Lion, and then the Wicked Witch of the West. When he'd come to the witch, Jacob would get furious, screw up his face, and pound on the page. "And this is the Wicked Witch—I HATE HER!" It was an unforgettable performance.

Well, Jacob finally got over that but kept us all fascinated by his emotional passion, temperament, and intellect as he grew up. Little did I know that my young friend Jacob would one day become a cheerleader for my writing, specifically my writing about food. And, as a result, this very book.

For the 2001 launch issue of *The New York Times Style Magazine*, my brilliant friend, the editor Billy Norwich, had the idea of reprinting an article I'd done years ago for *Cosmopolitan* about dining with Elizabeth Taylor and Richard Burton. I had mentioned the piece in my memoir, *Natural Blonde*, and Billy had looked it up.

Soon after the article was reprinted in the *Times*, young Jacob went to work for Norwich. Billy told me he hired Jacob not only because he'd been struck by the "promise of Jacob's journalist promise" but also because Jacob had raved about the *Cosmo* piece. Jacob went on and on in his special, enthusiastic way, deconstructing the article as "a triumph of high gossip." Jacob was a voracious reader. He said my take on the Burtons represented a kind of reporter's access to subjects that no longer exists in the celebrity world. And also it was about—of all things—eating.

For the next few years, long after young Jacob went on to jobs at *W* and *New York* magazines, Norwich, himself now at *Vogue*, assigned me more *Style and Entertaining* pieces and those selections form the skeleton for this book.

The Alpha and Omega of Starving Actors

In the year of our Lord 1962, an international entertainment scandal erupted in Rome that shook Hollywood, New York, and the Vatican to

---

* Jacob's parents are the writer–movie director Nora Ephron and writer Carl Bernstein.

their foundations. A very famous actress named Elizabeth Taylor, wed then to a very famous singer named Eddie Fisher, began co-starring with a not-yet-very-famous Welsh actor, Richard Burton, who was married to a famous, perfect wife, Sybil Burton.

Taylor and Burton were making the Joe Mankiewicz–20th Century Fox version of *Cleopatra*, a movie that almost bankrupted the studio and created seismic waves that still shiver down the cinematic pages of film history.

Miss Taylor and Mr. Burton were felled by a *coup de foudre*. That is, they fell in lust and then in love. Their marriages disintegrated. The Vatican condemned the actress. The paparazzi, invented largely by Federico Fellini's film *La Dolce Vita*, wouldn't leave them alone. "La Scandale," as the Burtons themselves came to term it, raged unabated until, and even after, they divorced their respective mates. They traveled the world trying to escape the notoriety that made them immortal, and married in Canada in 1964.

Soon after this, their genteel press rep John Springer advised them that I was the one and only journalist they should see, and arranged for us to meet in Paris on the set of an absurd movie they were making together called *The Sandpiper*. The Burtons and I, along with their costume designer Irene Sharaff, got acquainted in La Grande Cascade, a glamorous all-glass restaurant in the Bois de Boulogne. Here ensued an orgy of ordering, feasting, sending back, seizing tidbits from one another's plates, and the quaffing of much fine wine and Champagne. We gossiped and drank until four in the afternoon, with the director Vincente Minnelli pleading by telephone for the Burtons to please return to the movie set. He was all but spilling tears over his black velvet embroidered evening slippers, which he wore in the daytime.

I was then the entertainment editor of *Cosmopolitan* and in time I visited and interviewed the Burtons in what seems to have been every world capital, writing at least a story a year for my magazine and for newspapers. The Burtons and Liz, the reporter, were together in Paris, Rome, London, New York, Leningrad, and Hollywood. I adored the Burtons for what they were—good copy. And they liked me for what I was— sympathetic and mostly positive. But eventually I ran out of soap. What else to say about these overfed, overindulged, overpaid, overexposed stars?

Well, it came to pass in 1968 that I was sent again to Paris to link them in print. By now I was an intimate, admitted to their dressing rooms; I babysat their cats and picked up after their dogs. I carried makeup to Elizabeth from New York. I watched Alexandre, the Parisian hairdresser, turn both his and her curls into works of art. I saw them dress and undress, coo and curse, and I suffered through illnesses, diets, jealousies, drunken spats, the problems of their children, the perfidy of studios and press agents and producers.

One day in Paris, I tried to analyze what made the Burtons so much larger than life-size. If I could figure it out, perhaps I'd find a new angle for "covering" them. Indulging myself in a delicious order of raclette in a divine Left Bank café, I pondered my problem. Money, stardom, fame, and married sexual excess were not their gods, not at this point, anyway. Food was their ever-present reason for living. I discerned this later in a blinding flash as I opened one of the refrigerators in Elizabeth's dressing room. I said, "By George, I've got it." And soon I sat down and wrote what I still think is the best story I ever did on Elizabeth and Richard.

STARVING ACTORS

SCENE: TWA to Paris where 20th Century Fox was shooting, back to back, Elizabeth's picture *The Only Game in Town* and Richard's *Staircase* to accommodate the Burtons' togetherness. Darryl F. Zanuck (the head of Fox) sits across from me in the lounge, and I have visions of being discovered as a new "sexy" Estelle Parsons type. Over Nova Scotia it becomes obvious Mr. Zanuck is going to work on a script all the way, so I give up my career in films and let my thoughts drift to the last time I saw Elizabeth and Richard.

FLASHBACK (Zanuck influence, no doubt): Manhattan: The Plaza hotel's royal suite. The Burtons have summoned a waiter, who interrupts a discussion about a friend operated on for polyps.

RICHARD: "We'll have three orders of polyps on toast."
WAITER: "Sorry, sir, we have no scallops this time of year."
General hilarious laughter, led by Elizabeth: "Mabel [one of her pet names for Richard], you are too much. Now, we're all *dieting*, so no dessert. That's why we are ordering lima beans, corn on the cob, steak and kidney pie, and mashed potatoes."

When the waiter leaves, Richard begins a discussion with me about how waiters are all point killers. "They interrupt always just as you get to the punch line, or the most important thing you plan to say. It never fails. You are just on the verge of brilliance when they interrupt to ask, 'Is everything all right?!'" Elizabeth ignores him and begins eating pistachio nuts while we wait for lunch. When it arrives, she's disdainful of the white wine. "What is this, Richard? Are you saving money again? Really, I don't believe you, you are so cheap." She tastes. "Well, it's quite good, really. It's okay. We have this marvelous game we play when he's feeling good. I choose the most expensive wine listed. Richard pays. We've found some great wines that way. Remember, Agatha [another pet name], the one we got for $150 a bottle?"

Richard winces. One of his roles is to play cheapskate for his wife. He turns the talk to a pet rabbit they had in Switzerland.

ELIZABETH: "He liked martinis: with coffee, cream, and sugar. He was a wonderful pet; he slept in the bidet."

RICHARD: "Yes, if you sat on the potty, he'd hop up onto your lap and scratch you horribly with his claws. There were seventeen animals in Gstaad then—sheepdog, Yorkies, dachshund, cats, poodle, an Afghan, the rabbit. I finally said 'Enough!' and we gave most of them away. I couldn't bear it."

ELIZABETH: "Do you want any more of this? Good. I'm going to take all of this kidney-juice gook then. God, I love food—and wine, I adore wine. Listen, I think I'll have a hot fudge sundae." She does.

Then, while we wait for Elizabeth to have Alexandre do her hair, I overhear a secretary ordering lingerie from Henri Bendel. Someone is always ordering lingerie around the Burtons. You visualize a world of hotel suites with lovely once-worn panties, bras, slips, and body stockings left behind and delighted maids exclaiming over the windfall. Richard, on the other hand, claims to have only six sets of drawers to his name. He declares either he or his wife washes out a pair nightly.

The Burtons now sail "unobtrusively" out of the Plaza. Elizabeth is wearing a coffee-colored suede coat trimmed with a dramatic flounce of fox at the bottom and a matching explosion at the top. Her hair is in corkscrew ringlets and her eyes are flashing like "Walk" signs. Richard is very Southern California in a white cardigan and wraparound sunglasses. Alexandre has on something outré by Cardin, and there's a bodyguard who is neither introduced nor distinguished by tailoring. We pile into a blinding robin's egg blue Rolls to go two blocks. Richard admires my bare knees as I am trying to get out of the car, because he feels a day without complimenting a female is a day wasted. Then he asks, "Do you speak French?" I stammer, *"Un petit pois"* when I meant to say *"un peu."* He laughs; he thinks it's a deliberate joke. We are a real mob scene and all in all, we are as likely to escape notice as an orange tie on St. Patrick's Day.

Grand entrance into David Webb's jewelry emporium on 57th Street: "I am omniscient and triprescient," Richard murmurs, as the place dissolves into elegant pandemonium. People are springing to attention as if we were wearing stocking masks.

ELIZABETH: "I want to see some rings and things—nothing over $5,000."

Trays are brought. Still standing, she starts stuffing rings onto her fingers like a kid in a candy store. Alexandre is caressing and cooing over the jewelry. *"Très belle, très chic,"* he moans, jamming rings and bracelets onto *his* fingers and wrists.

ELIZABETH: "That's about all the French I understand."

RICHARD: "Yes, these rings are a steal at $4,000."

ELIZABETH (pityingly): "Richard, you don't understand, man. This stuff is not just ordinary diamonds-and-rubies junk. This is *it* now—it's very chic."

RICHARD: "It doesn't look real to me."

ELIZABETH: "Look, this is only $7,700. Don't you think it's kind of classy?"

RICHARD: "It's vulgar." He adds as an aside: "I like it very much."

ELIZABETH (ignoring him and turning on the patient salesman): "Well, look, Andrew, what will these three pieces be with my *spectacular* discount?" She indicates leopard, zebra, and serpent rings. "Never mind—send them to the hotel, and these, too." She points to a $2,500 lighter and a $29,000 shell purse.

We move out like Brink's bandits, leaving society ladies gaping out of the private showing rooms. Elizabeth gives us a dazzling non sequitur in the car: "I love that 'Dear Abby' column. Some of those things crack me up. Say, how can I get *Cosmopolitan*? I love that magazine. Oh, Richard, let's go now to Rumpelmayer's. And tonight we'll go to Gallagher's Steak House."

RICHARD: "When we're in Europe, we never talk of our friends in Amer-

ica, or plays we want to see, or films. We only talk about the food here—
pancakes, fried eggs, hamburgers, ice cream sodas."

ELIZABETH: "Speaking of film, if we buy a plane you have to install a
movie screen. I never get to see any movies. I'm starved—just because
you will never go with me."

RICHARD (patting her knee): "Quiet, Tubby, or I shall belt thee in thy tiny
chops."

FADE-OUT, DISSOLVE TO PARIS: The French have a saying (well, you
just know they do): "Love makes time pass; time makes love pass." In the
Burtons' case, love still seems to be around and only time has passed, along
with great wads of money. *Les Grand Deux* now own an elaborate yacht, the
$450,000 refurbished 110-foot *Kalizma*, a ten-passenger $1 million de Hav-
illand jet, the *Elizabeth*, complete with kitchen, bar, and movie setup, the
33.19-carat $305,000 Krupp diamond ring, a very rare lynx point Siamese
cat called Percy. Elizabeth has had a hysterectomy and is receiving daily
therapy for her back ailment. But, reunited with her early days *A Place in
the Sun* director George Stevens on *The Only Game in Town,* she is gamely
and gaily co-starring with Warren Beatty in a ridiculous contemporary story
about a Las Vegas dancer who falls for a gambling piano player.

SCENE: Morning: the Boulogne-sur-Seine studios. ETBs dressing suite,
freshly decorated in sunny yellows, whites, and greens. There is in the living room a well-stocked bar and a larder full of goodies from the Paris
American PX. The extra bathroom contains cases of Coca-Cola, Perrier,
and beer. Fresh mint is growing in the lavatory.

 Enter Mrs. Burton from the downstairs set, wearing a pink satin
bedspread and followed by Alexandre, a girl carrying a wig, a white
Pekingese, and five puppies to which she is gurgling, "Hello, snookums!"
The puppies frolic and do their stuff on the new cream carpets, which are
turning darker. The star is greeted by her longtime aide, Dick Hanley; her
PR man, John Lee; her secretary, George Davis; her makeup man, Frank
LaRue; her youthful designers, Mia and Vicky; her dresser, Jeanette; and a
young British nurse, Caroline, who is on hand to give her vitamin shots.
"What's that *shmatte* you're wearing?" someone asks.

ELIZABETH: "Well, I was naked in bed on the set. This is the love scene
day, you know. And I had to have something to wear upstairs. So I
grabbed this. Where's my ring?"

John Lee takes it off his finger. "Here," he winks. "I usually drop it in my drink at night. It makes the ice look better, and, besides, it cleans it."

"It's nothing really to look at," I say, stunned and almost blinded.

ELIZABETH: "No, it's not too much." Her cleavage shatters with laughter. "Princess Margaret said to me—how's that for a name-drop?—that she thought it was the most vulgar thing she'd ever seen. I said, 'Well, would you like to try it on?' She said, 'Yes, please.' So while she was admiring it on her finger, I said, in one of my rare brilliants . . . I tend to be mono-syllabic, you know . . . 'You see, it's not so vulgar now.' "

The smell of frying chicken rises from the kitchen, where John Lee is turning parts in a frying pan.

JOHN LEE: "I'm the publicity man for *poulet* today. Bettina"—the French model, Aly Khan's amour—"is coming for lunch, so we have to sock her with five thousand calories."

ELIZABETH: "Want a Blousey . . . a Blousey . . . a Bloody Mary? Now, what shall I drink . . . Salty Dog? Blousey? Hmmmm." In her vivid camera makeup, she is highly colored, flamboyant, larger than life.

She isn't fat, either. Her derriere and legs are slim. She has always had that top-heavy bosom, and now her pleasingly plump double chin is here to stay. But Elizabeth simply photographs heavier than she is. One can only assume she eats small portions.

Princess Elizabeth of Yugoslavia is calling. Clutching her slip-ping satin, Mrs. Burton takes the phone: "Listen, Sheba, how's by you?" They chat about flying to the yacht in Cannes for the weekend. "All right, Chicken Fat," says Elizabeth, hanging up. She beckons to me. "Come in. Have a cup of chili before Bettina gets here. Your friend Diane Judge made it here in the studio. She was in Paris last week. The longer it's in the fridge, the hotter it gets. Fantastic. Better than Chasen's. I sent Diane in the Rolls to Fauchon to buy the ingredients: the kidney beans cost ninety-nine cents a can here. I'd say, conservatively, this chili recipe for ten costs about two hundred dollars."

SCENE: Elizabeth is sitting, pinning up her hair to slip on a wig. "I'm let-ting my hair grow. Alexandre cut it off *that* short. He wanted me to look like a little boy, and I kept yelling, 'I don't want to look like a little boy!' " I hand her the special makeup sent from New York. She looks through the package. "Funny, they sent me false eyelashes. They must be kidding. I never wear them." She tosses them next to bottles of Femme, Jungle Gardenia, and a card reading: "Chicken Little Was Right."

Henri Chombert, the furrier, comes in with mink pelts for a coat Mrs. Burton is having made for her husband, a coat to be cut like a leather jacket. He also carries rare Siberian sable pelts for her. The Pekingese snaps at them, and Chombert, in *le beau geste,* tosses one to O Fie, the Peke, to play with. This enchants Elizabeth. "Now, I want the flattest-looking pelts for Richard's coat, not fluffy ones. What else do I want? Well, there was a convertible Rolls, the star of the English auto show, $30,000 I think it cost. Might get that one of these days. Richard says so far I haven't asked for the Super Chief."

John Lee is now frying bacon for an afternoon snack, and Elizabeth soon hovers by the stove waiting for a piece to be done. A tremendous pancake discussion ensues while I check the larder. It is crammed with Dinty Moore canned stew, Sara Lee cakes, Ritz crackers, Aunt Jemima mixes, Campbell's soups and pork and beans, Gebhardt's chili, maple syrup, Jolly Green Giant cream-style corn, B & B brown betty, Wilson's dried beef, Heinz pickles, V8 juice, Triscuits, Heinz ketchup, canned hominy, popcorn, Betty Crocker corn bread mix, Bumble Bee tuna.

SCENE: On the set, Elizabeth comes into view wearing a lavender djellaba and the eight-dollar beaten-gold native necklace I've brought her from Tunis. I had been in North Africa, where they were filming *Justine,* and Elizabeth wanted to know all about Anouk Aimée and Dirk Bogarde on location. "What did they have to eat there?" she asks after being assured that no romance was blooming. I told her that the only meal I remembered was served in cardboard boxes in the broiling sun and as Miss Aimée opened her box to reveal some kind of barbecued joint atop a bed of couscous, a swarm of flies landed on the food. She shut the box and we never ate a thing. Elizabeth makes a face! "Give me Paris hotel room service every time," she laughs.

She flicks her cheap necklace. "See, I can wear anything I like in this picture. Shall we give you jewelry credit?" Looking very pleased, she then triumphantly lifts the plate she is carrying to reveal a peanut butter and bacon sandwich. "So Elvis!" I wisecrack. She looks serious. "Well, I love Elvis."

The set is of an ordinary apartment looking out on a facsimile of the

Las Vegas strip. This movie has everything in it but Howard Hughes. War-ren Beatty comes and sits next to Elizabeth on a double bed as they wait for filming to start. He casually and tenderly massages her back as if he knows it's hurting. It is. Earlier, the star had emerged from her daily massage and exercise therapy, taken to relieve the strain on her disks. She looked white and pale. "Whew," she'd said. "That was lots of fun."

SCENE: Quitting time. Mrs. Burton pops her head out of her dressing room to the outer office, where her entourage is playing "Who Am I?"

ELIZABETH: "No one stays in here with me. You are all out there having fun." She saunters out wearing orange slacks. Sitting cross-legged, she smokes as if she just learned how and laughs when John Lee reveals that he is the Duchess of Windsor, after everyone has given up on his imper-sonation.

Enter Richard Burton. Kisses and greetings.

ELIZABETH: "Young Richard, hi." And she calls him by a vulgar term of endearment.

Then she takes him across the hall to show him an Op-Pop-Art room that has been specially decorated for him, even though he is shooting across Paris at the Billancourt Studios. The room is a riot of hippie posters, psychedelia, a red *E* and *R* on the wall, Day-Glo cards, and a dirty Walt Disney coloring book with Crayolas. He seems mildly amused.

RICHARD: "Today Rex [Harrison] and I had the greatest beef stew in the world."

ELIZABETH: "Yah, yah—my father can lick your father!"

RICHARD: "What did you have?"

ELIZABETH: "I had pancakes with strawberry syrup and bacon when I got here, fried chicken and chili for lunch."

RICHARD: "Tomorrow *we* are having stuffed steak. Your surroundings here may be grand, but the food is very common."

Elizabeth picks up one of the puppies and kisses it. "Hello, Florinda," she says softly in a sexy voice. She is obviously teasing her husband about headlines involving him with the South American model, Florinda Balkin. Everyone begins to talk of the girl's alleged statements to the Italian press that she could have Richard, but "he is too much of a bore."

ELIZABETH: "You know the Italians. I think Florinda has too much taste to have said anything so silly. Besides, Richard was in London at the clinic with me when they said he was in Rome. Weren't you, Luv?" (I wonder if this is for my benefit? Probably not.)

SCENE: Tout Paris at night. Posh party in a re-creation of Maxim's for the opening of A *Flea in Her Ear*. The Burtons enter in a crush. Elizabeth is wearing glittering emeralds and white egret feathers worked into her hair with diamonds. As she wedges her way past, I whisper, "You look like a fabulous chicken."

She blows a feather out of her mouth: "You mean I look like a chicken's behind." Then smiling demurely, she slips into place at a table next to Baron Guy de Rothschild. Photographers jam up to pop their flashbulbs as if no pictures of the Burtons existed. Elizabeth smiles, smokes a cigarette in her rather "high school" manner, and winks at me. I can see she is impatient for the photographers to leave and the waiters to bring the food.

SCENE: Morning after the weekend. John Lee is on the phone ordering lingerie in very bad French. Dick Hanley models the German-style, mink-lined leather trench coat Elizabeth has given him. He makes fun of me for having described him in an article as her "male secretary." ("Of course, I am male. What kind of a woman is called Dick?") Mr. Hanley has known Miss Taylor since her childhood. She now and then strays toward him and sits down in his lap as if she were three or four. Now he says to the minion who is shopping: "Get a dozen eggs for Madam. Also two frozen chickens. I just bought a dozen lemons. See if they have Crisco or Spry as I don't want oil."

Elizabeth comes out of the dressing room wearing a white lace mini dress. Her lipstick is vivid. She says, "The weekend was divine, but it has 'corpsed' me." She wiggles her fingers, saying "Bye, bye" as she goes down the hall like a delicious snowdrift on legs.

"I'm going to walk with you in case you drop any pearls," I comment.

"Or my stole," she cracks. "Listen, you know who's being an absolute pussycat—George Stevens. He said he knew I'd had an operation, and anytime I didn't feel up to it, he'd close down for the day. I got all sort of shy and started kicking my feet and said, 'That wouldn't be very professional of me, would it?' I was just adorable. You'd have loved me. It's extraordinary how good Fox is being to me. They had a wall knocked out to put this elevator to the second floor so I don't have to climb, because of my back."

We wait, but the elevator doesn't come. "Let's walk," she says. I cram in a question. "Would you forgive a man for being unfaithful to you?"

She gives me a burning look. "I sure *wouldn't*, sweetie."

I ask about Warren. "Well, he's marvelous, such a good actor and so nice. I must drive a serious actor like Warren Beatty up the wall. You know I don't take acting very seriously. It's fun and a giggle to me."

Stevens kisses her hand as we come on the sound stage and calls her "Lizbeth, dear." I can see she loves and respects him because I've seen her before with producers and directors. I once watched her inveigle a $25,000 bird pin out of a crafty Martin Ransohoff and then she wore it once. Now Warren leads her carefully onto the set. I whisper, "They sure think you're a fragile little flower."

Says Elizabeth, "But I am, I am." She bats her incredible lavender eyes to the strains of the Cole Porter music Stevens has had piped onto the set. She sits up straight, stretches her back, and yawns: "Gee, I wish I had a potato chip."

SCENE: *Après-midi.* Fox is getting ready to expose a planeload of grass-roots press to the Las Vegas gambling room set and to their stars. The blond press agent Pat Newcomb, who looks as if she might be a movie star herself, is upstairs talking to Elizabeth, who has given no guarantee that she'll appear for this magnificent clutch of rubes. Upon hearing that Richard gave them a tremendous time the day before, Elizabeth stands up and says, "Shall we go down? Here, Liz, take my Jack Daniel's. I don't want to drink whatever is being served there. Goody! It's a bottle party. I haven't been to one of those in years." She is suddenly gleeful.

Entering, she is besieged on all sides by men and women asking the same questions in varying U.S. accents. She laughs, she flutters her eyes— she toys with her drink as Miss Newcomb breaks up each group after ten minutes and guides her to meet press in other parts of the room. The reporters jostle and probe.

QUESTION: "What's this film about?"
ET: "A comedy with a light quality. It isn't like anything in my experience. The girl is warm, sympathetic, friendly. She's not neurotic or hysterical, for a change. This will be one film my kids can go see."

QUESTION: "What do you plan to do next?"

ET: "I hope, relax; or faint!"

QUESTION: "Are you still Jewish?"

ET (shocked): "Of course I am!"

QUESTION: "Are you raising your children as Jews?"

ET: "No, I'm letting them study several religions. They can decide later."

QUESTION: "Mr. Burton tells us that you are a nice girl."

ET: "I'm glad he decided that. Considering the part he's playing now in *Staircase*, where he's a homosexual, I think *he's* a very nice girl, too."

QUESTION: "He tells us he is very happily married."

ET: "I'm glad he is, because I am."

QUESTION: "He says you're extravagant."

ET: "I don't know why he says *that*."

QUESTION: "He says you can spend $1,000 a minute."

ET: "Wh-a-a-a-t? Why, that's cheap. I'm very good about my budget. I'm quite good—at times."

QUESTION: "Is that the famous diamond?"

ET (blowing on it): "Yes, it is. Mr. Burton gave it to me. It came from the Krupp people [she pronounces it "Kroup"] as in German munitions. I think it's rather nice that a little Jewish girl has it now."

The press is thoroughly beguiled. After the explosive laughter subsides, Miss Newcomb maneuvers the star out of the crowd to the door. Elizabeth eyes a tray of hors d'oeuvres over her shoulder and says quietly to me, "Schwartz, see if you can grab some of those for upstairs."

CLOSING SCENE: Las Vegas. A room service waiter emerges from the Burtons' hotel suite, where they are all but incommunicado during the location shooting here. He wrinkles his brow, "Jellied eels? Where am I going to find jellied eel in Nevada?"

FADE-OUT TO FINIS: When I sat down to write this, I was disturbed by reports that Elizabeth wasn't well, so I cabled Puerto Vallarta, Mexico (where the Burtons often stayed), to ask if she is okay. It took a while, as I think telegrams go in and out via burro. But, in time, the message came back: "ELIZABETH TAYLOR BURTON IS ALIVE AND EATING TACOS IN MEXICO."

Well, it figures.

Dining à la the Burtons

The Judge's Jailhouse Chili

¼ pound salt pork, cubed

4 pounds rough-cut or coarsely ground round steak

Four 4-ounce cans tomato sauce

4 beef bouillon cubes, or two 14½-ounce cans unsalted beef broth

4 tablespoons ground cumin

*6 tablespoons dried garlic chips (if you want fresh garlic, indulge yourself
   in slicing the same amount)*

1 tablespoon cayenne pepper

6 tablespoons salt

¾ cup chili powder

¼ cup masa flour (corn flour)

Four 19-ounce cans kidney or pinto beans, drained, optional

1. In a large heavy pot, render the salt pork and remove the cracklings. (To render means to fry the cubed salt pork at medium heat. Strain.) Brown the beef in the pork fat. While browning, in another pot bring to a boil the tomato sauce, 1 quart water, the bouillon cubes, cumin, garlic chips, cayenne, salt, and chili powder.

2. When the meat is browned, cover with the boiling mixture and add enough water or beef broth to cover the meat entirely. Cover the pot and simmer a minimum of 2 hours. Skim the excess fat and add enough masa flour to bind the juices, but not so much that the chili becomes pasty thick. Theoretically, the dish is now "done," but you can season to taste.

3. For chili with beans, add the kidney or pintos and simmer long enough to heat the beans. Stir occasionally so nothing sticks. The longer the chili cooks, the hotter it will taste.

4. Serve with soda crackers, Fritos, or tostadas. Chopped onions on the side and a bowl of shredded Monterey Jack cheese will be welcomed. The Burtons pronounced this "Hot stuff!"

8 TO 10 SERVINGS

Chipped Beef à la Krupp Diamond

Chipped beef
Flour
Butter
Milk
Curry powder
Hard-boiled eggs

Shred the chipped beef and dredge in the flour. Sauté in melted butter in a hot skillet. In a saucepan, make a white sauce using 3 tablespoons of flour, 3 tablespoons of butter, and a little more than 1 cup of milk. Add several pinches of curry powder. Serve over the beef. Add a few hard-boiled egg wedges to dip in the sauce or slice and place on top.

Serve this on toast.

When do you eat such a dish? Elizabeth says, "At high noon; eleven A.M., if it's ready!"

CHAPTER 4

DEATH

BY

MAYONNAISE*

I WAS DELIVERED out of Texas to Manhattan in late 1949, having escaped what I call American frontier survival cooking—barbecued or fried haunch of whatever . . . corn smoldering in its own husks . . . grain mashed into a flat sizzled cake . . . sticky rice . . . vitaminless mushy vegetables swimming in water and cooked senseless . . . a smattering of knowledge about "salads" that included iceberg lettuce, fruit, Jell-O, whipped cream, and nuts—all this appearing on tables forever decorated with red and yellow condiment bottles.

Well, the next amazing thing I knew, it was 1957, and there I was in Le Pavillon restaurant at 57th Street and Park Avenue being cautioned by the owner and creator, Henri Soulé, on how to test, taste, and eat caviar properly. Not for the great Soulé the subtleties of the horn or bone spoon to ward off the contaminating taste of (shudder) metal on fish egg.

---

* It was supposedly Cardinal Richelieu who invented this sauce made of oil and eggs. And here's hoping he gave some to Athos, Porthos, Aramis, and their sidekick, d'Artagnan.

M. Soulé would go to inspect the caviar he meant to buy with a fistful of regular old metal spoons stuck like a bouquet in his breast pocket. He used a different spoon on each tin, discarding them behind him as if they were plastic. Cautioning all the while, "My dear little girl, never never never never add anything to caviar. If you want the taste of egg and onions in your mouth, eat egg and onions, but don't offend caviar with them!"

Now, of course, up until my baptism by beluga under M. Soulé's tutelage, I hadn't had much of anything to do with caviar. And, of course, what little I'd had included small dots of inferior caviar from jars, dosed with chopped egg and onion and smothered in sour cream, not even crème fraîche. But I didn't tell that to M. Soulé. As he took me under his wing, opening the offered tins (he was making his selections for his important customers), almost everything tasted pretty much the same to me. *It was all great.* I just loved caviar! And I still love it and I'll eat it any way I can get it—plain, unadorned, and undressed—or . . . (Well, I'm so sorry, M. Soulé, you can take the girl out of the country, but . . .) I still love caviar with all the trimmings, too. I'll even eat it the more popular way atop a baked potato, though I think it's a waste.

Another benefit came my way because of M. Soulé. He would send to my humble East 38th Street brownstone apartment cases of a red wine he particularly favored. I unwittingly opened this as if it were soda pop, and my lowbrow friends and I gulped it down with everything from chicken-fried steak to chili. In my years of knowing M. Soulé, he made me one of the most popular girls ever to entertain in Murray Hill. Alas, I would be rich today if only I'd put M. Soulé's Château Pétrus away in a coolish dark place. But me and my Texas friends and my new New York friends were like the Mexican field hands who used to toil in the Rio Grande Valley.*

So like Pedro I suppose I am philosophical about all the great Château Pétrus I squirted down my throat just because it tasted so good and went so fast. But when I see bottles priced at $1,500 and $2,000 today, I gulp. I do also thank M. Soulé, now in heaven, for his generosity—and

---

* My father loved the tale of how Pedro worked so hard to save the money he made picking cotton forteen and sixteen hours a day. On Saturdays Pedro got into a big dice game, putting his earnings on the floor under a handkerchief, throwing a lot of snake eyes, and watching it all raked away in an hour's time. Then Pedro rose, shook his head, laughed, and said, "Come easy, go easy!"

for his belief in Pétrus. He put it on the map. And he certainly cured me of any taste for cheap red wine.

How did I come into the great Soulé's orbit? In 1955, I was a junior society reporter and my apprenticeship and friendship with M. Soulé was a gift from my boss, Igor Cassini, who was then the Hearst organization's famous society columnist Cholly Knickerbocker. Igor was willing to do everything for me except pay me a living wage and so he often took me to restaurants and nightclubs above my station. The first time we went to Pavillon, I was terrified, for Cassini had cautioned: "M. Soulé is kind-hearted but he doesn't suffer fools gladly. He has very strict ideas. He won't seat a lady at a table if she arrives alone. She may be a doyenne of society, but she must wait in the foyer until her companion arrives no matter how much she may need a cocktail. And he won't serve women in trousers—not even Hepburn or Dietrich. You must respect his French traditions and you must love food."

Fortunately, M. Soulé liked me. He was determined to educate my peasant qualities. I remained friends with him until he died in 1966 and I heartily recommend you read the Joseph Wechsberg book about him, *Dining at the Pavillon.* It's a classic.

BACK THEN, I often yearned for what my friend Tom Wolfe would eventually describe as "the glories of boiling lard."* In other words, I was addicted to the good side of Southern cooking, which I still love even if I eat it sparingly. But in my rarefied Soulé days I was in a separate, unequal universe of comfort food—haute cuisine.

I ate at all the great restaurants in those days, enjoying the remarkable soufflés at Voisin where one day the actress and my co-birthday friend Elaine Stritch and I were celebrating on February 2. As she sat down, looking voguishly smart and wearing a little hat with a veil, Elaine said, "Oh, Lizzie, Noel Coward is coming. He's trying to entice me to come to London and do *Sail Away* there, but I don't want to go." When the urbane master himself arrived, he was polite, cool, and fixated on Elaine. It mattered

---

* When I started writing this book I asked Tom Wolfe to tell me in which of his many colorful writings he had originated the phrase "the glories of boiling lard." He graciously wrote back saying he could not recall and had always believed the description originated with me. I'm not that clever. But it's still my favorite thing from the talented Tom.

not a jot nor tittle that this was my birthday, too; he kept plugging away at Elaine, whispering, cajoling, giving her a monogrammed passport case. I was having some extracurricular fun with martinis and finally he turned to me and said in his most understated charming voice: "And you, young woman. Will you please shut up!" I did. And Elaine did go to London.

Elaine and I first met in Chicago and later back in New York we became pals. She was already almost a big star, twenty-eight years old and fresh off the road from playing a forty-year-old ambassador in *Call Me Madam*. I lived through all her love affairs in which she attempted the acrobatics of staying involved with mature men who were divorced or trying to get divorced, while hanging on to her virginity with a vengeance, or until the Vatican would say she could wed. At some junction, she told me her New York apartment kitchen needed painting. I was between lowly jobs and it was before my "society" column career, so I painted her kitchen a Pepto-Bismol pink for her. And maybe it's still there, overlooking the East River with my signature, like Picasso's, down in one corner. Often we went with one of Elaine's many beaus to Sardi's and "21" and nice joints like that. But if we had to pay for ourselves we'd hit the popular P. J. Clarke's, made famous by the movie *The Lost Weekend*. We loved its checkered tablecloths and hamburgers. (We especially liked sneaking into the men's room when no men were there to observe the blocks of yellow ice in the troughs that constituted the urinals. Oh, we were low. We got our kicks wherever we could.)

We were given good tables most places because Elaine was a rising star and I was soon working in the fringes of journalism. I began to find out that food didn't have to have suffered the Inquisition; it could be treated kindly and gently and now and then arrive rare or merely sautéed.

We also frequented Pearl's, a Chinese restaurant unlike any other on the West Side. It had a spartan decor by the Broadway costumer Irene Sharaff, who believed in vivid colors. And it had Pearl herself, sometimes referred to as "the Chinese Joan Blondell" (a wisecracking comedienne from black-and-white films). Pearl knew China had had emperors but she never put on airs. She treated William S. Paley, Woody Allen, Lauren Bacall, Robert Mitchum, and Marlene Dietrich all exactly the same way she treated us unknowns, with a warm Cantonese contempt. Her *yuk sung* and lemon chicken were true Chinese comfort foods, often imitated, never rivaled. Nobody could make sweet-and-sour pork like Pearl and they should probably all just stop trying. And believe me, it was nothing like eating out of those cartons in *The Godfather.*

I couldn't go to Pavillon all the time, but I did have my favorite one dish there—lobster in champagne and lobster sauce. The more rosy sauce went on one side; the creamier one went on the other. This was a Soulé masterpiece and I ate it over and over, afraid to order too experimentally. And I began to branch out, not to M. Soulé's competition; he didn't have any competition. But I went to his imitators' restaurants.

I learned to eat orecchiette, a pasta that looks like ears, at the now long-gone Romeo Salta restaurant, and I discovered that while the "spaghetti red" my mother lashed together had been tasty, spaghetti called pasta had more class. It was better. I found that Le Veau d'Or served the best fillet of sole amandine in the world. At the Colony restaurant, where society's last valiants congregated, I struck up a friendship with a waiter from Montecatini Terme. So I rode the wave with Sirio Maccioni until he made his mark on New York with his several Le Cirques and Circo.

I lived through the sixties, when theme eateries arrived, courtesy of Restaurant Associates. These experiences involved one place called the Forum of the Twelve Caesars, where the waiters wore togas and served wild boar. The menu card was so large you couldn't handle it. I recall dining in Restaurant Associates' famed Tower Suite atop the Time-Life building. Here the staff always introduced themselves. The gent I went with was an Anglophile named Trumball Barton who fancied himself "Noel Coward in training." After a handsome young man said, "Hello, I'm John, your butler," Mr. Barton leapt up and said, "And I'm Trumball Barton, you may call me *Mr.* Barton. I am your customer, so no more personal chitchat if you don't mind."

It was here I first encountered the *entremets* sherbet with which to cleanse my palate. And here we were given a mysterious first course, a very small crab on toast. Another guest with us, the actress Kaye Ballard, looked down at it, glanced around, and then hit it a blow with her fist, mashing it flat. "I'll never wash it!" said Kaye, setting us off into hysterics. When the cleansing baby sherbets arrived, we found them as fascinating as the view from the top.

And long before Warner LeRoy put his pyrotechnics into the Russian Tea Room and it went belly up, I went to his psychedelic Maxwell's Plum as a guest of Woody Allen. Here we ordered more comfort food under the Tiffany glass decorations. Warner made a helluva shepherd's pie there, the kind of dish no one bothers to concoct anymore, originally made from leftovers.

These eating-out adventures kept me amused and busy. I often frequented the original Russian Tea Room on West 57th Street when it was owned by Faith Stewart-Gordon and one could not only enjoy Christmas decorations the year round but get a sense of Russia under the tsars, as well as a nice glass of tea while hearing how commie-baiter Roy Cohn had driven by during the Red scare of the fifties and put the café on his "watch list."

In spite of learning a lot about food, I still didn't cook. I didn't have time to prepare anything; I was too busy eating out and taking notes. This was a brave new world where baby veggies in strange combinations were described by Truman Capote as "the food of the rich" and Diana Vreeland rhapsodized over same in her fashion magazine pages. Taken to France on a tour by Mumm Champagne, I ate in a café outside Paris where the dessert included a hard-boiled egg dipped in chocolate. I could take Champagne or leave it, but I did like hearing Larry Gelbart's* theory that "Champagne is only ginger ale that knows somebody!" Eventually, I came to like delicate sauces and things blanched and buttered to perfection, eggs beaten and whipped to points of light.

Privately, when entertaining at home, I was still serving Southern comfort food in my apartment, which had once been the bathroom-dressing room of a town house owned by the swanky Millicent Rogers of Standard Oil. This had been turned into a living room with a vaulted ceiling, lots of bookshelves, and a fireplace. The only things I could make were fried chicken and chicken-fried steak, and I found if I bought the rest of the dinner and served a melting Brie first, no one cared, not when we had the Château Pétrus flowing.

I became faintly popular with the very crowd I admired and wanted so hard to impress—Helen Gurley Brown and her husband David, Gloria Steinem, Herb Sargent, Clay Felker, Tom Wolfe, Gloria Vanderbilt, Donald Brooks, Geraldine Stutz, Mica and Ahmet Ertegun, Barbara Goldsmith, Tommy Thompson, Nancy Friday, Gael Greene, Gay Talese, Mary Ann Madden, Joe Armstrong.

* The clever creator of M*A*S*H.

We ate our way through the Eisenhower recession, the Cuban missile crisis, Vietnam, the assassinations of JFK, RFK, Martin Luther King, Jr., and the American Nazi George Lincoln Rockwell—through Watergate, the Persian Gulf War, and the Clinton crisis. We ate and we ate well. And during the World Trade Center tragedy, a journalist friend was working in the street on the story. She ordered a sandwich, saying to an aide, "Don't bring me any fat-free mayonnaise. If the world is coming to an end, I want the real thing!"

In the early days of the Hamptons of Long Island, I became a permanent houseguest of Lee Bailey. He was not yet the Clarkson Potter cookbook king of food and entertaining, but he was on his way. We made our mark together in Bridgehampton by feeding people. Lee was constantly experimenting on his Bunkie, Louisiana, roots, and his own innate good taste. His mantra was for "homemade mayonnaise," which, frankly, I considered a waste of time. (I thought Hellmann's was just swell.*) But "Death by Mayonnaise" became our slogan. We talked about food and decor more than we did about drugs and sex. And, yes, we kept a little busy in all areas. We were young. (More about Lee later. His influence and fame deserve their own chapter.)

I never attained the finesse of many of Lee's other female devotees, who combined their super careers with being perfect cooks, hostesses, wives, and mothers. I just stuck to my elemental old favorites, fried chicken, for instance, in the classic mode. (All you need is a small, young chicken, salt, pepper, flour, and a paper bag to shake it in before depositing it in a hot skillet with about one-quarter inch of shortening or vegetable oil and a few spoonfuls of bacon grease.)

"Do you put a lid on the chicken when you fry it, Mama?" I used to ask. "You can, honey," she'd say, "but it won't make much difference." This very chicken, plus my other standbys—chicken- or country-fried steak and cream gravy—made me unpopular with women who were always dieting. But Lee would opine, "Men love it! Make it, Lizzie!" He would then hand over that main course to me while he did special vegetables, creamy mashed potatoes *using a ricer*, and beautiful desserts. I recall once broiling twenty perfect T-bone steaks on an outdoor grill while Lee

* We had and still have a friend, Suzanne Goodson, who always travels with her jar of Miracle Whip. She can't tolerate Hellmann's.

frothed up the rest of the dinner. This was a big hit, confirming what Alfred Hitchcock said, "There will obviously be a lot of drama in a steak that is too rare!"

One of the feats of entertaining pulled off at Lee's, where the cocktail reigned for years along with Lee's little spartan bowl of salted peanuts, was the main course constructed by our theater press agent friend, Diane Judge. Lee loved this meal, a New England boiled dinner dreamed up by the English-Dutch Diane, a perennial favorite because it could be made and "held" if the evening became too elongated or raucous. I am including Diane's recipe just as I gave her Jailhouse Chili earlier.

I opened this dialectic on comfort food high and low with a memory of Henri Soulé, who came to the U.S. in 1939 for the World's Fair and changed American food history. There is a story of how his biographer Joseph Wechsberg and Soulé drove back from Long Island to New York. (In East Hampton, Soulé had started a restaurant called The Hedges.) As they came west, Soulé, the man who brought French cuisine to the U.S., instructed the driver to stop at Grace's famous roadside stand. "Let's get out and have a couple of hot dogs—they're delicious here!" he told Wechsberg. M. Soulé, a man after my own dual nature.

I learned a lot about comfort and manners from M. Soulé. One weekend the elegant duPont-wed Francis Carpenter and her friend Shirley Maytag sailed into Sag Harbor, Long Island, on a yacht. "We must go to The Hedges," said Francis, so they rented an auto and set out. Arriving about 12:30, Francis was stunned to see only a few cars. The dining room was set up handsomely but empty. "Tell Mr. Soulé that Mrs. Carpenter is here for lunch," Francis said to a passing busboy. Soon, Soulé appeared in a bloody apron wiping his hands. Apologizing that he'd been butchering, he was charm itself, seating the ladies, asking what they'd like. "Whatever you want us to have," responded the gracious Francis. To Mrs. Maytag, she whispered, "Poor Henri. He has no customers."

Soulé served them himself—a fine lunch of fish and salad accompanied by an excellent white wine. When Francis asked for the check, M. Soulé bowed. "Oh, Mrs. Carpenter . . . there is no check. For, you see, there is no lunch at The Hedges."

So, who says there is no free lunch? If you are willing to dare to be lucky as *The New Yorker*'s E. B. White once advised, you can eat high, you can eat low. You can have a swell time between two worlds.

The Judge's New England Boiled Dinner

2 stalks celery, chopped
1 onion, quartered
1 bay leaf
1 handful mixed fresh herbs (sage, thyme, parsley)
1 palmful herbes de Provence
1 garlic clove, peeled and crushed
1 teaspoon black peppercorns
3 boneless smoked shoulder pork butt hams (about 2 pounds each), rinsed
8 large carrots, peeled and cut into 2-inch pieces
2 medium turnips, peeled and cut into 8 pieces each
9 medium russet potatoes, peeled and halved
2 parsnips, peeled and quartered
24 white onions, peeled
1 to 2 pounds fresh green beans, trimmed
2 large cabbages, trimmed and cut into 10 pieces
Melted butter, mustard, horseradish, applesauce, and rye bread for serving

1. Combine 2 gallons water with the celery, onion, bay leaf, herbs, garlic, and peppercorns in a 4- to 5-gallon pot and heat to boiling over medium heat. Simmer for 15 minutes. Wrap the hams in cheesecloth. Add the hams, and cover and simmer for 1 hour.

2. While the hams cook, prepare the vegetables; tie up the carrots in a piece of cheesecloth. Do the same with the turnips, potatoes, and parsnips. Tie up the onions and green beans together in cheesecloth. Leave the cabbage wedges as they are.

3. Remove the hams to a platter and while they are still hot remove the cheesecloth covering. Keep the hams warm.

4. Add the carrots and turnips to the simmering ham water; cover and simmer for 5 minutes. Then add the potato and parsnip bundles; cover and simmer for 10 minutes. Add the onions and green beans bundle; cover and simmer for 10 minutes. Cover all the vegetables with cabbage wedges, cover, and simmer for 10 minutes.

5. Using tongs, remove the cabbage wedges and lift each bundle out. Test for doneness. Slice the hams. Cut the bundles and arrange the vegetables around the sliced ham on a large platter, if you have one.

6. Spoon melted butter over the veggies. Serve with mustard, horseradish, applesauce, and some fine rye bread.

YIELD: AT LEAST 8 SERVINGS

I suggest Château Pétrus with this meal. Or a Coca-Cola or Diet Pepsi or diet Dr Pepper. Or decanted beer in a pitcher.

CHAPTER 5

AIN'T NOTHIN'

BUT A

CHOWHOUND

DURING THE ORGY of Elvis Presley mania that afflicted the press and public on the occasion of the twenty-fifth anniversary of the icon's death, I searched in vain for intimations and remembrances of Elvis that held meaning for me.

Learning that 7 percent of Americans believe Elvis is yet alive, and that his estate still earns $35 million a year, I was left unsatisfied, for nowhere in the overweening coverage and analysis did anyone mention the Presley impact on our continuing craze for the kind of all-American fattening food we are now told we should leave alone.

Everyone knows these days how overweight we all are, that obesity is a major health problem, and that some people still hope to sue McDonald's and Kentucky Fried Chicken for their addictions, just as others sued the tobacco companies. I try to take Mark Twain's advice and be very careful in reading health books, because I don't want to die from a misprint. But I'm like everyone else. Diet-guilty, we watch with our tongues hanging out as the current crop of celebrity anorexics slip into the Emmys and

Oscars in dresses that barely cover their vitals. These latter-day lovelies obviously have never been hit with the scent of boiling lard; the fragrance of ripe banana mashed with peanut butter and marshmallow; snap green beans and little new potatoes bubbling in water flavored with bacon grease or hog jowl; the flowery heat of beaten buttermilk biscuits smothered under cream gravy paste; the crispy curl of chicken or chicken-fried steak (Elvis called this "ugly steak"); the nutty smell of real overladen coconut cakes; the overwhelming cloud from homemade buttered popcorn—nothing like what emanates from modern cineplexes.

In other words, they are immune to Elvis—the Elvis that counts—not the king of rock 'n' roll, but the master of every fattening thing he desired. Elvis led a life in which he snacked without guilt. Just imagine that! Although he never heard of it, he lived to the max the Greek philosophy of *eudaemonia,* meaning "human flourishing."

As part of his legacy, Elvis has inspired several cookbooks and I highly recommend them to you: *Are You Hungry Tonight?*; *Fit For a King: The Elvis Presley Cookbook*; *The Presley Family Cookbook* (not to be confused with *The Presley Family & Friends Cookbook: A Cookbook and Memory Book From Those Who Knew Elvis Best*); *The I Love Elvis Cookbook*; *Elvis in Hollywood: Recipes Fit for a King,* and the one I love best and keep by my bed, *The Life and Cuisine of Elvis Presley.*

I don't really mind that Elvis has left the building. He and Marilyn Monroe would have made simply horrifying old people. It's better for them—and for us—that they're gone, save from the screen and CDs and memories. But when I think of Elvis living and roaming those overwrought rooms in Graceland, I find myself transported like Marcel Proust in *Remembrance of Things Past.* Elvis himself is my madeleine, that tea-soaked bit of cake that took Proust back to his Aunt Léonie and childhood at Combray. The mere mention of Elvis is enough to set off a mnemonic combination that takes me straight to the food of my childhood. (And my adulthood, when I can get it!) You needn't make fun of this. In the *New York Times' Books of the Century,* writer Rose Lee assays that this shift to another scene at an instant's notice "justifies M. Proust in dilating upon the most minute occurrences, so long as he maintains the air of spontaneous recollection. It injects dignity into otherwise trivial perceptions. . . . It is a constant means of affirming Proust's belief in the essentially subjective nature of human experience."

I don't really expect that I can inject any dignity into the Elvis diet, but I don't see any difference between Proust's madeleine, allegedly named for Madeleine Paulmier, a nineteenth-century pastry cook, and my Elvis-of-the-demanding-short orders-to-his-cook Pauline Nicholson.

On a recent vacation in Martha's Vineyard, I dragged with me only two books: Benita Eisler's life of Lord Byron, which weighed a ton and which I read with overwhelming pleasure, and the aforesaid, rather high-toned Elvis *Cuisine* title, by David Adler. I needed the latter as an antidote to all the Vineyard's rare tuna, seared swordfish, dandelion green salads, and other healthy offerings that came with the uncorking of vintage bottled water. I would retire to bed with Lord Byron, entertain myself with his "mad, bad, and dangerous to know" behavior for a while, and then put myself to sleep reading Elvis recipes.

Sometimes I would daydream, wondering what Elvis would have thought of a dessert trifle sent me by my brother Bobby for fried Snickers bars. Or I'd suddenly remember going to the local Dairy Queen in Gonzales, Texas, and asking for a Frito Pie. The boy in the paper hat would seize a bag of Frito-Lay's best, slash the side open, pour hot Texas chili over the insides, hand me a plastic spoon, and ask for fifty cents. Quick, cheap, crunchy, hot with fire and pepper, and totally satisfying.

I was encouraged to read a recent book, *Mr. S: My Life with Frank Sinatra,* by his former valet George Jacobs and William Stadiem. This book was a guilty pleasure from sex to nuts, yes, and from soup to nuts, too.

It's nice to think of a slim Sinatra enjoying his olive oil and fried egg sandwiches and eating his Campbell's pork and beans right out of the can. (That's how I like mine: cold, with a bag of potato chips.) Then there is the joy of reading Jacobs's take on Ava Gardner: "Ava drank Cokes with peanuts in the bottle. Very Southern. Also Ritz crackers. We cooked Southern feasts—the glory that was grease, we called them—fried everything, vegetables obliterated in pork fat, rich cakes made in Crisco, pecan pie. She was one of the rare women who could gorge on everything she wanted and never gain a pound."

Well, so I'm not the only one sitting in fine avant-garde restaurants these days unable to find a single thing listed that I really want to eat. There is plenty to eat, more than enough, in fact, of what I call Discomfort Food. I recall that the author James Dickey offered an opinion I could go along with: "Here is supper!" He wrote of black-eyed peas with ham hock, fried okra, country cornbread, sweet potato pie. "You talk of supping with the gods. You've just done it, for who but a god could have come up with the divine fact of okra?"

Let's add, off the top of my head, turnip or collard greens in bacon grease, grits, hominy, crowder peas in butter sauce, fried chicken/rabbit/squirrel/catfish, fried corn, chicken and dumplings, coconut pie, rice pudding, fried green tomatoes, hot-water corn bread, barbecue, ribs, chitlins, candied yams, watermelon rind pickle—and, yes, let's just not forget about the desserts.

On the Vineyard, which keeps a comforting look of being like America used to be, I'd wander through the farmers' markets and always be taken by the handsome fruit pies, advertised as "homemade." When I'd get them home, they'd seem bland and nothing "like Mother used to make." Actually, my mother didn't make pies; she bought her pies from a neighbor, Mrs. Norris. I recall going home to Texas to visit with my mouth watering, asking my brother James, "Does Mrs. Norris still bake her excellent pies?" He looked sad and said that this local paragon of pastry had died, but before she left he'd discovered her secret. "The real reason you liked her pies? She used a lot of sugar with her fruit. She didn't skimp. Nowadays, people make pies and stupidly cut down on sugar and that's why they're no good."

My brothers were like most Texas men from the "good old days." They could outcook any woman they'd ever met. They loved to expound on how to fry catfish. "It has to be in bacon drippings, and you lightly cover the fish with cornmeal—not that tacky crappy batter that cafés now use to make their orders look bigger. This also applies to frying oysters and shrimp."

Brother Bobby keeps harping on bacon. When I told him Joan Crawford's way with wilted spinach was to "just pour bacon grease over the spinach leaves until they sag," he started to laugh. "I knew that old girl had more talent than she showed in her early porn movie! God bless Joan!"

James always wanted me to alert him when I was coming home so he could fix me a Southern Hunter's Feast: "A little quail cooked inside a dove cooked inside a guinea hen cooked inside a turkey. You have to just watch out for buckshot in the teeth." This sounded like some Greek and Roman feasts I'd read about in M. F. K. Fisher.

But it was too complicated for me. Like Elvis, I want to call down to

Pauline and order the way he did. (He had cooks on duty at Graceland twenty-four hours a day.) How about a fried potato sandwich? Elvis could eat five of these at a sitting—half a pound of bacon, two sliced fried potatoes, sliced onions, white bread, and mustard! No wonder Elvis used a towel for a napkin when he ate at home via Pauline.

Actually, he was fastidious in other ways. He used a knife and fork to eat his peanut butter and banana sandwich.* He was superstitious, too. No New Year's passed in which Elvis failed to eat black-eyed peas and ham hock for good luck. I try always to follow the King's example. (If I can't find black-eyed peas to make from scratch, I open a can. It's better than nothing. What I really prefer is the black-eyed pea and hot chorizo sausage soup made at the Hudson Place Restaurant on Third Avenue and 36th Street. There isn't a Southerner in sight in that café, but it's full of lucky eaters!)

Some things Elvis liked are too much even for me. I have yet to try fried dill pickles, invented in Mississippi. I'm afraid I'll like them. Elvis craved gelatin made with a Shasta drink, canned fruit cocktail mixed with raisins/coconut flakes/mini-marshmallows, bologna cups—remember those from the Great Depression? He loved "The Elvis Special," which he invented himself, consisting of peanut butter and cheese on Wonder Bread, and the famous "Fool's Gold Loaf," a whole slab of Italian bread filled with a pound of bacon, peanut butter, and grape jelly. Then there was the Elvis version of the Fluffernutter—peanut butter, sweet Marshmallow Fluff, bananas, and Wonder Bread, all rolled in crushed peanuts.

Of course, I can't excuse my own food cravings. Elvis could. He had psychological reasons, being born a twin whose sibling died, and having a father who went to jail for forgery when Elvis was only three. (The separation was more or less lasting.) Elvis also became famous too soon, was exploited by Colonel Parker, and never got over losing his dear mother.

Food for Elvis represented Mama and safety. He often compared his African-American cook Pauline to his mother, saying they had looked alike and he admitted he wanted to be cooked for and mothered. His problems about loss and motherhood were reflected in his feelings that as soon as women became mothers they could no longer be sex objects in his eyes.

---

* This recipe opens *The Clinton Presidential Center Cookbook*, sold at the Clinton Library in Little Rock, Arkansas.

(Priscilla discovered this to her dismay as she produced one of the two fabulous-looking female offspring, Lisa Marie and Danielle, who today bear the Elvis name and look like dear old daddy/granddaddy.)

Another legacy from Elvis would also have delighted him. His heirs created Elvis Presley's Memphis restaurant, devoted to some of his special cravings. Why don't they franchise that near me, I wonder?

Well, Elvis might have lived longer if he'd eaten only fish, tofu, and vegetables. But can one call that living? I can't see Elvis getting off food any more than he could get off drugs. Linus had his blanket . . . Proust his madeleine . . . Elvis had his Pauline on duty . . . and I, well, I have the Elvis recipes and menus for unbelievable meals. Sometimes I just go to bed hungry and read this book.

Time magazine once wrote that Elvis moved "as if he'd swallowed a jackhammer." Maybe he tried that, too.

Elvis Fried Potato Sandwich

½ pound bacon
2 small russet potatoes (about 3 ounces each), peeled and sliced
     ¼-inch thick
2 small yellow onions (about 2 ounces each), peeled and thinly sliced
     into rings
Salt and pepper to taste
2 large slices country-style white bread
Mustard to taste

1. Fry the bacon in a heavy cast-iron skillet to desired doneness and drain on paper towels. Heat the bacon drippings over medium heat, add the potatoes and onions and sprinkle with salt and pepper. Fry until the potatoes are browned and crisp on the outside and tender on the inside and the onions are tender, too. Do not turn the potatoes until they are crisp. Taste for seasoning.

2. Grill or broil the bread until it is toasted on one side. Smear the untoasted sides generously with mustard and layer on the bacon and the potatoes and onions on top of one mustard side. Cover with the remaining bread, mustard side down.

YIELD: 1 SANDWICH (I love these "cooking instructions.")

Deep-fried Snickers Bar

In honor of Elvis Presley

1 sheet puff pastry
1 Snickers bar (2.07-ounce size), frozen
Oil for deep-frying
1 scoop favorite ice cream
Hot fudge or caramel sauce
Powdered sugar

1. Unfold the pastry and cut a 5-inch square. Cover and refrigerate the remaining pastry for future use. Unwrap the candy bar and place diagonally across the pastry sheet. Fold one of the long points over the candy bar. Lightly wet the other points with water until gummy. Fold up the short sides of the pastry onto the candy bar and press to seal them, making sure not to leave gaps at the corners. Bring up the remaining side of the pastry and press gently to seal the edges of the covered candy bar. Place in the freezer for 1 hour.

2. In a small, deep saucepan, heat 1½ to 2 inches of oil to 375°F. Carefully slide the prepared candy bar into the oil and fry until it is crisp, golden, and floats. Remove with tongs. Drain briefly on paper towels. Place the bar in a shallow serving bowl. Place the ice cream to one side of it, drizzle the sauce all over, and sprinkle with powdered sugar from a fine sieve.

YIELD: 1 SERVING, which will never be forgotten

Hudson Place New Year's Soup

4 cups chicken stock
1 tablespoon white wine vinegar
2 bay leaves
6 ounces dried black-eyed peas
1 tablespoon virgin olive oil
1 onion, finely diced
2 garlic cloves, finely crushed
1 large carrot, finely chopped
1 stalk celery, finely chopped
1 small red bell pepper, finely chopped

6 ounces (or more to your taste) chorizo (or hot Italian) sausage, oven-
cooked and thinly sliced
Parsley or cilantro
Salt and pepper to taste

1. Mix 4 cups chicken stock with 6 cups water, and add a tablespoon white wine vinegar and the bay leaves.

2. Boil the black-eyed peas in plain water until soft; drain and sauté the peas in the olive oil with the vegetables until brown. Add to the chicken stock and water, bring to a boil, then turn down the heat and simmer for 20 minutes; remove bay leaves. Add the pre-cooked sausage when serving. Sprinkle some chopped parsley or cilantro on top, or salt and pepper if you prefer.

6 SERVINGS

CHAPTER 6

WATERMELON

DAZE

When one has tasted watermelon, he knows what the angels eat.

—MARK TWAIN

IT TOOK YEARS of living in Manhattan, the isle of my Texas dreams, before I realized my favorite food was politically incorrect. Yes, the watermelon—the sheer delight of my childhood—was and perhaps still is almost never the melon of choice for most people. Any other melon is acceptable, but not watermelon.

This reality came as "a shock to my nervous system" as they say below the Mason-Dixon. Recently I was having dinner at one of the city's best private dining rooms in the Park Avenue apartment of the former ambassador to Austria, Henry Grunwald, and his divine spouse, Louise, a friend of mine since her salad days in the Hamptons of Long Island. A platter of casaba, honeydew, and cantaloupe appeared.

"Why don't people here ever serve watermelon?" I asked, disappointedly eyeing the yellow and green slices. No fetching red slashes were visible. The ambassador, a man who was the last of *Time*'s great editors, said calmly, "Because I despise watermelon." The ultragentlemanly Henry even added a subtle "Ugh!" after his statement. I was stunned. My idol Henry didn't like watermelon, didn't crave it the way I did, didn't even allow it at his cosmopolitan table.

Louise, her eyes dancing, started laughing. "Henry is just a hopeless Austrian Mittel-European elitist, Liz. He doesn't like peanut butter either. Or Coca-Cola." I exclaimed that this was downright un-American, and Henry, who had taught himself to speak English by going to the movies on 42nd Street after coming to this country to escape Hitler, indignantly insisted that he *did* like Coca-Cola! But he added, "Watermelon is simply beyond the pale."

As I taxied home full of fabulous home cooking that had been devised for a couple who don't cook and are seldom home, I pondered the watermelon enigma. Why had it taken me so long to see that Yankees (a breed which I fully believed I'd become one of after living in New York City for fifty-four years) find watermelon so non-U? (This was the brilliant Nancy Mitford's way of separating Britain's social sheep from the goats. She invented the designations U vs. non-U.) I realized that down deep I knew that watermelon wasn't held in regard in the East, even though fruit stands were now full of melons, even out of season. I knew this because I always ate my watermelon surreptitiously.

Desperate with craving, I usually bought a piece and ate it when alone. I was tired of being ragged about loving watermelon. Even my office staff, a genial tolerant bunch, always had something to say if I brought in watermelon. They wouldn't think a thing if someone put salt and pepper on cantaloupe, but when I sprinkle salt on watermelon to bring out the flavor, they flinch. And they carp, "Yes, yes, we know—what you buy in the East is not a patch on the big long green watermelons of your childhood."

So there it is. Like the flag of the Confederacy, the watermelon, too, had become politically incorrect. It is a food that by its very proliferation, fecundity, and simplicity casts "lower class" aspersions on those who eat it. Back about the time the Ku Klux Klan was running things down South after the Civil War, the watermelon became an African-American symbol, a nasty joke, the food of former slaves and poor white trash who couldn't find anything better to eat.

So the watermelon is a staple of no-longer-acceptable humor, possibly because Southern food expert John Egerton believes it was brought to these shores by slaves. I suppose that since the end of the Civil War, black people and watermelon avoid juxtaposition for fear of aspersions and unkind humor. (Books about the Frank Sinatra "Rat Pack" tell us that most members of the pack liked to hound and torment their pal Sammy Davis, Jr., by leaving watermelons outside his hotel room door.)

My elegant performer friend Bobby Short collects a kind of Southern kitsch—Aunt Jemima mammies in head scarves, minstrel actors with painted lips, and little black faces framed by a slice of red watermelon. He and I both recall back in the fifties and sixties that the nightclub bar of a Southern charmer named Goldie Hawkins was decorated with watermelon paintings. Some black performers didn't feel comfortable there. Bobby says that some years ago, Hollywood's Beverly Wilshire Hotel had a kind of all-night café-drugstore. There during the heady days of civil rights marches, he saw a well-dressed black man sitting at the counter eating a large watermelon slice with a knife and fork. "It was definitely a political statement in the sixties."

Of course, the magnificent watermelon has a long thirst- and hunger-relieving history, having come from subtropical Africa thousands of years ago. Some pinpoint its origin as the Kalahari Desert. Watermelons were being harvested five thousand years ago in Egypt and can be seen in hieroglyphics. They were placed in burial tombs to nourish the dead in the afterlife. In the tenth century, this fruit spread to China, all of Asia, and was in Central America by 1516. The Moors were taking watermelons along with tiles and algebra all through Europe in the thirteenth century. The American colonies were growing watermelons from seeds in the early 1600s.

The watermelon was always an important fruit because it traveled well in its own oblong or round "container" and it would keep for several weeks. The Japanese improved on this several years ago when they learned how to grow square stackable melons, developed in tempered glass cases. These unique melons are still so special that they sell in Japan for as much as eighty dollars apiece.

The watermelon is a perfect natural, like the egg. The writer David Margolick describes it as "one of those foods like raisins or olive oil or maple syrup that is very nearly perfect as is. Tasty, sweet, crunchy, nutritious and fun—cotton candy without the calories and cavities." Enrico Caruso called it a good fruit. "You eat, you drink, you wash your face."

Watermelon's moist and easy nature has launched many legends
and myths. Daniel Wallace wrote a novel around one of these themes in
his book *The Watermelon King.* Set in Ashland, Alabama, it tells how com-
munities would annually crown a king who is always the town's oldest virgin. He would then wear a carved watermelon rind crown and carry a
watermelon vine scepter. And he must mate before the festival ends. (I am
intrigued by the idea of a small Southern town finding a male virgin to be
the king. In my experience I'm not sure I ever met any males down South
who were virgins!)

But never mind that. Today there are watermelon festivals all over
the nation, including the famous Luling Watermelon Thump in Texas,
the annual Hampton County Festival in South Carolina, the Mize Annual
Hope Festival in Mississippi, and the Vining, Minnesota, Watermelon
Day. There are scores of others.

In an article for *Harper's,* "Fruit As Remembered by the Dead,"
John Berger* writes of watermelons as

the fruit of drought . . . we ate them as you might draw water from a well in an
oasis. They were improbable, they comforted us. . . . Even before they are open,
melons smell of a sweet enclosed water. A heavy enclosing smell with no edges to
it. . . . The taste includes both darkness and sunshine . . . when small and green, a
melon may suggest youth. But quickly the fruit becomes oddly ageless—like a
mother to her child. The blemishes on its skin—and there are always some—are
like moles or birthmarks. They do not imply aging as blemishes do on other fruit.
They simply confirm that this unique melon is and was always itself.

If I could have just one food, I'd select one of those old-fashioned oblong
two-foot Mississippi melons, which were such a dark green, they looked
obsidian on the outside. We would gaze longingly at these dark blobs lying
out in summer fields. We listened as children to many Texas tales of watermelon thieves. Someone left a sign in a raided field reading "One of these
melons is poisoned." When they came back, the farmer had added a sign:
"Now another melon in this patch is poisoned."

My friend Helen O'Hagan, who defined fashion at Saks Fifth Avenue for years, tells me that she and her friends always staked out water-

* Mr. Berger lives in Paris. He gave me permission to use his words about melons if I would
also include the information that he is a pacifist, especially as it pertains to Iraq, which he calls "a
country of drought."

melon patches during the day, then returned at night to thump and select only the best, hold them high, drop them, and sit down on the ground to devour the "hearts" in the dark. "It was my favorite kind of date," says the inadvertent criminal, Ms. O'Hagan. My brothers used to boast manfully about puncturing long melons, and injecting them with rum or gin for wild parties. All this was sacrilege to me.

The watermelon was a star of my 1930s childhood Depression-era entertainment. The radio was new and daring, television hadn't yet been invented, no one had air-conditioning. Moving picture shows were only for rare occasions or Saturday mornings. In the heat of Texas evenings, our big entertainment was to visit one of the burgeoning watermelon "gardens" that sprang up around Fort Worth in the summer.

These were Italianate in nature, al fresco tables under strings of colored lights. The melons were deep in steel vats of so-called iceman's ice — big blocks. A large slice of watermelon cost a nickel and my father would make them cut a new melon before he'd pay. "Are you sure your knife is clean?" he'd ask the server. "That's important." We would veer between the standard reds and the unique yellow-meated melons. If the rind was thick, my father gathered up the remnants to take home for watermelon rind pickle. My grandmother always complained, "A thin rind won't make a good pickle."

Our other big treat was to drive from Fort Worth to nearby Weatherford, the hometown of Mary Martin. There on the courthouse lawn was the town's raison d'être, a plaster-of-paris watermelon. We knew that Mary was now (1938) on Broadway singing risqué songs, but we also knew that once she'd actually been here. We thought of the watermelon as hers. Such outings were big deals to us. We'd go home with sticky juice dribbled down our summer clothes, wearing the "watermelon teeth" Daddy had cut for us from the rind. Of course, we looked grotesque. My mother, who came from a family of educated Mississippi doctors and teachers, would always look at us askance after such excursions with Daddy, chugging along in the old Model A Ford. She would shake her head, letting us know even then that the watermelon had "no class." When we had it at home, I remember her making us undress and get into the bathtub naked to eat. Or we could stay out in the backyard and have the garden hose turned on us after.

Watermelon once saved my life. I was traveling for five weeks in Greece. The all-natural menu of fish, feta, and grape leaves became tiresome. But I did learn the word for watermelon. Wherever we went I said,

"*Karpouzi.*" No one in Greece found this odd, and so I came, more than ever, to consider watermelon the nectar of the gods.

In the summer of 2003, the Hebrew University in Jerusalem claimed it was developing a less-fattening watermelon that would still retain its sweetness. In a "breeding program," Professor Shmuel Wolf had encouraged a melon with more fructose than glucose or sucrose (calorie culprits). This dietetic baby is coming.

Then, both the *Times* and *The Washington Post* offered encouraging updates. The aforesaid David Margolick did an op-ed piece on the deseeding of watermelon. He noted that the venerable watermelon was at least five thousand years old, and "the one with seeds has died of entirely unnatural causes . . . conventional watermelons will not disappear entirely; a few farmers will still grow them, catering to the carriage trade. You will still be able to find them abroad. Perhaps Restoration Hardware will carry them, alongside the likes of Ovaltine and Ipana toothpaste." Margolick deplored a society that wants seedless melons. "Seeds, it seems," he mourned, "are inconvenient . . . what is summer without spitting out watermelon seeds, either on a plate, or on the ground, or at your brother, or an inch farther than anyone else?"

About this time I was heartened by a letter from style maven Billy Norwich. He and a buddy, Patrick McCarthy of the chic *W* magazine, had gone to Biarritz to weekend with the designer Karl Lagerfeld. Billy noted that "the newly slenderized Karl served watermelon after every meal, with fruit and sorbet." He added, "Is this the democratization of chic? The democratization of fruits?"

Then the *Times* brought us a front-page story on the new pint-sized watermelon. Reporter David Barboza said the Syngenta Seeds company is producing what they call PureHeart melons in Arizona that are the size of cantaloupes. In Oxnard, California, the Seminis Vegetable Seeds people are also producing the Bambino, another small melon. These seed producers say their melons are "pricier . . . but are flying off the shelves. . . . This makes it easier in a hectic lifestyle with limited space." (I can only assume that David Margolick and I won't like these "improvements" either.) But it's nice to know people are still into watermelon. In 2003, someone also began painting watermelons as graffiti all over the town of New Rochelle. It rated a news story . . . "Watermelon Terrorists."

The most interesting melon news comes from *The Washington*

Post. They say Asians and Asian Americans top the list of watermelon lovers, according to the National Watermelon Promotion Board's survey. Next come Hispanics, non-Latin whites, and, finally, blacks. They write, "The sound you just heard was yet another racial stereotype going *ker-splat!*" The survey claims two in three Americans bought a watermelon in the last year. They preferred seedless, while college grads bought more than less well educated Americans. I liked their final sentence: "The super-smart also were the most likely to be heavy watermelon consumers."

I had a watermelon experience recently at the Sip-Sip beachfront restaurant on Harbour Island in the Bahamas. This open-air spot overlooks a pink beach where the sand is like pastel talcum powder. Seeing the word *watermelon* on the simple menu, I ordered it. The plate arrived with three manageable triangles of melon, already glittering under a rough scattering of sea salt that sparkled in the sunlight like diamond crystals.

At the bottom rim of the plate lay three round white circles of peppered-and-herbed goat cheese drenched in olive oil, which had run down onto parts of the melon. When I overcame my initial aversion to this "dressed up" melon, it turned out to be interesting and tasty. It was another version of "eating against" the differing sweetness of the melon with the tang of cheese and the slick of oil. What inspired this? Probably Italy's buffalo mozzarella with fresh tomatoes. Or maybe it's a bit like the Savory Watermelon Salad, which we offer you here.

That same evening I had cocktails at the Bahamian house of New York decorator Tom Scheerer. He launched a sudden discussion of one of my favorite things—butter! "Name something that can't be improved or enhanced by a bit of butter?" he asked. His guests finally decided that only the eternal watermelon is exempt and is the most likely answer.

To end—nowadays when I go to the Henry Grunwalds for dinner, they invariably serve me watermelon for dessert. It's their little inside joke. Henry sends me, instead of flowers, enormous green watermelons and I note, with rue, there is no way to cut and keep them in the refrigerator of my modest apartment! But still, I think watermelon is a wonderful idea for dessert. If you can't produce something chocolate, then why not slices of watermelon on a platter with forks, spoons, knives, to anyone's best uses. And pass the salt, please!

Savory Watermelon Salad

One 3½-pound slice of watermelon, rind removed, chopped into
*   1- to 2-inch cubes (approximately 4 cups)*
12 red radishes, washed and thinly sliced
½ pound feta cheese, crumbled
15 mint leaves, finely chopped
3 tablespoons balsamic vinegar
3 tablespoons extra-virgin olive oil

Combine the watermelon and radishes on a serving platter. Top with the feta cheese and mint. Drizzle with balsamic vinegar and olive oil, and serve.

4 SERVINGS

From The Lobster Roll, *by Jodi della Femina and Andrea Terry (Clarkson Potter, 2003)*

Watermelon Granita

½ cup water
5 to 7 tbsp sugar
½ large watermelon (5 lbs of flesh)
Juice and zest of 2 limes

Put water and sugar in saucepan and bring to a low boil. When sugar has dissolved, remove pan from heat. Cut rind off the watermelon, then cut flesh into 2-inch chunks. Puree melon chunks in batches in food processor. Press puree through sieve; discard seeds and fibers. Stir syrup and lime juice and zest into melon liquid. Pour liquid mixture into wide, shallow container. Cover with lid, foil, or plastic wrap and freeze for an hour or two, until it has frozen around edges. Take out container and scrape ice with fork, mixing it from edges into center. Repeat scraping process every half-hour or so until entire mixture has turned into small ice flakes. (At least three times will be necessary.) Serve in attractive glasses or bowls, preferably immediately. You may leave granita in freezer overnight. If you do, let sit for a few minutes to soften, and rake with fork to lighten texture just before serving.

SERVES 4 TO 6

From Granita Magic: 55 Ices for Every Reason and Every Season—Always the Perfect Thing to Serve, *by Nadia Roden (Workman Publishing, 2003)*

CHAPTER 7

WATCH

YOUR

MOUTH!

They dined on mince and slices of quince,
Which they ate with a runcible spoon . . .

—EDWARD LEAR, "THE OWL AND THE PUSSYCAT"

WHEN I CAME to New York I was full of Texas beans and gusto. I
guess I thought this enthusiastic approach was what would pay off
for an ambitious Southwestern girl. I had done very well at the University
of Texas, learned some rudimentary journalism skills, raised my consciousness, and made good grades. I had become a big fish in a little pond
and now I yearned to put myself into the arena of the finer and larger
things in life. But I already knew I wouldn't ever be able to fake it and do
away with my down-home roots. I was a terrible actor.

On the outside I still resembled the characters Annie—Annie Oak-
ley in *Annie Get Your Gun* or Ado Annie in *Oklahoma!*—but a certain part

of my growing up concerned itself with a lot of hopeful pseudo-intellectual wannabe pretension. This was probably engineered by reading *The New Yorker* and *The New York Review of Books*. Whatever was out there, I only knew I wanted more of it, whether it had to do with books, art, films, dance, theater, ballet, international news, even history and the mores of High Society. I was deep into everything that had ever happened in either New York or Hollywood. For me, Texas and Middle America stretched like a great Saul Steinberg desert between the two coasts. I wanted to take my little Annie personality on the road to both oceans, where I felt surely I could combine "doin' what comes natur'lly" with some upper crust. Did I have a presentiment about the two blue coasts of Bush America? No.

My mother had been a kindhearted, good soul. I was wild, spirited, and nothing like my beautiful mother and I wasn't ladylike, no matter how I tried. But I decided to try to be good-hearted. This seemed enough for me to aspire to since I didn't resemble Sarah Elizabeth McCall. I would try to combine just being myself with being good and the world would surely embrace me.

My mother had her problems adjusting to Texas. She had to cope with her feisty, largely self-educated and temperamental husband—my father—and then with my rambunctious brothers and with me trying to act just like them. She also had to contend with all of my father's Smith relatives, his seven siblings, each one as eccentric as he was. She often had in residence one or both of his hardscrabble, religiously fanatic, narrow-minded parents—two people who had married at ages sixteen and twenty-one and hated each other cordially. On top of this, there soon arrived her own downtrodden Mississippi relatives, droves of them, seeking a better life in Texas. And most of them lived with us and on us, off and on.

So though she disliked cooking, meals were always thrust upon her. Feeding people became her major ordeal. While she plugged away at inspiring and nagging her children, correcting their English and making them go to Sunday school, I think table manners came to be the least of her survival worries.

I had been raised on the Golden Rule of doing unto others as you wanted to be done to. But somehow, in the family confusion and competition, I believed that all bets were off at the table. We had no servants, so I knew nothing of being served. Food was set down in big bowls for people to help themselves. Then it was every man, woman, and child for him/her/

itself. The old boardinghouse reach was a given. "Family, hold back" was a Depression slogan for when the preacher came to Sunday dinner and there wasn't quite enough on the table. I knew what it was to fight for my chicken wing or "the Pope's nose" or anything left over. So, lacking active guidance and imitating those round about me, I suppose I substituted eating with positive gusto for my missing manners.

In New York, when I actually entered the so-called higher reaches of the big city (working for the society columnist Cholly Knickerbocker), I saw that I was among the socially disadvantaged. I had already found myself elbowed out of jobs by glamorous debs from Vassar and Smith and now I endeavored to improve myself by watching how others lived, ate, and behaved. But the school of hard knocks doesn't always sand off those raw edges, especially if your friends encourage you not to abandon your "amusing" roughneck self.

I got by on energy, ambition, curiosity, and enthusiasm. I thought this covered my deficiencies. I didn't realize what a failing grade I'd kept getting as I clawed my way to the middle. And it wasn't too long ago that two of my most loving and admirable friends finally told me, within months of each other, that I had the worst table manners they'd ever seen for one in my position.

This hurt my feelings but I knew they were right. I blushed to recall being at lunch in Mrs. Vincent Astor's house, sitting next to her, when I realized I didn't know how to handle the finger bowl issue. These things have pretty much gone out of use, but growing up as I did, I'd never actually encountered a finger bowl. I dabbled my fingers in it, but had no idea I was to move it from its plate and set it aside. The butler was standing helpless, waiting for me to move it for the next course. (Green beans, as I recall.) Finally, Mrs. Astor just reached over and moved it off my plate, continuing to chat all the while. I had no choice then but to go on impersonating the absentminded professor, pretending that the conversation was so riveting that I hadn't noticed what was going on.

Only months later one of my critics sent me a clipping. It advertised children's classes in etiquette and table manners at The Plaza. The accompanying note read: "You should sign up for this." And so I did. It's never too late to try to improve.

The Plaza hotel, which Bob Benton and David Newman selected for their *In & Out Book* of the sixties as something "classic and great," remains at the center of Manhattan's universe. It is just off Fifth Avenue between 58th and 59th streets, although I regret to say that most of New York's foreign-born taxi drivers now haven't a clue where or what it is.

This famous hotel is the one where Cary Grant feuded with room service because they always charged him for two English muffins and sent him only three halves for breakfast. (He demanded and received the fourth half.) . . . It's where the great choreographer/performer Kay Thompson created a rambunctious little girl named Eloise, who still captures our imagination. . . . It is the hotel that was frequented by F. Scott Fitzgerald and the one to which Ernest Hemingway is said to have bequeathed his heart. Bought by Donald Trump in 1988 and sold by him later, it is where much of the headlined news of his split with his wife Ivana took place. . . . It is a landmark. Fairmont Hotels & Resorts insisted that the Plaza will "reinvent tradition for the twenty-first century." And we can only hope that the Israeli developer who bought it from them in August 2004 for $675 million will carry on the Plaza's traditions.

Now the hotel has a "Young Plaza Ambassadors" program for children from six to eighteen, offering them cooking classes, dancing with the Radio City Music Hall Rockettes, and "A Complete Etiquette Workshop," taught by Ms. Sara Gorfinkle, a professor from the New School. These lessons at lunch in the State Suite are offered monthly at a cost of $35 a session. The one I signed up for was "Basic Dining Skills," taught by Ms. Lyudmila Bloch, who directs the Young Ambassadors program. (The Plaza decided to overlook the fact that I was more than eighteen!)

The parents who attended my Saturday class, mostly young good-looking mothers, sat in little gold chairs in an anteroom. There were a few fathers. "We children" sat thirty strong at a U-shaped table before a big cardboard printout of a perfect table setting. Across from this was a clock set with hands at 4:20.

Standing inside our U, Ms. Bloch asked questions, took answers, asked more questions, and showed us where we were going wrong as waiters served a roll and butter, a bowl of chicken with vegetable soup, a plate of sliced chicken with french fried potatoes, and finally a dessert of ice cream with cake. It was all quite delicious. And I had to restrain myself from gobbling it up and wiping my mouth with my sleeve. (As you know, Napoleon supposedly had buttons sewn onto his soldiers' uniform cuffs just to stop such a process.)

I didn't have a parent, so I made my longtime friend Suzanne Goodson go with me. She is from Tennessee, so I figured she had as much to learn as I did. But then, Suzanne was once wed to a demanding rich man, so maybe not. The children and Ms. Bloch were quite tolerant of us, the only two adults in class as we went up the road to learned etiquette.

In the opening moments, Ms. Bloch, who had an attractive European accent, told us about the rules of civility. She said that when men were busy settling America during the Revolution that separated us from British table manners, it was the women who had to enforce etiquette. This nice redheaded lady noted that we need etiquette to be "respectable" and "to behave well." She asked, "What is the worst thing we can do to others? I want volunteers," she said. A pert little eight-year-old piped up, "We can hurt someone's feelings!"

I don't know if this was the answer Ms. Bloch expected or not, but she nodded. She had the charming way of telling the children, "Ask me," when she meant to say "tell me." She went on to say we could think of etiquette as a cake. Because I was busy observing the children instead of learning, I lost track of why this is so. But I did note that one-third of the children were African-American. All of them looked charming and self-possessed, but most attractive to me were three little boys sitting on Suzanne's left. They'd arrived late and breathless. Their little boy clothes were simply sensational.

Ms. Bloch was discussing as urgent the fact that we must learn how to do introductions. (1) Stand; never remain seated during an introduction. (2) Smile. (3) Make eye contact. (4) Say your name. I missed number 5, which was no doubt crucial.

I had been distracted by a little girl who said her name was Sojourner and I wondered if she'd been named for the famous abolitionist and suffragist Sojourner Truth. This little Sojourner was feisty and smart. She could always answer whatever Ms. Bloch threw out and at the relief break later, she came and demanded to be photographed with me. I said, "Okay, but first show how you do an introduction and what you learned today."

She was already standing. She smiled. She made eye contact. She said, "Oh, I am Sojourner So-and-so. This is my mother. [She paused.] Miss Smith — my mother. Mother, this is Miss Smith."

We had already had a tussle with Ms. Bloch over procedure. Initially, she told us to say the name of the most important person being introduced first. As in "Mr. Mayor, this is my mother." I pointed out that she'd actually said, "Mother, this is the Mayor. Mr. Mayor, my mother." Ms. Bloch said I was right but she seemed puzzled. I offered, "Perhaps one's mother is more important to one than a mere mayor." It's a thought.

Later, we ate the lunch offered by The Plaza as we learned. "Elbows off the table. Sit straight up. Never, ever, use your napkin for anything but wiping your mouth carefully. Keep your table napkins low on your lap. Eat from the outside in; that is, the outside cutlery is used first and you discard it. Keep your bread and butter on the bread plate, not on your dinner plate. . . . Cut one piece of meat at a time and eat it. . . . Never lick your fingers. But it's okay in fast-food restaurants to eat with your fingers. (I thought, It better be!). . . . Don't load your fork. . . . Salads are always on the left, glasses on the right. If you want more food, wait until it's offered. . . . Chew and swallow before answering people. . . . Do not correct your parents or siblings at the table. (I must confess I wondered, Why not?)

"What is the very first thing we do at table?" asked Ms. Bloch. A little blond beauty stuck up her hand and answered, "We say grace." I think this surprised Ms. Bloch, who had meant we should unfold our napkins onto our laps. But she acquiesced to a spiritual nicety. "Yes, and then?"

Then the napkin. Ms. Bloch used this time to advise that we must never "explain" why we are leaving the table if we do. "Simply get up and say, 'Excuse me,' and fold your napkin across the back of the chair so the waiter will know you plan to return."

This was a new one on me. I'd never seen a napkin folded on the back of a chair. But what did I know? One child then asked, "But what if the napkin is greasy and the chair is upholstered and very nice, like these chairs? It might make a stain." Ms. Bloch didn't seem exactly nonplussed by this, but I felt she wasn't used to such smart kids asking about the vagaries of life. She recovered nicely, "In that case, fold the napkin and leave it on the left side of your plate." I whispered to Suzanne, "That's what I thought one did in the first place." Suzanne dug me in the ribs to be quiet. We almost lost track then of advice that we must pass food to the right at table because the guest of honor sits to the right of the host. Ms. Bloch said this was a courteous acknowledgment of the guest of honor.

When soup was served, I tried to impress Suzanne with poetry:

"Like little ships gone out to sea, I push my spoon away from me." I was thrilled that I knew one thing before it was actually announced. But Suzanne was riveted by Ms. Bloch's advice never to turn the spoon over and leave it in the empty bowl when the soup is gone. Merely leave it on the side of the bowl. I said, "Well, I learned something right there." Suzanne hissed, "Shut up!"

I didn't think "Shut up!" was good manners, but then I've known Suzanne a long time. As Ms. Bloch advised us to keep our elbows close to our sides while eating, sixty-odd elbows clanged into thirty little waistlines, as well as our larger ones. We were learning like crazy—never pass salt and pepper separately; they always go as a pair.

Just as Ms. Bloch told us not to blow on our soup but just wait until it cools, I sneezed in a prelude to my often irritating "eating allergy." This was horribly embarrassing because all the children chorused "God bless you." I begged their pardon, which was more than I had done at Mrs. Astor's lunch over the finger bowl crisis when the charming Patsy Preston looked at me as if I had slapped the queen.

Now we were served a terrific piece of grilled chicken with some yummy french fries. This caused a frisson of pleasure among the children—and between Suzanne and Liz as well. You'd think none of us had ever seen a french fry before; I guess we just weren't expecting them at The Plaza. Suddenly, my favorite Ralph Lauren–attired little boy on the left said he'd dropped his napkin. Ms. Bloch was delighted. "Leave it right there. Just ask for another." She pointed to the artificial clock, saying that 10 and 4 are the two places you must rest your knives and forks between courses. She added that we should sit between courses with hands in our laps.

While waiting, I fear I zoned out on Ms. Bloch. I was thinking of my godson, five and a half, comparing him to these children. I feared he might have trouble in this class because of his limited menu palate— peanut butter, jelly, macaroni and cheese, hamburgers, occasional pizzas, occasional force feedings of peas, broccoli, and fruit, but very little interest in ever trying anything new. The chief ingredient at every meal, even breakfast—ketchup. Then there was the period of not eating his "friends." He wouldn't eat Goldfish, Gummy Bears, or Animal Crackers. "Friends don't eat friends!" he said. When I mentioned lamb chops, he screamed, "Who would eat a lamb?" I shuddered thinking what might happen when he discovered where hamburger came from.

Now Ms. Bloch had our attention again. She was discussing cutting up food and transferring the fork to take it to the mouth. So I spoke up and asked whether she thought it was important to show the children how differently Europeans handle a knife and fork. And I popped off that surely she meant to explain to them that Europeans consider it okay to leave your hands balanced on the table at the wrist, which American etiquette says is a no-no. Ms. Bloch paused, but then said, yes, it was important to show the two ways of handling cutlery. "Both are acceptable!" Beside me, Suzanne now gritted her teeth. "You're going to get us kicked out of here." But I preened even though I knew I'd never be the teacher's pet.

My Favorite Boy now lost his napkin for a second time; then a third. This was delightful, as it stopped our proceedings cold. Time flew anyway and we came to dessert, where the waiters brought us each a fresh knife and fork. "We will explain eating ice cream with a fork," said Ms. Bloch while the children murmured in unrest. What appeared was a scoop of ice cream with some kind of cake under it. The intricate manner of eating this dish with two hands was then explained.

Then we took a break. "Return for the tea lesson," advised Ms. Bloch. But Suzanne and I were full to bursting and also full of the virtues of etiquette. We went over to Bergdorf Goodman to try to spend some money instead. "Did you notice, she never said anything about eating with your mouth closed?" I said to Suzanne as we walked by the Plaza fountain. "Hmmm, well, I guess the whole lesson then was lost on you," she said sarcastically.

Suzanne never hurts my feelings because she is like family and I couldn't always get along with them either. Now I just keep imagining my Favorite Boy at home, asking for a new napkin every time he drops one. As one of the rather distracted mothers remarked to me when we were leaving after the etiquette lesson: "Honestly, I'm usually running back and forth between the kitchen and the dining room. All I'm really hoping for is to encourage them to eat. To please eat something. They're so picky. I usually just don't have much time for all the niceties."

It reminded me of my own dear mother. And then if mother fails, "they" can go to etiquette class—just like I did.

CHAPTER 8

FRIED!

IN THE BACKSEAT

OF CARS

WELL, there's a title for you. Several of the happiest experiences I've ever had involve eating and cars. It's just like sex and cars—so very all-American.

The Martha's Vineyard town of Oak Bluffs always has a slight carnival atmosphere, but every little village on the Vineyard has its own complexities and peculiarities. Oak Bluffs is famous for its Chautauqua-like, mostly African-American neighborhood of soulful singing and Protestant gospel gathering together. This happens in a neighborhood clutch of crowded-together, brightly painted patchwork Victorian wooden houses situated just a step from the picturesque harbor. As you drive through this community, you see that the owners must have bought up all the pink, lavender, baby blue, mauve, purple, red, and maroon paint for miles around. There is nothing like this unique community anyplace else I've ever been. Oak Bluffs is Diane Sawyer's favorite place to show to visitors who come to this Massachusetts resort island.

On the particular outing I remember, we are a sedan full of adults and kids—the adults waiting in Oak Bluffs at the oldest indoor merry-go-round in the United States. A clutch of screaming children is inside trying to catch the brass ring. My visitors, the San Antonio–born Ernie Pomerantz and Marie Brenner suddenly spy a sign across the street: "Voted Three Years in a Row—the Best Fried Clams on the Vineyard."

Marie, a distinguished reporter for *Vanity Fair*, says: "When you see a sign like that where it emphasizes 'three years in a row,' then I think one should take a chance on truth in advertising." (As Marie is always dieting, very health conscious, and apt to actually try to make "healthy" Tex-Mex food if you don't stop her, I was surprised that she was interested.) But because Marie has blown the whistle on the tobacco companies, reminded us of anti-Semitism in France, and done many other award-winning feats of journalism, I always take her advice.

So we buy two cardboard containers of fried clam strips and a couple of Diet Cokes, and as soon as we collect our kids, we pile back into the car and are rolling toward the more upscale and citified Edgartown. We stuff our faces as we speed along enjoying what we now term the "first course" before an intended al fresco lunch at the more conventionally New Englandish Edgartown wharf. Our only problem with the first course is sharing tartar sauce between the front and back seats and getting our traveling packets to yield up their salt in the damp atmosphere.

I have to admit we didn't go right on to lunch when we got to Edgartown. First we decided to take the world's shortest ferry ride across to Chappaquiddick, but we were bitterly disappointed in it as a famous U.S. tourist attraction because they seem to have tidied up the Teddy Kennedy scene and just about erased the infamous Dyke Bridge.

Martha's Vineyard is typical of many northeastern shore locales catering to summer tourists and depending on tiny shacks and jump-up cafés serving fried seafood, grilled hamburgers, hot dogs, and the like. Many such also now feature lobster rolls. These are the unfranchised true fast-food spots so dear to American hearts, though in truth while their food is "fast," it's usually good because it's cooked to order. Such places range from real true restaurants such as the great Cook's on Bailey's Island near Brunswick, Maine, to shacks up and down the Atlantic seaboard. You find them, too, along the Texas and Louisiana coasts. And everywhere else land meets sea.

In Vineyard Haven, for instance, John's Fish House serves fish and chips that would make any Britisher gasp with pleasure. The gifted movie and stage director Mike Nichols took me to his favorite place on the

Martha's Vineyard road out of the little fishing village of Menemsha.* This tiny culinary miracle is cleverly called The Bite. It has already been immortalized in all of crime expert Linda Fairstein's detective novels. And it is here that Linda brings the forensic-minded best-selling author Patricia Cornwell for lunch. Patricia sits down at The Bite to eat with people she doesn't know. Personally, I've never had the luxury of sitting down at The Bite. Handed steaming, crackling onion rings, clams, shrimp, and the works, one dances about looking in vain for a seat. Usually you dine at The Bite standing, eating off the hood of an automobile.†

In the elegant Litchfield County section of Connecticut where the elite live in their magnificent gardened hills and dales, usually without benefit of water views, there's a more *raffinée* version of The Bite. It is called Clamp's, on Route 202 at Sawyer Hill Road, near New Preston.

Spending a weekend near Washington, Connecticut, with my adman-painter pal Peter Rogers, I was treated to one glorious servant-served, chef-created private dinner party after another. But nothing came up to the crunchy goodness of an outdoor lunch at Clamp's.

The lunch was "hosted" by realtors Seymour Surnow and Dennis Kyte and they brought along their own thermos of Bloody Marys. We were joined by Casey Ribicoff, the merry widow of the distinguished Connecticut senator Abe Ribicoff. Also sitting with us were the Shubert Theatre king and queen, Gerald and Patricia Schoenfeld. I suppose if Oscar and Annette de la Renta and Nancy and Henry Kissinger hadn't been in the Dominican Republic, they'd have been there with us in all our fluttering paper-napkined splendor as we crunched, ate off each other's paper plates, and exclaimed!

Another Connecticut boiling-oil fast-fry place I love is in Old Saybrook on the former Boston Post Road. Johnny Ad's is its own phenomenon, always crammed and crowded with people standing, waiting to have their numbers called. There they sell the T-shirts and aprons that read "Frankly, Scallop, I Don't Give a Clam!"

What is the true secret of the best of these ubiquitous fry palaces with coleslaw and pickles and the works to go? They all do frequent changes of

---

* Here you will most likely see among the little sailboats the enormous motor yacht of the tycoon Maurice Tempelsman, the man who enlivened Jacqueline Kennedy's life after she divorced Aristotle Onassis.

† As this book went to press, Linda introduced me to the sisters who own and run The Bite, Karen and Jackie Flynn. They emerge from their sizzling fried chicken wings, clams, oysters, zucchini, onion rings, and "chips" to shake hands with their own lovely floured fingers. And for once, *I got to sit down.*

their frying oil! If you don't like commercially fried food, probably the seller is reusing his oil. But let's talk about frying things at the end of this chapter. For now, let me say I don't think you can beat this type of open-air informal eating experience so long as you don't do it too often. And keep your Tums and Maalox handy. Look, all kinds of things are labeled these days as being un-American and unpatriotic; I'm afraid that always happens when there's a war or a terrorist threat "on." But what I think is truly un-American is for one to be so vain, narcissistic, and intent on health, thinness, and living forever that you never stoop to eating this kind of all-American food.

Keep on Frying

Deep-frying requires care. But it produces sensational results. I am going to give you the highlights, but I suggest you buy Rick Rodgers's book, *Fried & True*. It is full of the very best tips for how to deep fry, with excellent recipes for unusual fryable items, *www.chroniclebooks.com*. Or write 85 Second Street, San Francisco, CA 94105.

SUGGESTIONS FROM RICK:

A Dutch oven, 5-quart capacity, enameled cast-iron. It would hold 3 pounds of melted vegetable shortening. An uncoated cast-iron pot would also serve. Electric skillets must be at least 3 inches deep, but they just aren't deep enough for big pieces. They are fine, as are small deep fryers, for bite-size food.

You don't want to crowd food that is frying. Pieces should not touch one another. So cook in batches if possible.

Have an oven heated nearby to 150°–200°F for keeping food warm.

Electric deep fryers are excellent because they come with special filters that soak up odors. They should have nonstick interiors.

A deep-fry thermometer with a clip to hang it on the pot is helpful. Don't let it touch the bottom of the pot. Never leave it in the frying fat longer than necessary.

Your fry temp should be about 350°F.

When draining deep-fried foods, put them on a rack of some kind. They'll stay crisper longer.

The sooner you serve fried food the better.

Regarding oil, do yourself a favor and change it after every outing. You'll get better results and hang the cost. Vegetable shortening is better than vegetable oil. Lard is the most flavorful and gives an old-fashioned taste. But the trick is to buy professional-grade deep-fry oil, easy to find at wholesale grocers and price clubs. Get five quarts. It has a long shelf life.

Olive oil is good for cooking Italian dishes as it adds flavor to the food. But it is expensive. A moderate-priced golden olive oil is okay for frying. Corn and safflower oils are too heavy for deep-frying. The best oil for frying is the more expensive grapeseed oil.

Again let me recommend Rick's book with its beautiful photos by Christopher Hirsheimer. It will tell you how to make Saratoga potato chips, double-cooked fried chicken, General Tso's chicken with its three dips in hot oil, okra fritters, artichoke sandwiches, Roman artichokes, and deep-fried Cornish game hens! (Rick says these are much less difficult and dangerous to make than frying whole turkeys! Nevertheless, I am giving you the way to deep-fry a turkey, as done by the late tycoon and ambassador to the Court of St. James, Walter Annenberg, and also by that Hollywood hostess nonpareil Betsy Bloomingdale.)

And yes, in this fry chapter we mention lobster rolls because they are ubiquitous these days on every shore. Buy the Jodi della Femina–Andrea Terry book, *The Lobster Roll,* or just take their advice as to how to make a perfect one at home. Buy fresh lobster meat; it's much simpler than cooking and cleaning lobsters.

Lobster Rolls

2 pounds lobster meat, chopped into chunks
1 cup chopped celery (3 to 4 stalks) (Don't let the celery
water down your salad. Wrap it chopped in a dry
clean towel and put in the fridge for 20 minutes.
The towel will absorb the moisture.)
¾ to 1 cup Hellmann's mayonnaise
½ teaspoon salt
¼ teaspoon freshly ground black pepper
6 tablespoons (¾ stick) unsalted soft butter
6 hot dog buns

Mix together everything except the butter and buns. Butter the buns lightly and toast in a skillet for 2 minutes per side. Stuff those rolls. And that's all, folks.

YIELD: 6 SANDWICHES

Deep-fried Turkey

The thing to wear if you use this recipe is a black apron from the *Casual Living* catalog with the slogan REAL MEN FRY TURKEYS!

8 ounces bottled Italian dressing
4 tablespoons Worcestershire sauce
4 ounces (half of an 8-ounce jar) Dijon mustard
6 to 7 tablespoons Konrikos or other Creole seasoning
10- to 12-pound fresh turkey (no larger than 12 pounds)
Vegetable oil

1. Make a marinade with the Italian dressing, Worcestershire sauce, mustard, and 4 to 5 tablespoons of the seasoning, and liquefy in a food processor.

2. Inject the liquefied marinade into the turkey breast and all through the turkey, using a syringe with a large-mouth needle. Sprinkle and rub the remaining 2 tablespoons of the Creole seasoning all over the turkey.

3. Heat the vegetable oil (enough to cover the entire turkey) to 350°F, checking the temperature with a deep-fry thermometer.

4. Deep-fry the turkey 2½ minutes per pound. The skin will turn quite dark.

5. Let stand at room temperature for 30 minutes, then slice thinly and serve.

from Entertaining with Betsy Bloomingdale

I WANT TO SALUTE HERE the Ocean Grill restaurant on Columbus Avenue on New York City's Upper West Side. In their fried clams–shrimp–scallop platters they include the thinnest of thin slices of fried lemon rounds. Delicious!

CHAPTER 9

HIGH

TIMES,

HIGH TEA

Back in the mid-fifties I was participating in Manhattan life as an "outsider" who was "in." Working for the *Palm Beach Social Pictorial* as a columnist of happenings in New York and also acting as a ghostwriter for the Cholly Knickerbocker society column, I was forever encountering situations that were totally foreign to me, above my station, out of my ken. And I did have one experience that still causes me to shake my head in wonder.

Now there are, of course, social legends just as there are film, theater, literature, and art legends. One of these was the late Mrs. Joseph Verner Reed of Hobe Sound, born a Pryor, wed to a descendant of distinguished early American revolutionary forebears.

Mrs. Reed was the most fearsome of all the WASPy doyennes. But when I met her, I didn't know that she was the standard-bearer who kept the "wrong" people out of Hobe Sound where her family owned the Jupiter Island Club. Her word was law and her law was self-created. *Town & Country* magazine once opined that one might visit Hobe Sound, but if you didn't belong to the Reed-owned Jupiter Island Club, you couldn't play golf; you couldn't even get your hair done on Hobe Sound.

The fact that Mrs. Reed would one day be listed and described in a book called *The Best Families* never occurred to me in those early days. I knew a lot of show biz trivia—that Clark Gable had false teeth, that Esther Williams had been a very big moneymaker for MGM—but I didn't know that just one hundred miles from Palm Beach, Mrs. Reed had beat out the Greek god Janus, the keeper of the doors to heaven, by keeping the un-wanted * out of Hobe Sound.

Her friend Betty Sherrill insists to this day that Mrs. Reed was not anti-Semitic. But Mrs. Reed had the dreaded black sweater rule. It all began when someone visited the Sound and was rude to the African-American help. So Mrs. Reed sent her old retainer, Robuck, with the person's bill and also a black sweater. Her note read: "You are going to need this up north!"

At the time of my Permelia Reed experience, I didn't know any of this. I had never heard of Mrs. Reed. My friend, theater press agent Shirley Herz, called one day asking me to freelance on the side and help her with a charity event. Shirley was Broadway to the core and said she needed me as a go-between with another world. I would be the person in touch with this formidable dowager, Mrs. Reed, who was her new and momentary employer and who would convey her wishes entirely through me while Shirley's hardworking office minions performed the scut work for a money-raiser. (Frankly, I forget what the beneficiary of this charity was; suffice it to say that it was something worthy and important.) But Shirley said she just knew that Mrs. Reed, who she had barely met, would be taken by my "genial, gentle personality." She wisecracked, "And, no doubt, by your genial gentle GENTILE personality, too!"

I met Mrs. Reed and found her unimpressive. It never occurred to me to feel terrorized by her. She reminded me a bit of those spare, sparse, land-rich, hard-driven women of West Texas. She put on no airs. She wore a simple skirt, a pastel cashmere sweater set, and good pearls. She asked me to her East 61st Street apartment, which was tastefully but not lavishly furnished. What impressed me the most was the tea she had set up so we

---

* "Unwanted," meaning perhaps the wrong look, race, creed, political affiliation, manners, or someone who was simply below the salt, NOC—not our crowd, not comme il faut, or just someone who didn't make the cut.

could get acquainted. Even in those earlier days, "tea" wasn't a big-ticket item with most of the upscale people I met. I noticed rich * people gave you a stiff drink and some crudities, but most of these souls didn't bother with tea. Mrs. Reed's offering, via a Mary Petty–attired silent maid, was just too England-for-empire for words. I recall Mrs. Reed's sandwiches—little bite-size cucumbers on buttered white bread. Thin brown bread boasting thinner slivers of ham or chicken. No crusts, please, we're hoping to be British. Beautifully deviled eggs with just a touch of curry powder. Scones (I had never seen a scone before, but I'd certainly heard of them). Clotted cream—the works. And the tea. I love tea and Mrs. Reed's was delicious. I managed not to drop anything. I waited until she left the room to cram a few sandwiches in my mouth. I mostly left the scones alone because I knew I'd be covered in crumbs. I patted my lips with a beautiful tiny Porthault napkin. I didn't ask for a doggie bag, though I was tempted by some of the fragile cookies and little cakes.

Mrs. Reed conducted our business in a very upfront manner. She didn't ask me personal questions, nor did she comment on my Texas accent as so many did. She asked a few polite curriculum vitae questions, such as where had I gone to school. A state university? Well, that was just fine. Mainly, we were there together to do a job. She had straightforward, simple requests for the charity event and relayed them in a down-to-earth manner. Invitations, an orchestra, caterers, and so forth were needed. I took down her instructions, asked what I hoped were clarifying, insightful questions, and we sorted things out. As I was leaving after our second meeting, where once again we'd had a marvelous tea and chatted a bit about the weather, she said to me. "Liz, please don't continue to call me 'Mrs. Reed.' My name is Permelia and I want you to call me that."

I didn't want to. Mrs. Reed was considerably my senior and I felt it wasn't fitting. And she was the boss. I also didn't know if I could remember "Permelia," a rather odd name. But I said, "Thank you, Mrs. Reed—I mean, Permelia." Then I said good-bye and went about the real business of seeing that a bunch of energetic and ambitious Jewish girls under the command of Shirley Herz could carry out wishes expressed to Texas trash by Hobe Sound royalty!

For the rest of the short time I worked with Mrs. Reed, I tried to re-

---

* Never say "wealthy"; it's non-U, as I had learned reading Nancy Mitford.

member to call her Permelia. And when I failed, she'd firmly correct me as she ladled out the tea. "Mrs. Reed is the wife of Ambassador Joseph Verner Reed, but you and I are friends working on an important charity project. So to you, I must always be Permelia."

Years passed. I became ridiculously cognizant about so-called society, not ambitious for myself (that was impossible), but I liked knowing who was who and what was what and where the bodies were buried and who had been who in the recent historical past. I began to hobnob with the admirable Cleveland Amory, who had written *Who Killed Society?* I got myself on speaking terms with Angelo Zuccotti, the great maître d' of El Morocco. The *Social Register* people put me on their mailing list and I received the new edition annually for my library.

So I finally came to realize who Mrs. Reed really was—one of the true queens, the most formidable guardian of a private club on that exclusive and particular barrier island off the Florida coast. People practically committed suicide because she wouldn't give them the time of day. Her thumbs-down could send you straight to the social guillotine. Her yes was a ticket to heaven. Everything about Mrs. Reed seemed to be first-rate. Her son, Sam, was wed to the amazing Annette of the Engelhard diamond and platinum family. (One future day, Annette would divorce Sam to marry my friend, designer Oscar de la Renta, and she'd be heading up New York society. Mrs. Vincent Astor herself would pronounce that Annette was her chosen heir, but Mrs. de la Renta wasn't—and isn't—interested in a life of servitude to what is left of the crème de la crème. She prefers her divine children, gardening, and reading and talking with her host of pals.)

At any rate, I went merrily down the years running into Mrs. Reed now and again. She'd always greet me like a long-lost friend. "Liz did some wonderful work with me in the past," she'd say fondly introducing me, bearing down on the "with" instead of saying "for."

I would say, "Aw, shucks, Permelia, it was the Shirley Herz office." But she ignored that.

"You call Mrs. Joseph Verner Reed by her first name?" asked the social butterfly Jerome Zipkin, incredulous! "How do *you* know Permelia Reed?" asked my socialite friend John Galliher who knew every well-dressed international name. Others would just be openmouthed, wondering. "Yes, I call her Permelia," I'd say. "I've known her quite a while. She insists on it . . . It's no big deal."

The world that wanted Mrs. Reed's approval looked on aghast. It was years before I understood that Mrs. Reed's treatment of me was simply her version of noblesse oblige. After all, I hadn't made any waves. I had expressed pleasure and gratification for the lovely high teas she'd laid out for me. I'd been respectful, shy, and I'd done good work with (for) her. And then I never tried to go to Hobe Sound. That would probably have been a different matter.

Permelia's High Tea

Well, I have already described her tea, but I would never have asked Mrs. Reed how her help made scones. I'm sure, however, that the following, adapted from *The Duchess of Devonshire's Chatsworth Cookery Book*, published by Frances Lincoln, will be right up to snuff. And we can be fairly sure that had the duchess wanted to go to Hobe Sound, Mrs. Reed would not have sent her a black sweater.

Scones

8 ounces self-rising flour
½ teaspoon baking powder
Pinch of salt
2 ounces butter
1 tablespoon sugar
2 ounces golden raisins or sultanas, as the English call them, optional
1 egg, beaten
½ cup milk, plus extra

1. Preheat the oven to 425°F and line or grease a baking tray.

2. Sift the flour, baking powder, and salt together. Rub in the butter with your fingertips until the mixture resembles fine breadcrumbs. Stir in the sugar and sultanas, if desired. Beat the egg and milk together, pour into the crumble, and mix to a soft dough.

3. Roll out the dough to a thickness of ¾ inch on a lightly floured surface. Using a pastry cutter or the rim of a glass, stamp out 2-inch circles, rerolling the trimmings to use all the dough. Lift the scones onto the prepared tray, brush the tops with milk, and bake for 15 to 20 minutes, until they are well risen and golden.

4. Serve the scones warm with butter and strawberry jam, or let them cool and fill them with thick, fresh cream and jam.

12 TO 15 SCONES

HIGH TEA IS BRITISH, of course, and evidently got its name not from the high and mighty, but from working-class people sitting on high stools or standing at counters, trying to ward off hunger pangs before dinner. Traditionally, then, as they took their tea, they ate leftover meats in sandwiches.

But others say high tea was introduced by Anna, the seventh Duchess of Bedford, in the early 1800s, as a means of filling the gap between early lunch and late dinner. Possibly the best book on the entire business is *Taking Tea at the Savoy*, which offers dazzling recipes for everything from honey and ham biscuits to roast beef in horseradish sauce to passion fruit and chocolate shortcake. (You can order this little Anton Edelmann gem from Pavilion Books, the Chrysalis Bldg., Bramley Road, London, W10 65P, or via Amazon.com.) The serving of tea with trimmings evolved into a more snobby and upscale deal, what some call "the Queen of Alternative Events," and first-rate hotels the world over still make a stab at presenting it with scones, crumpets, biscuits, toast, Cornish pasties,* Welsh rarebit, Scotch woodcock, cucumber or ham or chicken sandwiches, custards, fruit tarts, cream puffs, various cakes and pastries, plus the 20 million daily cups of tea it takes to fill out the ritual each late afternoon.

In the U.S. many business types have begun meeting over tea as an alternative to cocktails before the workday ends. And some people get together at teatime just because it's "different" and unusual. After all, Thomas De Quincey called it "the flavored beverage of the intellectual."

---

* Not sweets, but tiny meat pies. These are not actually to be confused with the glittery costume bits of the same name, covering the nipples of striptease artists. I don't know why, but "pasties" remind me of Billy Rose's Casa Mañana, which opened in Fort Worth, Texas, back in 1936. It boasted Sally Rand's Nude Ranch and no kids were allowed into a compound where all-but-naked beauties twirled guns from holsters artfully placed over their private parts. They also had on cowboy hats, boots, and bandanas around their neck under which their breasts were visible. It was downright raunchy for the times and for Texas. One tourist accidentally was allowed to enter with a babe-in-arms who suddenly piped up, "Look, Mommy, they've got their dinners showing!" The crowd broke for the exit en masse. Okay, so that wasn't about tea pasties. Sue me!

Tea makes people seem "civilized." I'd say 4:00 P.M. is the operative time to have tea. Use whatever china amuses you and the good silver and cloth napkins. Believe me, if you invite someone to come to have tea, high or low, they probably will never forget you.

The singer Carly Simon has made tea into a big habit at her permanent home on Martha's Vineyard. She says of tea, "It is the perfect choice for an afternoon social event. Tea is civility at its least threatening . . . to make a good tea, there has to be an infusion process. You must let the leaf open and brew in the hottest of water." *

Mrs. William S. (Babe) Paley used to make a big deal out of high tea because everything about food diverted and amused her famous husband, the head of CBS. She had a giant silver tea service with a big hot silver kettle atop Sterno to hold roiling water. The best of imported Hu-Kwa black tea † was used, one heaped teaspoon per person. It was, naturally, loose tea, and if you use that, you need silver tea infuser balls or a strainer of some kind. But I figure in these terrorist times you can keep a selection of tea flavors and simply let people choose from the types in tissue with a string. (Let's don't go too crazy and grand here.)

Because I have used the scones recipe from the duchess, who was one of the famous Mitford sisters (Deborah), I might as well tell you she called them "receipts." And her book on the manner in which her family has provided food over the years for hundreds of tourists and visitors at the stately home Chatsworth is among the treasures to be found wherever women admit they don't like to cook. The duchess herself stopped cooking during World War II and never took it up again. When she was asked to write her book, someone said, "That's rich. It's like a blind woman driving down the M1 highway." So I have a soft spot for the duchess.

Her book brims with nostalgia for childhood goodies—fresh fruit and vegetables in season . . . eggs from hens you've raised yourself . . . stock made from scratch . . . her mother's Scotch collops ("of all the receipts in this book, this is probably the easiest and quickest") . . .

---

* Carly's charm is resident in a book by her business partner Tamara Weiss, who has put together the best, most informal cookbook of its kind anywhere. You can buy *Potluck at Midnight Farm* at the Midnight Farm store in Vineyard Haven, Massachusetts. Or order from Clarkson Potter publishers or from Amazon.com.

† Used by the Rockefellers, Philadelphia bluebloods, et al. Available at William Poll, 1051 Lexington Avenue, New York, NY 10021, 212-288-0501, and also from its importer, Mark T. Wendell Tea Company, 50 Beharrel Street, P.O. Box 1312, West Concord, MA 01742, 978-369-3709.

caramelized chicory . . . Devonshire cream fresh from the milking . . . her mother's brown bread . . . Cheddar cheese and curried cheese biscuits . . . lemon drizzle cake . . . chocolate fudge pudding . . . and the famous Malva Pudding of Dutch South Africa, a super-nursery treat for a winter's day.

You may never prepare many of the Chatsworth recipes, say, Leek and Stilton Soup, Vichyssoise of Cucumber, Lady Gage's Smoked Haddock à la Crème, Salmon Piccatas with Sorrel Sauce, Stir-fried Guinea Fowl in Garlic and Whisky with Stir-fried Vegetables, Deviled Pheasant, Oxtail Daube with Parsnip Puree, etc., etc., but you will have one hell of a good time reading this delightful book. And here's something that the duchess seems to really recommend.

Scotch Collops

3 ounces butter
½ pound beef fillet, freshly ground
2 tablespoons all-purpose flour
½ cup beef stock or water
3 slices bread
Flaked sea salt
Freshly ground black pepper
1 tablespoon chopped parsley

Melt the butter in a large pan over moderate heat, tip in the ground meat, and stir until browned. Add the flour, mixing it well to soak up all the juices. Cook for 3 to 4 minutes and then add the stock or water. Season and cook for another 5 minutes. Meanwhile, toast the bread, cut off the crusts, and cut into ¼-inch dice. Transfer the collops onto a hot dish, surrounded with snippets of toast, sprinkle with salt, pepper, and chopped parsley, and serve piping hot.

Hey, that was quick and easy. Thank you, Duchess.

2 TO 3 SERVINGS

Malva Pudding

This was brought back by Diana and Pamela Mitford from a visit to South Africa. The duchess says, "I remember their enthusiasm for this, a sort of super-nursery pudding." Making this dessert with a gang of kids is sheer magic. The pudding bubbles like a mad science project and changes consistency before your eyes.

> 13 ounces all-purpose flour
> 3 teaspoons bicarbonate of soda [baking soda]
> 1 ounce salt
> 1¼ pounds caster sugar *
> 3 eggs
> 3 tablespoons apricot jam
> 2¼ cups milk
> 3 tablespoons butter
> 3 teaspoons white wine vinegar

> FOR THE SAUCE
> 9 ounces double cream
> 9 ounces milk
> 1¼ pounds caster sugar
> 9 ounces hot water
> 9 ounces butter

1. Preheat the oven to 375°F.

2. Sift the flour, bicarbonate of soda, and salt together. Beat the sugar and eggs together until light and fluffy. Then beat in the apricot jam followed by the milk. Melt the butter and vinegar together and add to the mixture. Gently fold in the flour and pour into a well-buttered pie dish. Bake in the oven for 1½ hours.

3. Toward the end of the cooking time, bring all the sauce ingredients to a boil in a deep pan. When you take the pudding out of the oven, pierce it all over with a skewer and ladle over a few tablespoons of the sauce. Allow this to soak in before serving and hand out the remaining sauce separately.

6 SERVINGS

---

* Not as fine as confectioners' sugar, but superfine, with grains small enough to go through a sugar "caster" or "sprinkler."

CHAPTER 10

"OF ALL THE

GIN JOINTS IN ALL

THE WORLD . . ."

I F M A N H A T T A N —like the famous movie *Casablanca*—has a Rick's, where everyone goes, it must be Elaine's on Second Avenue between 88th and 89th streets. Many characters have shown off, many dramas have taken place, many deals have been dealt there. It has attracted Jacqueline Kennedy Onassis and Woody Allen and Michael Caine and Gloria Steinem. West Coast VIPs always make a beeline for Elaine's. Hundreds of writers consider it theirs.

The owner of this unpretentious spot is a big-hearted closet intellectual, a sexy charmer and a red-hot plump and powerful mama, who isn't a pushover and who is, indeed, a hard taskmaster for phonies and fakes. Elaine Kaufman has put her stamp on New York City café life in a long-running utterly focused career and there is no one else even vaguely like her. If she is your friend, you hardly need other friends. If you misbehave around her, she could throw your ass right out into the street. But I'd say she's too soft-hearted.

She started her salon-saloon-café back in 1963 way up in the low-rent district. The Second Avenue address was never chic, smart, or easy. But it became a mecca for visiting movie types, sports figures, tycoons, Broadway hot shots, wannabes of all types and writers of all stripes—both those on the best-seller lists and those still eating at Elaine's on the cuff (one of her failings).

If I want to run into Tom Wolfe, Norman Mailer, Bill Styron, Lewis Lapham, James Brady, Gay Talese, Carl Bernstein, Steve Dunleavy, Dan Greenberg, A. E. Hotchner, Nora Ephron, Jay McInerney, Nick Pileggi, Frederic Morton, Erica Jong, Pete Hamill, Jimmy Breslin, Mary Higgins Clark, Dan Jenkins, Bud Shrake, David Halberstam, Larry L. King, Kurt Vonnegut, Bruce Jay Friedman, Michael and Alice Arlen, Herb Sargent, I go to Elaine's. And in the past I went there for "the lates": Tommy Thompson, Willie Morris, Peter Stone, Noel Behn, Mario Puzo, Joseph Heller, Peter Maas, George Plimpton, Terry Southern, Truman Capote—you name them. Elaine throws away the reason for her special regard for these giants. She says all that the men among them want to talk about is "baseball, money, and pussy." (Why, that reminds me of the men in the Lone Star State where I grew up!)

About the only queen this city has really ever had is the Statue of Liberty. But if it had to crown a live one, I expect the diadem would go to Elaine Kaufman, the woman with the curly smile. Her café is the natural heir to Bleek's Artists & Writers Saloon of the twenties, thirties, and forties, where the *Herald Tribune* gang hung out, the Algonquin Round Table with its hard-drinking twenties-era literary lights, or the clubby "21," the speakeasy that went legit after Prohibition ended. Elaine is a legend to rank with John Perona of El Morocco, Sherman Billingsley of the Stork Club, Tim Costello, Toots Shor, or Danny Levezzo of P. J. Clarke's. Her contemporary, Joe Allen, who has his own famed saloon-cafés—Joe Allen's and Orso on both coasts and in Europe—notes that Elaine never went the franchise and expansion route. She remained faithful to her one address and her big dream.

In 2003, Elaine was made a Living Landmark by the New York Landmarks Conservancy. While others showed off with songs, poetry, and self-aggrandizing remarks, she made a typical Elaine acceptance speech. "Thank you. I accept this for the late George Plimpton." (The Landmarks people have honored many rich and famous New Yorkers, but I believe Elaine was the first one ever to have three sets of friends buy tables in her honor! Then George Steinbrenner topped her; his pals bought eight tables.)

I knew Elaine back in the early fifties when she was a waitress at Portofino in Greenwich Village. She was then in love with the café owner, Alfredo Viazzi, a charming Italian guy who was soon outstripped when Elaine left him and became a restaurant legend on her own. We have had many adventures since 1953, or was it 1954?

I have enjoyed a lot of caviar and smoked salmon from Elaine Kaufman over the years, but it was a Tex-Mex evening that almost did us both in. Elaine and I once left the confines of New York to go to Fort Worth, Texas, where our pal, former TCU beauty queen June Jenkins, was opening a restaurant in the newly refurbished by Sid Bass downtown of what is fondly called "Cowtown." (June is wed to the writer Dan Jenkins, who I call "the chicken-fried steak novelist." All of his wonderfully funny books contain prominent mentions of this Texas delicacy. His wife's restaurant at the time also featured C.F.S. but leavened in some hot Tex-Mex.)

This was a great night for me. I had been born only a few miles from downtown Fort Worth. We were near the very legendary place, a bank, where as a child I was often told the story of a robber who came in with a bottle of nitroglycerin and threatened the bank with extinction. (I think he had Listerine in the bottle, but, anyway, it was a big childhood deal!)

June Jenkins's restaurant, near this very spot, opened with a highfalutin bang because of the backing of the Midaslike Bass family. At the opening, I ignored social climbing and simply ate everything in sight. Tacos, hot jalapeños, enchiladas, lashings of chicken-fried steak and gravy, buckets of margaritas. Elaine was more reserved. She was fascinated that the café had no desserts — only massive frozen Dove bars. As the TV genius Chuck Barris says, "A balanced diet is a Dove bar in each hand!" Anyway, Elaine's resolve crumbled. She ate two — or three.

The next day we were two very sick puppies. "Bad idea to come here," moaned Elaine. I said, agreeing with the first Tom Wolfe, "You can't go home again!" June Jenkins didn't take our implied slight on her café easily, but she's a forgiving person, having lived with a football and golf fanatic for a lifetime. She put us on the plane to New York, so we went back to Manhattan on our shields, so to speak. Then we made a pact. We'll only go back to Texas to rodeo, not to eat!

Now, there are several things they always say about Elaine, who is still going strong after forty years in the business. She plays favorites. Yes, she does. What's the point of creating your own fiefdom from scratch and working it every day of your life and then not giving your friends and "family" a break? Then there are the people who denigrate Elaine's food. I think they are dead wrong. I would never order a veal chop anywhere else in New York—except maybe at Le Cirque. I want to quote two things about the food at Elaine's from A. E. Hotchner's delightful book *Everyone Comes to Elaine's*. Here is cookbook maven Barbara Kafka:

Well, what about the food? It isn't fancy but if one stays within the strong points of the kitchen, it is possible to have a really excellent meal . . . The steaks are good, particularly the T-bone, the spinach is impeccably clean—creamed, leaf or with garlic and oil. A first-rate Caesar salad or roasted peppers with fresh anchovies can start a meal, or try an artichoke with all the work done—the leaves arranged like petals of a flower and the cleaned heart at the center. On the right night of the week there is an ample chicken-vegetable soup with large tender chunks. There is a good Oreo cheesecake and these are just a few of my favorites. There are splendid wines.

Barbara also recommends rock Cornish game hens stuffed with rice.

Then Helen Gurley Brown, who toys with a lettuce leaf now and then but loves food in spite of her dieting, says emphatically, "I never had a bad meal at Elaine's. Spinach and bacon salad, calamari, clams, and linguini are my special friends."

Humorist P. J. O'Rourke makes a recognizable plea: "I'm safe from the food. Every other place in New York seems to be specializing in some horribly gustatory fad! Elaine never serves me a fish that isn't dead yet, or a Bolivian guinea pig terrine."

I liked something else I read about Elaine's and a special of mashed potatoes made with *greibenes*—onions fried in chicken fat. When someone ordered this, the chef said, "*Greibenes* have killed more Jews than the Holocaust." That may be true but I'm ordering it the next time I go up to Elaine's where everybody goes.*

* In his terrific book *City Room*, *New York Times*man Arthur Gelb more aptly describes *greibenes* as "bits of fried chicken skin that tasted like bacon. Nutritionally appalling and absolutely delicious. Hungry kids playing in the Depression-era streets of the Bronx on Friday nights shouting up to tenement windows for snacks. Indulgent mothers would toss down brown paper bags containing sandwiches, usually an onion roll cut in half, lathered in chicken fat with chopped liver and something called greibenes."

Many interesting things have happened to me at Elaine's. The first time I ever tried to go there I was with a duPont heiress. But Elaine's then partner, Don, wouldn't let us in—they didn't care for unescorted ladies. (Funny, a lot of guys think they are the best kind.) I never told this to Elaine, however, and I kept going back because soon another friend of mine, Elaine Stritch, was tending bar because she liked to be around booze and theater life was slow in the summer. (Ms. Kaufman attracts show biz types. She once had the giant Jackie Gleason do his bartender number behind her bar.)

It was in Elaine's that I asked best-selling author Sally Jenkins (she cowrote Lance Armstrong's book) how it felt to introduce her famous father, Dan, at events where he was being honored. "Liz, I'll tell you. Now I know how Frank Sinatra, Jr., always felt!"

It was in Elaine's, just as the documentary *Pumping Iron* was being released, that I met the young Austrian bodybuilder Arnold Schwarzenegger. Those were less PC times and I asked if I could sit on his lap and feel his muscles. He naturally said yes and now every time I see the new governor of California, I find myself inappropriately feeling him up. (It's a trade-off.) It just seems silly to stop now.

It was in Elaine's where one night I sat between two VIMs (very important musicians) at dinner and both were blessedly much older than I. So it was great fun to be flirted with and treated like a kid by Skitch Henderson and Isaac Stern. That sort of thing doesn't happen to me often.

It was in Elaine's that the only extant photo of all the functioning gossip columnists of New York City was taken. I am standing by the sainted late Neal Travis of the *New York Post*. They had tried to get us all together for weeks, but it took the magic words—"be at Elaine's"—to make it happen.

It was also in Elaine's in the early days when one of my favorite anecdotes happened. The governor of New York, Nelson Rockefeller, met informally with a clutch of disgruntled labor leaders to hear their grievances. The meeting lasted several hours in an afternoon when the café was deserted. There was much grumbling from the union bosses about low wages and take-home pay. Rockefeller, the scion of one of America's richest families, sat there nodding sagaciously.

As the meeting ended, the union guys left. The governor stood to have his coat placed over his shoulders. He seemed rueful. Finally, he said to an aide: "Take-home pay! They kept talking about take-home pay. What the hell is that?!"

And, oh yes, lest I forget. I love the waiters at Elaine's. Most of them have been there for years and they are great.

Now, for tourists, wannabes, and celebrity chasers—you *can* get into Elaine's. Just make a reservation. But don't expect to sit at the best tables along the wall. (Actually, all of the tables are perfectly fine.) Behave, don't table hop, don't annoy the lions. Leave a good tip. Don't ask for hamburger—Elaine doesn't like it. She doesn't serve them.

She's the queen and that's that!

The Elvis Potato Sandwich

James Wojcik

Only columnist ever to appear in
three major newspapers in a single
metropolitan area. With the monkeys
in the first Le Cirque.
Photo courtesy of Matthew Rolston

Al Hirschfeld's 1989 caricature of Liz.

*©Al Hirschfeld/Margo Feiden Galleries Ltd.,
New York. www.alhirschfeld.com*

My darling mother in 1910,
age 18, eating one of those fabulous
Mississippi watermelons.
Liz Smith Private Collection

Married to Captain Ed Beeman,
living in Galveston, Texas, as
World War II ended. I read
The Joy of Cooking every day and for
dinner each night I made—reservations!
Liz Smith Private Collection

High cotton and hair in 1962. The urbane Jim Mitchell, Palm Beach's Mary Sanford, a smitten Liz, and stockbroker Jack Monroe occupying the Aristotle Onassis booth at the glamorous El Morocco.
Photo by Jerome Zerbe / Liz Smith Private Collection

Gloria Safier, my dad, café owner Romeo Salta, me, and my mother (circa 1963), New York City. Sloan said after this lunch, "I et and I et and I didn't know a thing I et until I et an olive!" quoting Will Rogers.
Liz Smith Private Collection

Sixties big hair! Liz with El Morocco flack Jim Mitchell in the
Latin Quarter nightspot. We're in a Jet Set group: Laddie and Mary Sanford,
Robert Lion Gardiner, Dolores Littman. Some had never crossed
Fifth Avenue to the West Side before.
Liz Smith Private Collection

Lunching with the boss, the
columnist Cholly Knickerbocker
(Igor Cassini) at the old Colony
restaurant in 1961 before he was
indicted by Attorney General Bobby
Kennedy and we all lost our jobs.
*Impact Photos / Liz Smith
Private Collection*

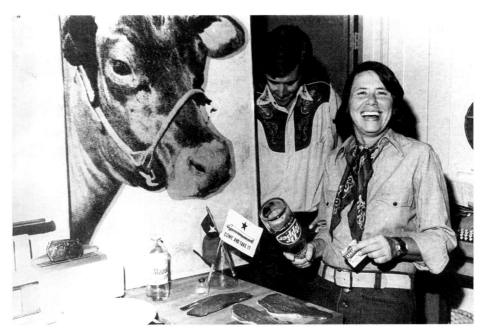

Texans Joe Armstrong of Abilene and Liz Smith of Fort Worth beat round steak with a
Dr Pepper bottle and pose with fake flour trying to be authentic.
Photo courtesy of Allen Frame

Here's the group shot that made the restaurant Michael's on West 55th Street
famous in 2003. Billy Crystal, Ann Richards, Liz, Joe Armstrong, Marsha Garces, Bill
Clinton, Robin Williams, Diane Sawyer. As we posed for a "private" photo, a *New York
Post* paparazzo whizzed in uninvited and snapped us. We went world-wide. And so did
Michael's. I'll never forget that day. President Clinton ordered extra French fries.
It was before he had to stop.
Photo courtesy of Patrick McMullan

Actor Dirk Bogarde fancies himself in this shot, and I fancied him too. He called me "Sardine" for all the wrong reasons.
Tom Murray

Iris Love and Liz in a Houston charity cook-out. The chicken-fried steak was fine, but Iris's biscuits became concrete. Lynn Wyatt and Jimmy Galanos won the prize.
Photo by Mary Ellen Gordon / Liz Smith Private Collection

Red hot chili peppers! And a great big wooly dog. What more can one desire?
Liz Smith Private Collection

Eating al fresco with my love Lee Bailey, actress Elaine Stritch, and Peter Brown, who repped the Beatles. We made the food ourselves, but God made the Sagg Pond Hamptons scenery.
Susan Wood / Time Life Pictures / Getty Images

Lee Bailey and I kick off his franchised store for food, wine,
and gracious living in Saks Fifth Avenue. He went on to cookbook glory,
a forerunner of Martha Stewart.
Photo by Camera 1 / Liz Smith Private Collection

Frying chicken with Lee Bailey in his Sagg Pond house where we fed and fueled
a generation of talented actors, artists, writers, directors, and other food mavens
in the sixties, seventies, and eighties.
Liz Smith Private Collection

The god of food critics: Craig Claiborne of *The New York Times*. I appreciated him more as a kind, charming human being. This is at a Warner LeRoy party shortly before Craig left us for that big restaurant in the sky.
Liz Smith Private Collection

A rare sit-down at The Bite in Martha's Vineyard. Mystery writer Linda Fairstein is across from her lawyer hubby Justin Feldman. Next to Linda: Henry and Louise Grunwald—stars in these pages; Liz with a chicken wing; Emily Baird, my intern; Billy Norwich of *Vogue* in his hat; former Governor Ann Richards.
Liz Smith Private Collection

Back to my red pepper roots at the famed La Posta on the border between Mexico, Texas, and New Mexico. Here's where they shot Billy the Kid.

Liz Smith Private Collection

Dan Rather and his chicken-fried steak "co-anchor" as we hunkered down before a dinner of corn bread, collards, black-eyed peas, and cream gravy.

Marc Bryan-Brown www.bryan-brown.com

Judging a barbecue sponsored by Jack Daniels in Lynchburg, Tennessee, with *Daily News* food critic Suzanne Hamlin. We ate lots of smokey ribs, drank lots of J.D., and went to a pig race. What else?

Liz Smith Private Collection

The one-time governor of Texas, Ann Richards, fries at the Elizabeth Peabody dinner.
Here they discuss how high one can go on the hog.
Liz Smith Private Collection

Two old-timers, Liz and Elaine Kaufman, the famed restaurant queen.
We met in Greenwich Village, late fifties, and went on to
eating glory ever after.
Joe Vericker / PhotoBureau

Two of my favorite things—coconut cake! This was dessert for our Peabody C.F.S.
dinner. Sony chief Sir Howard Stringer looks on amazed; he was born in Wales!

Liz Smith Private Collection

Beating a chicken-fried steak with a hammer in the kitchen of fashion's Arnold Scaasi.
At the same time I seem to be advertising the Italian hotspot, San Domenico,
which certainly has better food.

Liz Smith Private Collection

Here's how they serve watermelon on Harbor Island in the Bahamas—with feta cheese, olive oil, and herbs. As they say, watermelon is one thing that can't be "improved" by adding butter.
Liz Smith Private Collection

Blowing out a candle at the Four Seasons Grill where their idea of fun is cotton candy after you've paid $9.50 for a baked potato. I asked owner Julian how much a potato cost. He said, "Depends on who you are. We charge Peter Peterson more!"
Liz Smith Private Collection

Here I am front and center with Richard Nixon in the Robert Cenedella painting that hung in the second Le Cirque. I never sat down to eat with Richard Nixon in my life, but he did sometimes send me a bottle of wine.
"Le Cirque, the First Generation" 1996, mural by Robert Cenedella
Image courtesy of RCenedella Gallery www.RCenedellaGallery.com

Liz engineers the Bloomberg food critic Peter Elliott and Le Cirque king Sirio Maccioni into producing the latter's memoir about cooking and masterminding one's way to the top.
Liz Smith Private Collection

I flew in this Malcolm Forbes "Fabergé" balloon over the fields of Normandy. Later I would breakfast with Malcolm and some of his "egg" collection over an extraordinary meet in New York.
Photo courtesy of Paul Beirne

Liz and Iris, the odd couple—one from the modern world, the other from antiquity—en route to fun and games on the Malcolm Forbes yacht *The Highlander*, photographed by Jill Krementz.
Photograph © by Jill Krementz – used courtesy of the photographer

Having fun on the conga line with Sam Donaldson and Diane Sawyer.
New Yorkers love to party! Washingtonians too.
James F. Clements

Hosts-creators of my eightieth birthday party at Le Cirque. Ellen Levine, Ann Richards
behind her, my wax self from Madame Tussauds, Joan Ganz Cooney,
Gayfryd Steinberg, Suzanne Goodson, Louise Grunwald, Cynthia McFadden,
and down front Barbara Walters, Joni Evans, Marie Brenner.
They pulled out all the stops.
Photo courtesy of Mary Hilliard

Julia Roberts and Mary E. Smith—two Southern girls with very big mouths who like to eat. We're at the famed 100 Wooster Street café where Julianna Margulies was our waitress, believe it or not!

Liz Smith Private Collection

You caught me!

Photo courtesy of Tom Gates

CHAPTER 11

THE MYSTIQUE

OF C.F.S.,

ITS OWN SELF

ALREADY IN THESE PAGES I have mentioned chicken-fried steak, but now let us consider this "delicacy" as an entity deserving its own chapter.

This once Depression-era poverty meat is no longer so cheap, and no longer depressed. Once, at twenty-five cents a pound, it was still a much-to-be desired meal, but few in the slipping middle and underclass of the thirties had a whole quarter of a dollar to spend on the main course.

The upper classes, of course, never dreamed of C.F.S. and today, in yearning-to-be-fat-free America, many are squeamish at the very mention of such a thing. The true elite has never even heard of C.F.S., or considered it. If they did, they would simply make it an extension of Bubba's lower-class, somewhat distasteful legend. Poor Bubba, he has had a lot to answer for since Bill Clinton took over his name.

Well, all I can say is these C.F.S. detractors don't know what they are missing. Running down the back alley from 1811 Jennings Street in Fort Worth as a kid, with a rare and valuable quarter clutched in my fist, is one of my happy childhood memories. That very coin meant "shake and shavey" * for dinner.

When I had more or less inspected in passing all the neighboring garbage cans, greeted the friendly next-door cats and dogs, and found a few discarded bottles and other artifacts dropped by Fort Worth's busy garbage men, I'd wend my way to the Liversey Grocery Store, where they made me show them the quarter before they would cut the meat, which usually had a big round bull's-eye bone full of marrow in one corner. Then, after I'd paid (for they wouldn't let the Sloan Smith family charge there any longer because we owed them a fortune), they'd let me select a big free dill pickle from an enormous vat of brine. Holding on to the pickle and the brown paper–wrapped "pound of round," I'd skip home. It was steak, cut thin to fry, red meat after all.

My mother, the non-chef who hated to cook, could put together a C.F.S. dinner in about fifteen minutes. She found it easy. (She would think this entire chapter was just ridiculous.) She'd throw the meat onto the butcher-block counter and beat it to one-quarter inch, bashing it with a plain old hammer, or a wooden mallet, the dull backside of a big knife, or, as my Georgia friend Chuck Howard used to say, "Mama would just hit it with a Coke bottle!" This was "tenderizing" at its best. She'd then cut it into small four-inch pieces, although some people preferred it as a large flounder-sized entity. Some C.F.S. is served, in the words of expert Gary Cartwright, "as big as a hubcap and twice as chewy" in roadside diners and cafés. But not in the Smith house.

The bacon grease that accumulated in a coffee can on the stove was already bubbling in a black cast-iron skillet that my grandfather, Jerome Bonaparte Smith, had made by hand in his foundry. The tenderized meat was dredged through beaten eggs and then through flour and thrown into the frying pan with a thin layer of bacon grease. Now, most people believe meat should be salted only after cooking to keep the juices in. But Mother just wanted to get the whole thing over with. She salted and peppered before or during the frying.

When the meat was crispy and golden brown it was turned over, cooked on the other side, and later transferred to a flat brown paper grocery bag to drain. (Some people use paper towels, but back during the De-

* "Steak and gravy" in the Texas palaver of Lone Star State cooking. We'd never heard of Cockney rhyming slang, but we were doing it.

pression we'd never seen a paper towel and, in any case, I think the brown paper bag is superior.) The excess skillet grease was poured back into the stove's coffee can and a measured bowl of milk was added to the drippings, after first lashing the frypan with flour to make gravy. Lots of salt and pepper needed here to taste. (Not enough simple seasoning is why most cream gravies fail the taste test. And a lot of recipes call for kosher salt, minced or salted garlic, minced fresh sage, Tabasco, and so on. Well, you can, but I think it's just a lot of bother.) *

Constant stirring over a reduced heat produces "cream gravy," which many of the elite effete refer to as "wallpaper paste." But if you can get it off the heat at the exact right moment—taste bud nirvana! (Today there are modern improvements! It'll all be easier if you use Wondra flour, which shakes out looking like sugar and does not clot and bunch up. You also need a good whisk for stirring, and don't forget tasting and last-minute salt and pepper.)

We always sat down in a kind of rapture for C.F.S. It always made the "trimmings"—biscuits, corn bread, mashed potatoes, black-eyed peas, collard greens, or anything else—taste better. (Especially the vinegary taste of the greens eaten "against" the hot meat and gravy.)

Okay. Okay. I know C.F.S. is what used to be characterized as "corny" . . . today, some would say "gross." Dieters wouldn't eat C.F.S. on a bet, although Ann Richards, the former governor of Texas, says she fed C.F.S. "fingers" and "strips" to her five children throughout their childhood. "It was their favorite and not one of my kids grew up to be fat." Still, slim women are repelled by the very thought. Vegans are revolted. In the lexicon of the Upper Crust, this crusty, tasty main dish is very L.C.

So, I ask you, why is C.F.S. always such a big success, making an unexpected hit out of any dinner featuring it? I have seldom had a C.F.S. failure in spite of Mary Ann Madden (the onetime super-gameswoman of *New York* magazine) pronouncing that it "tasted like burnt nurse's uniforms." And my late agent Gloria Safier, a cook given to an overuse of dill in all her cooking, termed it "burnt shoe leather." (Both of these women had a lot of problems with their love lives.)

Robb Walsh of the *Houston Press* has written a treatise defending

---

* Satan is said to hate salt. Yet Malcolm de Chazal wrote, "Salt is the policeman of taste." So let that be a lesson to you. Plutarch called it "the finest condiment of all." Salt is a symbol of hospitality the world over. We need it.

the honor of C.F.S., which you can grab off the Internet under houston press.com (Dining, Café, January 11, 2001). In it Robb questions the origins of C.F.S, saying the *Lone Star Book of Records* has the dish being invented in 1911 by Jimmy Don Perkins of Lamesa. He thinks this is just a myth. And we certainly were eating C.F.S. in Cowtown, Fort Worth, Texas, after the stock market crash of 1929 and on through the Depression and World War II. The Pig Stand drive-ins of San Antonio were serving it in sandwiches in the forties. *Gourmet* columnists Jane and Michael Stern speculated in their *Eat Your Way Across America* that C.F.S. was invented in the Hill Country of Texas by immigrant Germans. Robb writes, "My own guess is that the dish existed as beefsteak Wiener schnitzel long before its catchy Southern name was coined." Texas pioneers, familiar with tough meat, learned early on to tenderize and bread their beef into C.F.S. The late great foodist James Beard says C.F.S. was patterned after the Austrian Wiener schnitzel and the Italian veal Milanese, popular in the U.S. for 150 years. So perhaps C.F.S. was forged on immigrant European favorites in a manner to make tough cuts of meat tender—just as Robb Walsh says Texans also, for practical reasons, invented the hamburger, chili con carne, and barbecued brisket. This is the "cook tough meat until it gives up" philosophy.

As this book went to press, there were 153,000 listings of C.F.S. recipes on Google, which gives you an idea of how popular our dish really is. We can't begin to give all the various approaches to C.F.S., but here's an odd one that is famous all over the South and wherever they still worship the King.

Elvis's Ugly Steak

1 pound sirloin steak, pounded with a meat tenderizer
1 garlic clove, cut in half
½ teaspoon salt
½ teaspoon pepper
½ teaspoon onion powder
½ cup all-purpose flour
Mazola or other vegetable oil

Rub the steak with the garlic halves, and discard the garlic. Sprinkle the salt, pepper, and onion powder on the steak. Dredge both sides of the steak in the flour.

Heat the oil in an iron skillet, using enough to cover the steak. At 350°F, throw in the steak. Fry until brown, then turn and brown on the other side. Remove to a warm platter. For Elvis, cut the steak into tiny bite-size pieces.*

THE ELVIS IDEA of using sirloin instead of round steak has been epitomized today by Houston's Rio Ranch Steakhouse, where they dip a sirloin in buttermilk batter and fry it. I call this gilding the lily to no purpose. The great C.F.S. novelist, Dan Jenkins, who knows where every good C.F.S. is made in all of Texas, including his childhood favorite café, Massey's, in Fort Worth, insists it should be eaten when drinking beer. Dan deplores the Rio Ranch trend, which has led to chicken-fried venison, chicken-fried rib eyes, chicken-fried tuna steaks, and, he says, the worst of all, flattened pieces of chicken-fried chicken! "Let fried chicken be fried chicken," says Dan. "But let chicken-fried steak stand on its own."

But back to my question as to why the C.F.S. dinner almost never fails. One of my best C.F.S. dinners offered up in the recent past happened in the posh East River apartment of the socially acceptable Elizabeth Taylor Peabody. Her building once was home to Greta Garbo and her own apartment had been a pied-à-terre for comme il faut doyenne Mrs. John Barry Ryan. Ms. Peabody herself, a scion of the famous Peabodys of Massachusetts and a niece of the late Marietta Tree, is a social revolutionary working mostly pro bono in psychiatric medicine at Memorial Sloan-Kettering Cancer Center. She spends her days setting up support groups for cancer patients and counseling the ailing and dying.

So she likes to put a little fun in her life after hours. When I introduced her to the Honorable Ann Richards, Elizabeth was determined to show Ann off to her boss, Dr. Jimmie Holland, one of the legends in psychiatric medicine and a native Texan herself. Together, we decided on a C.F.S. dinner. This amused Ann, who by then, I think, had had more than her fill of barbecue, fried things, and hot sauce. Ann watches her weight, exercises like a demon, leads the fight against osteoporosis, and has developed an elevated international taste for French and Italian cooking and

---

* There's no heresy here; this was Elvis's own baby pleasure. But it seems to me anyone who can afford sirloin might enjoy it for its own self and have some C.F.S. later. Almost all C.F.S. is made from cheaper cuts of meat, usually round steak, in big curly pieces that sometimes cover the plate. And many cooks insist you must dredge the steak through a shallow dish of beaten eggs first, before you flour it. (That's what I do.)

fish. But being a great sport, true to her Waco, Texas, roots, she agreed to go along with our idea.

We bought all the side dishes for the dinner from The Pink Tea Cup in Greenwich Village—black-eyed peas, collards, corn-okra-tomato mix, beaten biscuits, corn bread sticks. To be on the safe side, Elizabeth also ordered some expensive smoked salmon for the nonexperimental and vats of ice cream and a big white coconut cake for dessert. (Why not add insult to injury?)

A grand gang attended—the Welsh-born Sir Howard Stringer, who now runs Sony in America . . . those transplanted New Yorkers Dan and Jean Rather, who are C.F.S. connoisseurs from the wilds of mid-Texas (Dan may still hoke up his conversation with Texas flavor, but one of the greatest lunches I've ever had was one of unpronounceable French delicacies served to us by Daniel Boulud in midtown Manhattan, with Dan doing the ordering and selecting) . . . the best-dressed Joan Ganz Cooney of *Sesame Street* fame and her Nebraska-born Greek husband, Pete Peterson of Blackstone finance. (His father ran a Greek diner and wanted Pete to come into the diner business, so Pete knows "down-home" ethnic cooking. Still, he'd never heard of C.F.S.) There was also the Carlisle clothes company's Tom Fallon, once aide to fashion's Bill Blass and a fashionista himself, to the max. You just know that Tom, who used to dine in Paris with Hubert de Givenchy, had no C.F.S. wisdom to fall back on. And we had Helen O'Hagan, a devotee of Southern cooking, but the refined kind. Even Helen perhaps felt she wasn't quite ready for C.F.S. We added also the suave international Henry Grunwalds of Park Avenue, Southampton, Vienna, and Martha's Vineyard. There was also portrait painter Peter Rogers of Mississippi; he knew enough to be enthusiastic. The others, in fact, most of the guests, were equally ignorant of high fry and we led them like lambs to the slaughter.

Dr. Jimmie was in the kitchen early on attacking the steak from the butcher. Governor Ann arrived and fell to with a will. Though she was the guest of honor, Ann no longer drinks, so she avoided our margarita cocktail hour and joined Jimmie. Together they fried up the thin-cut round steak, put it in a warming oven, then made the gravy and stunned the glitterati with a dinner that defied convention. (So we bought a lot of the dinner ready-made, so what? We are working women; we can't do everything from scratch. And The Pink Tea Cup put everything in big metal rectangular containers that just slid into the oven to warm.)

Grease spots soon appeared on Ms. Peabody's Porthault linen. Her grandmother's famous china had never boasted so many delicious C.F.S. crumbs, nor been wiped so clean by crumbling biscuits and swipes of corn bread. "I think I'll try a second helping of that, that, er, schnitzel," said Ambassador Grunwald. Even the most delicate palates tried the "horrible" cream gravy. We offered Pepcid tablets with dessert.

Dan and Jean Rather said we had hit the C.F.S. bull's-eye. Ms. Peabody said she had never given such a successful dinner. People talked about it for days and still bring it up to her as she is passing the usual caviar and delicate poached fish and ravishingly acceptable salads at her ordinary dinner parties. "Say, when are you doing the C.F.S. dinner again?" ask her famished guests.

Barbara Walters once grew so weary of hearing me talk about C.F.S. that when she gave one of her own famous catered dinners in my honor, she asked Glorious Food for one of its usual uppity menus. But during the cocktail hour, she had them serve only hors d'oeuvres of C.F.S. with toothpicks to dip into a slimmed-down cream gravy sauce. It was a big hit. This reminded me of the nouveau riche Dallas matron when asked what she intended to serve at her coming party. "Oh," she said breezily, "just fried meat and whiskey."

I have had a couple of misses with my C.F.S. Once the Texas tornado, Joe Armstrong, who works in New York media but never lets us forget his Abilene roots, asked me to pose with him cooking C.F.S. in a photo for a little newspaper called the *New York Texan*. Although the fashion paper *W* had just pronounced that C.F.S. was "out" and white grapes and white wine were "in," we forged ahead. I wore Neiman Marcus western denim and Joe was dressed in his vintage Roy Rogers yoked shirt. When I got to his bachelor apartment with most of the ingredients—Wesson oil, steak, and a big Pepsi bottle to beat it with, I asked Joe for flour. He looked but didn't have any. He shrugged. "You know I don't cook here!" The photographer was already there, what to do? Joe scoured around and came in from the bathroom with some Johnson's baby powder. We put it on a plate and it lives forever as "flour" in our photo. Of course, we couldn't eat the C.F.S. after our great deception.

On Joe's refrigerator that day was a clipping from a movie review of something titled *Truck Driving Woman*. It asked, "What does Jackie Onassis know about the wonders of chicken fried steak?" We recalled that Hollywood had saluted C.F.S. in the movie *The Last Picture Show*. Actor Ben

Johnson enters the town's local café with an imperative: "Chicken fry me a steak." (In an instant, C.F.S. had become a verb!) Although Archer City, the movie's locale and the home of writer Larry McMurtry, is in West Texas, the gifted Larry himself recommends The Ranchman's Café in Ponder, north of Dallas, as home of the best café C.F.S. And as we went to press, those experts *Semi-Tough*'s Dan Jenkins and his *Sports Illustrated* sidekick, Bud Shrake, recommend Mac's Steak House in Arlington, Texas, for the best.

We hoped for a general C.F.S. renaissance after food critic Gael Greene published her novel *Blue Skies, No Candy,* for although most of her story was about a woman obsessed with sex and French cooking, she had fallen for a handsome Texan who loved C.F.S. After that we desired more understanding in the cultured world. But in spite of novelist Dan Jenkins's constant mentions of C.F.S. in all his books from *Semi-Tough* to *Baja, Oklahoma* and on, I don't see C.F.S. catching on. Who knows? The little town of Crawford near President Bush's ranch has only one café, The Coffee Station. It is an outpost for the White House press in residence. *The Washington Post* printed that reporters have been "slowed by a month of chicken-fried steak." Nonsense! They are just lucky.

Another time I was invited to a Houston charity cook-off in the Astrodome, where amateurs did their bit in open-front booths on small stages. Each contestant, and a helper, prepared their contest entree, as the well-heeled guests milled about drinking and cheering them on in bejeweled or tuxedoed splendor.

My entry was, of course, C.F.S. with gravy and biscuits. I had made the mistake of bringing my New York friend Iris Love along as sous chef. Iris, a child of Manhattan privilege, could not understand that biscuit dough must be handled lightly and touched as little as possible. By the time she finished kneading, forming, patting, pulling, and showing off to the crowd, our biscuit dough had turned gray with handling and the biscuits came out like lead bullets. Unable to control Iris, I concentrated on my C.F.S. and before you knew it, its delicious sizzle drew a gang of Texas tycoons and millionaires, all looking up over their black ties, begging for a taste. "Just gimme one bite," they importuned. I started cutting the finished steak into small pieces and passing them out on paper napkins. Our crowd grew larger, hungrier. Tuxedo ties were torn loose as eager hands reached up. In the end, we barely had enough meat left for the six judges to try, but we had putty-colored biscuits aplenty. Naturally, we did not win anything. But we were the popular hit of the night. Men had loved us!

The winners had made an impossibly outré dish. Lynn Wyatt, the Texas beauty, and Jimmy Galanos of Hollywood and world fashion had concocted some kind of pineapple "thing" with a glazed meringue topping. It looked very handsome, and once I got the meringue smeared on my velvet evening jacket, it hardened like cement and I could never get it off.

Frankly, I found the winning recipe very much in a class with Iris's gray flannel biscuits. But then Lynn and Jimmy were friendly competitors, so we couldn't be poor sports. (This reminds me that recently I sent to Mrs. Wyatt in Houston two photographs of myself with her at the Wyatt villa in the south of France. These were taken thirty years ago. In one of these, I am actually wearing a ridiculous T-shirt that reads: "If you are good and say your prayers, when you die you will go to Texas." I suppose I thought that would amuse Lynn's fine French guests. Then I ran into the Wyatts when we sat near one another at Ronald Reagan's funeral in Washington. Oscar opined, "Liz, you know those pictures of you and Lynn? Well, it's a helluva note, but you two look much better now and more attractive than you did as girls years ago." Oh, those Texas men. They love C.F.S. and I love them!

How to Make Great C.F.S.

This is a matter on which the experts always disagree. We've given you the Elvis version, but intend to offer some true options and highlights:

Governor Ann's C.F.S.

Ann includes bacon in her recipe because she feels one needs bacon grease for flavor. (Throw the bacon itself out or save it for sandwiches tomorrow!) But Wesson oil is better for the major part of frying, so mix the two.

Bacon grease combined with vegetable oil should be about ¼ or ½ inch deep in the skillet. Ann also includes a cup of milk to beat into the eggs for dipping the peppered/salted meat in before dredging it through flour. She says C.F.S. must not be overcooked and gives it about 6 minutes in the hot grease. She prefers to cut the meat into smaller steaks "about the size of your hand. It is virtually impossible to write an exact recipe because it's more about PROCESS than it is about PROPORTIONS."

P.S. The gravy! Ann says, "One must drain the bacon grease and Wesson oil out of the skillet, leaving 4 to 6 tablespoons of fat. Keep the heat on medium and add ½ cup of flour. Stir it around so that the flour cooks but doesn't brown. Add 2 to 3 cups of milk to the roux and whisk until thickened. If there are crumbled bits of steak in the grease, all the better. Salt and pepper to taste and serve in a bowl separate from the steaks because it should be poured over the steak and potatoes at the table if possible."

Dr. Jimmie's C.F.S. Ideas

The good doctor differs from Ann only in the omission of the milk-and-eggs dredging before flouring. She just cooks her meat with flour, salt, and pepper. This technically makes it a bit different. This is what rural folks call "country-fried steak." Jimmie does say the secret is "thin slices . . . you can put it in cold water beforehand if you pat it dry before cooking. . . . Thin-bottom frypans don't cook as well."

Texas Monthly's C.F.S.

Via Gary Cartwright
Gary adds 2 cups of buttermilk to his recipe, which otherwise seems to follow the Ann Richards dictum. He believes your C.F.S. should marinate in buttermilk for only 20 minutes. Gary removes his steaks, pats them dry, then dredges them in flour, dips them again in buttermilk, dredges them in flour again. He says cook them 8 minutes total. (Well, they may need a little longer—all that soaking, patting, double dredging! But he is the unchallenged king of all C.F.S. cooks to the Bud Shrake–Dan Jenkins crowd.)

Liz's Tips for C.F.S.

I'd say in a burst of enthusiasm, buy half a pound of round steak for each person. I always cook as much as I have patience for, because leftover C.F.S. is delicious so long as you haven't put it in the refrigerator. Just leave it overnight covered with foil or Saran Wrap on the kitchen counter. (You'll be lucky to find any left the next morning.) In the recipe I send out to my six fans worldwide, I pretty much follow the Ann Richards rules and regulations. (But I intend to experiment with Gary's buttermilk. I hate to be narrow-minded.)

In the matter of gravy I do say: put the milk into the gravy bowl or boat you plan to serve from before you start—that will be your measure for how much cream gravy you make. You can use a mixture of milk and water, skim milk, whole milk, evaporated milk, half-and-half, or heavy cream; it depends on how rich you want to make it.

I always say drink beer with C.F.S., or some kind of soda pop, or Puligny-Montrachet '71, or Château Lafite Rothschild '67. Whatever!

Heaven save us from people who make real batters or coverings of corn-flakes or potato chips for their C.F.S. Virgil's barbecue café near Times Square has the potato chip abomination. The rest of its food is fine. But God save the simple C.F.S. from adornment.

CHAPTER 12

CHILI

TODAY,

HOT TAMALE!

Two things happened often on the streets of Fort Worth when I was growing up. First, we had newspaper extras. When big stories took place—such as Will Rogers and Wiley Post's plane crash in Alaska—the *Star-Telegram* and the *Fort Worth Press* put paperboys out in the residential districts with special editions carrying the story. They'd be shouting "Extra! Extra!" and we'd rush out with a few pennies and buy the newspaper, lingering in the gutter to read the latest. Daddy would be standing on the front porch yelling for us to bring it to him. This was desirable in an age where there was no television and radio was a sometime thing.

Second, we had food vendors plying the streets. Old Mexicans came by weekly shouting out their wares. "Tamales! Hot tamales!" We would rush to the pushcart with maybe a nickel or a dime and take a dozen tamales in their cornhusks wrapped in an old newspaper that was dripping with grease. This was the most delectable fast food ever. In those days, no one talked about quesadillas, fajitas, burritos, or tacos. Hot tamales were hot! Although my father would laugh and tell us they were made of ground-up cats and dogs and sometimes rats, we didn't believe him. They were fabulous and pretty soon we'd all (even Daddy) be sitting around in the backyard or even the front porch swing, peeling off the cornhusks, dripping with orangy-looking sauce, breaking the tamales into bits, eating with our fingers. Fort Worth was far north in Texas and had only a small Mexican population, but what we had there was choice. (Or "cherce" as Spencer Tracy would have said in the movies!)

So whatever happened to tamales? They seem to have gone the way of the dial telephone or the buttons on men's flies. Even some of the best Mexican restaurants don't bother to offer them and if they do, you're lucky to find a good one. I believe what happened is that Mexican women emerged into the general workplace and there vanished a phalanx of older señoras who had the patience to make this dish.

After I married during World War II and was living in New Mexico, I discovered a lot more Mexican culture than I'd ever encountered in Texas. And one of my best encounters was to find the famous La Posta restaurant in the very southwestern corner of New Mexico. This beautiful adobe building, situated under enormous cottonwood trees, stood at the junction of New Mexico, Arizona, and Old Mexico. Its reputation included having been a stop on the Butterfield Stagecoach Line, as well as the place where they were said to have shot Billy the Kid. But its more modern success came from the imagination of the late owner, Katy Camunez, who turned it into a great restaurant. Every December they hang the outdoor trees with huge oversize wrapped Christmas gifts, which swing there in the green branches as if to lure a race of giants. Inside they decorate the rooms with every imaginable Mexican Christmas image— ravishing Nativity scenes, fir trees, cacti, beautiful flowers holding gorgeous ornaments. And in one room, exotic birds fly about unencumbered, with parrots and macaws screeching and enjoying themselves in a jungle of bushes and trees.

I visited the kitchen, where an old woman sat on a stool next to a cooked calf's head. She was slowly scraping off small amounts of colorless headcheese and feeding it carefully into a large, turning mixing bowl. She was making tamales, creating them from the headcheese and fine masa (cornmeal), to be shaped around shreds of beef mixed with spices and peppers. The masa had to be carefully massaged around the beef. Although she had the advantage of the electric mixing bowl, she was still making tamales by hand. And that care and detail is what makes the tamale great. When I saw that old woman, the diamonds on her fingers glazed over by the greasy headcheese and masa, I knew why machine-made tamales are usually not worth eating. You can order them from Neiman Marcus and out of the *Cowboys & Indians* magazine and so forth, but they are frequently disappointing.

The advertising genius Jane Trahey, who once helped put Neiman's of Dallas on the map, used to have a saying that I sometimes still hear: "Bad Mexican food is better than no Mexican food." But if you have eaten real Mexican food in the Zona Rosa of Mexico City or in Acapulco or along the Texas-Mexico border, or even great Tex-Mex in San Antonio or the Rio Grande Valley and points west, you know it very well when you get it and the bad is not beautiful.

Here I must side with Helen Bryant, whose funny book *Fixin' to Be Texan* is full of useful glimpses of southwestern mores. She asks, "Making Mexican food at home? Are you Mexican? If so you know how. If not why would you want to attempt it. Mexican restaurants are good, plentiful, cheap. And their plates are hotter than yours."

I also agree with Ms. Bryant about the wonders of chili. She makes one hard rule: no beans in chili. And she suggests if you put too much tomato sauce or tomatoes in chili, that turns it into an Italian dish. But her chili advice is first-rate if you haven't the patience for Diane Judge's recipe (page 22). Here's Helen's solution: "Go to the grocery store. Buy a pound of lean ground beef, an 8-ounce can of tomato sauce, and a Wick Fowler brand chili kit. The result will be chili as good as anybody else's."

In New York we do yearn for Mexican food. I'm lucky. I happen to live over El Rio Grande restaurant in my building at Third Avenue and 38th Street. This double-duty café makes the same food for the Texas side of the restaurant as the Mexican side. That includes first-rate margaritas and the best, freshest tostadas anywhere, as well as passable guacamole, fajitas, and enchiladas. Two longtime favorites of mine are El Charro in Greenwich Village and El Parador on East 34th Street. Again, they have the knack with margaritas. For a special treat I go to Rosa Mexicana on the Upper East Side where they still make good tamales. There is a sister Rosa Mexicana on Ninth Avenue near Lincoln Center. Here, with hundreds of tiny Acapulco divers in miniature poised to plunge down a wall of running water, you can dine in splendor and have a perfect guacamole made right at your table in a matter of seconds, in an authentic black volcanic bowl. But—no tamales at this Rosa. My, how I miss them and the authentic real cornhusks they come wrapped in!

When you don't lower yourself (and I mean physically go down South, as opposed to any social strata) to the border or its environs in the country, you miss a lot of things happening cuisinewise in America.

Recently, I was having a delightful time in San Antonio, strolling along the River Walk until someone told me that only tourists do that. (I went on doing it anyway!) I bought every kind of colorful Mexican object in the market around the Mi Tierra café. This may be the most fun of any Mexican restaurant left in North America; I'm not sure, but it comes close for sheer spectacle. You have to wait to get a table. You can clear out the tourists, and it is still great with its suits of lights from bullfighters on the wall, its armadillos, its jackalopes,* its spurs, its saddles, its blankets, its artwork, and the rest of it. It's worth the wait to get in for the superior food and goodies to take away, including exotic baked goods, and candy.

But the thing I enjoyed the most was breakfast in the Four Seasons Hotel along the River Walk. There I had *migas* for breakfast, and breakfast being my favorite meal, I truly loved this. How to make four servings of *migas*:

Alamo Migas

½ cup diced yellow onion
½ cup diced red pepper
½ cup diced poblano pepper
2 teaspoons minced garlic
Vegetable oil
10 eggs
½ cup crushed tortilla chips
½ cup Monterey Jack cheese
1 tablespoon chopped cilantro
Salt and pepper

* Half rabbit, half antelope.

[98]

Sauté the onion, red pepper, poblano, and garlic in scant vegetable oil until the onion is translucent and the peppers are tender. Add the eggs and tortilla chips and stir over the heat until the eggs are scrambled. Remove from the heat, add the cheese, cilantro, and salt and pepper to taste.

4 SERVINGS

CHAPTER 13

LE CIRQUE

DE MY

SOUL!

PEOPLE OFTEN ASK ME to name my favorite New York restaurant. I am always hard-pressed because I don't want to admit that if I have my "druthers," I'll be down at the vintage long-playing Pink Tea Cup on Charles Street in Greenwich Village, working away at their deep double-fried bacon,* sizzling chicken wings, collard greens, black-eyed peas, plus okra with tomatoes and corn. I know folks have expectations that I'm out every night eating in the best French and Italian places with white damask napkins and rotating wine stewards.

Working for years in the society column vineyards, I did learn a bit about eating high off the hog. I have been overfed, overentertained, overstimulated, and living beyond my means for years. My friend and office aide Diane Judge describes this as "better living through publicity." So it is true that since the mid-fifties, when I started toiling for the old, now-defunct Cholly Knickerbocker column, I have eaten well above my sta-

---

* It was Mark Twain who said bacon would improve the taste of even an angel. He would have loved the Tea Cup's crisp, dry, greaseless, and alert slabs of pork-fried heaven.

tion, been exposed to wondrous things, and great restaurants have grown accustomed to my face.

But being out and "with it" in New York City is more than just the attraction of fine food itself. There's something to be said for dressing up, making an effort, and experiencing the best.

Thus, giving it true and serious consideration, the fact that I have been feted, saluted, seated, and treated awfully well also has something to do with favorite places. So my favorite restaurant for the here and now— early twenty-first century—has been Sirio Maccioni's Le Cirque 2000, which some have described as having "perhaps the best social connections of any restaurant in the world" and also as "the most famous restaurant in the world."

This makes me sound a bit pretentious and snobby. But I loved Le Cirque when it was first situated in the Mayfair Hotel on East 65th Street off Park Avenue. And I loved it when Sirio moved it to the landmarked Villard Mansion adjoining the Palace Hotel on Madison Avenue, between 50th and 51st streets. And I will love Le Cirque in its next incarnation, for by the time you read this, I am practically certain that a new Le Cirque III will soon open, probably on Central Park South or in a Bloomberg building.

Sirio closed the Madison Avenue Le Cirque 2000 on New Year's Eve 2004 with a giant party of caviar, fois gras, and champagne at $500 a head.

Actually, I was always "in training" for Le Cirque since way back when. I have written elsewhere in these pages about my scholarship under the maestro Henri Soulé, who made French cuisine what he wanted it to be in America. But I had a second mentor. In the fifties, when I started working as a ghost writer for Igor Cassini, who had inherited the long-running Cholly column,* we had an office in a town house on 61st Street near Madison Avenue. Cassini had no wish to trek down to Hearst's New York *Journal-American* newspaper offices at 220 South Street. He needed to be midtown for romantic assignations and quick getaways. This was very convenient for him and working in midtown Manhattan spoiled me early on. As a result I have never been quite as ink-stained as other journalism wretches.

---

* Commenting on the names dropped by Cholly's column, columnist Leonard Lyons wise-cracked: "They can't be Society. *I* know them all!"

Just across the street from the Cassini town house office was the popular Colony restaurant, a place that may have taken its name from the exclusive, prestigious, and hard-to-get-into Colony Club. It sounded good, at any rate, and the restaurant attracted what was left in the *Social Register* and others from latter-day café society, as well as people from the international set. (Both Cassini and columnist Earl Wilson were always coining catchphrases and each man claimed he had originated the phrase "the jet set.")

In the Colony, one might find the Duke and Duchess of Windsor . . . the social queen Mrs. Lytle Hull . . . the untouchable "La Grande Mademoiselle," a rich spinster named Beth Leary . . . Prince Aly Khan . . . either Ari Onassis or Stavros Niarchos . . . one or both of the Morgan twins, Gloria Vanderbilt (mère) and Thelma, Viscountess Furness . . . occasionally the heiresses Doris Duke and Barbara Hutton . . . even "Jackims" Astor, whose mother, pregnant with him, had watched the *Titanic* sink from her lifeboat . . . and, my personal favorite, the sexy Broadway producer Leland Hayward, to name just a few regulars.

Cassini himself dropped into the Colony almost every day when he wasn't off to the Deepdale Golf Course in Long Island. On golf days, he directed me to go over for lunch and "take some notes." When I protested I hadn't the clothes or the wherewithal, he laughed and took me himself to meet the genial owner, Gene Cavallero. I say Mr. C. was "genial," but perhaps he felt he had no choice. The Cholly Knickerbocker column wrote him up constantly. And Cavallero's modus was never to give anyone from our office a check. In fact, Mr. Cassini's rather formidable mother, known as the "she-wolf," would go to the Colony, admire the china dinner plates, and tell the headwaiter to send a dozen to her apartment. They did, without a murmur.

"Just tip well," said Cassini, "and don't go around in the Colony saying 'Oy vey!,' which is a bad habit I see you've picked up from your theater friends." He handed me a wad of bills. So I went and dropped the Yiddish slang I'd gone to so much trouble to acquire. As I didn't understand anything about the food listed on the big elegant menu, I invariably ordered the one thing I did understand—*goujonettes de sole frites*. Later I was to realize they had a lot in common with Mrs. Paul's fish sticks. But at the time, they just made my coverage of the high life easy while I improved my meager French and Italian.

As I've said, it was Henri Soulé who brought major French haute cuisine to the U.S. during the World's Fair of 1939. Then he opened Le Pavillon, a temple to gastronomy such as even those Francophiles Ben Franklin and Thomas Jefferson could never have dreamed might happen in America. Henri Soulé inspired many Francophile imitators, and some of them were first-class Italians like Cavallero.

I wasn't really eating in the Colony; I was observing and working. I kept busy, noting that the Windsors, who had given it all up for love, had very little to say to each other . . . that the spinster Mlle. Leary had everyone intimidated as she barked orders . . . that the truly social Mrs. Hull had dropped the word that she'd never pose for a photo unless it helped her charity, the Musicians' Emergency Fund. (In that case, said she, "I'd pose with a barrel of monkeys!") . . . I was told that Prince Aly Khan was the kindest and most genteel of all ladies' men and, indeed, when I later really met him, I fell just like every other female who'd ever touched his hand . . . I also saw that the famous Mr. Hayward—rumored to have been in love with Katharine Hepburn, then wed to the delightful Margaret Sullavan and later to Slim Keith, the former Mrs. Howard Hawks (he still had Pamela Churchill in his future)—would always sit at the same table in the blue-and-white striped awning bar. They placed a fifth of Johnnie Walker Black Label on his table and Leland finished it during lunch. (Don't ask how people got any work done in New York in those harddrinking days. Many souls drank like this and the three-martini lunch was not a myth.)

So I knew who a few people were in the Colony, but not nearly enough to effectively write about them. A young waiter there befriended me and though I seldom understood what he was saying because we had differing concepts of what constitutes English, his manner was perfect and friendly. He understood that I was out of my depth and he determined to help me.

This young fellow was fresh from Montecatini, Italy, though he'd had a stopover in Paris where his boyhood pal, the actor Yves Montand, had helped him make his way. But Paris was not for Sirio Maccioni. He wanted New York, a restaurant-loving city open and welcoming to service people who spoke foreign languages and were willing to brave the frontier to teach us about sauces and sorcery. In time, my Sirio graduated to maître d' at the Colony and along the way he collected some very important admirers: Frank Sinatra, Cary Grant, Princess Grace, the William S. Paleys, the Gianni Agnellis—everyone loved Sirio.

It was his patrons, Mr. and Mrs. William Zeckendorf, who later lured Sirio into taking over a restaurant in the Mayfair Hotel in partnership with the Colony chef, Jean Verne, in 1973. This was the first Le Cirque. Decorated by Ellen McCluskey as a kind of playful mock version of the Singerie Room at Versailles, it boasted aristocratic monkeys and candelabra and was an instant hit.

So why do I love Le Cirque and all of its offshoots and manifestations? Not because it's grand and exclusive and expensive, but because it constitutes the great immigrant success story in its creator, Sirio. I also love it because they kept a Robert Cenedella painting in their entrance showing me sitting with others, above the salt. (Actually, I'm next to Richard Nixon, who I never sat down with in my life.) But anyway, I love Le Cirque because Sirio continues to push the envelope of his story, opening successful branches in Mexico City and Las Vegas, holding London and Paris at bay while they beg for him.

I always have to explain the Le Cirque idea to people. Why did Sirio desert his smaller digs in the Mayfair? This little hotel was a mecca, especially for rich Texans. Why did he use the circus decor in Le Cirque 2000? Why so many rooms? Was the large lavender dining room better than the smaller red room? Is Sirio the autocrat he seems to be?

Well, I can explain. After twenty years at the Mayfair, Sirio began to find his successive landlords impossible. Sirio elected to relocate. The Sultan of Brunei, richer in the nineties than now, spent an estimated $10 million to fit a larger restaurant for Sirio into the landmarked Villard Mansion adjacent to the Brunei-owned Palace Hotel. Sirio could not touch a lintel of this Villard house. His designer, Adam Tihany, spent several million on the decor but had to leave fireplaces, wall carvings, windows, intact. So he devised an insertable, removable Art Deco circus theme for the carpets and furniture, and used neon hangings in the bar. He brightened up this noli me tangere library atmosphere with a colorful bold decor and Sirio had a second hit.

But there was no difference between the red room and the lavender one. It was only what the customer made of it. While Le Cirque sometimes alters, Sirio never does. Is he an autocrat? No, he is a man with a sense of humor. Unlike most restaurateurs, he knows how to have fun.

When Italian olive oil was still new to most Americans, Sirio was asked, "What is the meaning of virgin olive oil?" He smiled and said, "They are olives that have never been with a man." * When Jerome Zipkin, the social arbiter and friend to Nancy Reagan, used to sneer and ask why he was charging eight dollars for asparagus, Sirio would only nod and say, "Well, of course, Mr. Zipkin, we will only charge you five dollars." Sirio denies being a snob but says he does believe in "an elite." And he bosses around only his family and his staff, and saves his chief exasperation for the occasional customer who refuses to wear a necktie or jacket. "Should I let them in wearing Levi's?" he moans, shaking his giant head.

He is a perfectionist, a fussbudget, funny and vulnerable at the same time, bemoaning his fate while counting his chickens and his success. I still understand only a fraction of what he says. But I find his heart so tender, so large. He is generous, irascible at times, and entirely human.

If I give him the opening, he'll give me chapter and verse about how he doesn't understand his customers. "They liked me on Sixty-fifth Street but they said Fifty-first Street was too far downtown. I am told they won't like Central Park South either. Are they crazy? What do you think? Should I let them come in here wearing those polo shirts and awful Hollywood clothes?" If I sympathize, he sets off on the offers bombarding him from abroad. "They think I am triplets!" (Watch him overcome those painful memories of his early days in Paris and open Café Sirio in the Ritz Hotel at any moment.)

I love this guy. There is nothing I wouldn't do for him. And because he has trained me so well over the years, I have often enjoyed Le Cirque's pièce de résistance and recommend it to all newcomers—the black sea bass wrapped in a crust of potatoes . . . or the seared foie gras to make my arteries clinch . . . or the Dover sole meunière . . . or risotto with young vegetables and lobster sauce . . . or one of my favorites, which no one quite believes is on the menu: crisped pigs' feet with jellied fruits. (The Duchess of Devonshire would have loved this item. I do!)

Sirio himself invented the now-standard pasta primavera, or as it was originally called, "Spaghetti Le Cirque." This is pasta with cream sauce and fresh vegetables. Once upon a time it was so despised by his elit-

---

* Actual definition: "Oil from olives solely through a purely mechanical (nonchemical) process. The oil has no treatments other than washing and filtering, nor has it been mixed with anything else."—Ben Schott's *Food & Drink Miscellany*.

ist chefs that Sirio would make it himself outside the kitchen for customers. Today it has became a standard, but when the *Times*'s Craig Claiborne first tasted it, he pronounced it a new masterpiece. It has been called "an Italian dish made in a distinctly French way and that is Sirio's genius." I also give Sirio credit for introducing Americans to white truffles. He thinks he brought in the first ones,* and I think of him standing behind a waiter who is shaving them onto my plate over potatoes, pasta, or scrambled eggs. Sirio is saying to the waiter, "More! More!"

We needn't go into Le Cirque's famed desserts. They are masterpieces, ever changing, acrobats in chocolate and cookie lace, new fantasies in berries and spun sugar and orange rind, sherbet set in its own lemon, soufflés to die over, and the old-fashioned dessert most restaurants don't bother to make anymore—that myth in beaten egg whites, floating islands.

Sirio's wife, Egidiana, has contributed greatly to his success and to raising his three amazingly good-looking and talented sons. (Mario runs Le Cirque in Vegas and Mauro and Marco run the less formal Osteria del Circo on West 56th Street.) Signora Maccioni now has her own *The Maccioni Family Cookbook*, all about the early days in Tuscany, with recipes that have helped make Sirio famous. And he recently finished his memoir with the Bloomberg food critic Peter Elliot, titled *Sirio—The Story of My Life and Le Cirque*.

Well, yes, yes, I know now you are saying they are extra nice to me at Le Cirque in all its incarnations because I write about them and that affects my "favoritism" and maybe also it's because Sirio and I go way back. But actually, the people who work the various Le Cirques are all warmhearted Italians (with a sprinkling of French and Swiss) and they'll be just as nice to you if you go in a few times, pay your bill with the realization that you're in a first-class place, make yourself presentable, and express a real interest in eating well. After all, they are artists who have made food and drink and congeniality their very lives.

P.S. They do want you to wear a jacket and tie and not show off your

---

* But the almost one hundred-year-old Barbetta, on Restaurant Row, West 46th Street, also imported truffles early on. The owner, Laura Maioglio, is a fanatic on this specialty. This is a great northern Italian restaurant with class, full of antiques, with fabulous Champagne risotto and one of the most beautiful outdoor gardens ever for dining al fresco in season.

navel piercings, in order that you may complement their very fine offerings of civility, service, and effort.

Tuscan Fried Potatoes

I know, I know—right here is where I should give you a recipe for something they make at Le Cirque, which you may duplicate. But don't be silly. I couldn't and you probably couldn't either.

But here is Egi Maccioni's way with Tuscan fried potatoes and she says, "The secret is taking a long time to make them so they get soft on the inside and crusty and flavorful on the outside."

1½ cups olive oil

4 medium yellow potatoes, peeled, cut into wedges

4 cloves garlic, finely chopped

1 sprig fresh rosemary, or 1 teaspoon dried

1 teaspoon salt

Pepper

Heat the olive oil in a large, heavy skillet over high heat until hot. Add the potatoes, garlic, rosemary, and salt. Spread the potatoes out in a single layer. Cook for 5 minutes on high heat, turning the potato wedges once to cook both sides. Reduce the heat to medium and cook the potatoes, stirring and turning occasionally until crispy and golden brown, about 25 minutes. Carefully remove the potato wedges to a platter covered with paper towels. Season with pepper. Eat immediately.

SERVES 4

CHAPTER 14

SOUP

TO NUTS

TO NORA

. . . and from each chapter rises a reek, a heady stench of truffles,
Château d'Yquem and quails financière.

—M. F. K. FISHER, *THE ART OF EATING*

THIS PORTION came to be known by me as "The Decadence
Chapter." I wrote it in a white-hot burst of enthusiasm and exuberance after a fabulous evening in the apartment of my longtime friend Nora
Ephron. I sent it to her thinking she'd burble her thanks and mutual admiration. Instead what I got back from Nora was her usual high-minded attention to detail, a literary tongue-lashing for my carelessness and pages of
corrections and chiding. (But also some glorious tips.)

Nora felt I had decidedly done her evening wrong in that I'd taken
from it an aura of, yes, decadence. But I love decadence, so perhaps that's

how my mistakes happened in the first place. At any rate, to be edited and corrected by the marvelous Nora is not something that can happen to just anyone. I have known this incredible female for about thirty-five years. I admire everything about her. Thus I decided I'd write for you my original version of the evening at Nora's and then I'd just let Nora put me to shame. So, here it is—chapter, verse, original, and Nora Ephron's corrections!

Liz: Original MS

One never approaches a dinner invitation from the gifted writer–movie director Nora Ephron with any hint of reluctance or boredom. She is a cook-entrepreneur who began making her reputation for loving food and its ramifications by arbitrarily including recipes in her witty and acerbic books (*Crazy Salad, Heartburn*, etc.). Many writers now include descriptions of meals and feats of cookery as therapy for their beleaguered fictional protagonists. (Patricia Cornwell's forensic heroine Dr. Kay Scarpetta comes to mind. Kay is forever easing her angst by whipping up something Italian to erase the strain of all those tortured dead bodies. This not only gives the good doctor a break, it gives the reader a break. Then there are the Robert Parker "Spenser" private-eye novels, exercises in sandwich and body building, beguiling pages of perfect food and drink while we wait for the regrettable vigilante violence and for the crime to be solved.)

When Nora lived in Washington in the seventies, she became so well known for her mania and expertise on food, its preparation and presentation, that a popular restaurant opened, using her name. This drove Nora a little crazy. "I was an amateur," she says, "this was unfair competition." It also caused a hell of a lot of confusion with people saying they were going to Nora's and no one being quite sure whether they'd see them at Nora's house with Sally Quinn and Ben Bradlee, or find them paying a check at the café. When an acquaintance named her dog "Nora," it was the last straw and Nora went back to live in Manhattan where no one has ever mistaken her for anyone or anything other than herself since.

Nora's correction:

The reason a restaurant called Nora's opened in Washington was not because of me or my cooking (which was mostly famous in my own home), but because there was, incredibly enough, another person called Nora living in Washington. And she opened a restaurant that all of us liked to go to. So obviously I never said the quote you made up: "I was an amateur. This was unfair competition." Shame on you.

But it *was* thoroughly confusing. You're right about that. I like being the only Nora insofar as it's possible. And when these people I thought were my friends named their dog Nora, it really did make me nuts. But the dog wasn't the last straw; the last straw was that the marriage that had brought me to Washington ended with a bang and gave me a reason to go back to New York.

Liz:

It's best to arrive at Nora's hungry, adventurous, and full of anticipatory glee. It doesn't hurt if you also act smart, interested, interesting, and you are full of inside gossip about crimes, *The New York Times*, the Hamptons, and stuff like that.

On this particular night, I was seeing the relatively new Chez Ephron–Pileggi apartment. Nora is wed to the talented Mafia crime expert and writer Nick Pileggi, who gave us the immortal movie *Goodfellas*. I took along a gag bottle of red wine with my picture on the label and the words "Château Texas—bottled in Fort Worth" underneath. This had been a birthday gift from the brilliant *60 Minutes* man, Morley Safer. I thought I'd get a big rise out of Nora with this bottle, but she was distracted by greater wine considerations. She was uncorking a grand Cristal Champagne and her other guests were arriving. (I now daydream that one night, Nick and Nora will snatch up that bottle of red from their wine cellar and suddenly see they are drinking the mysterious "Château Texas." I can just imagine hearty laughter or I hope for it at least.)

Nora:

I feel really bad that I didn't pay any attention to the bottle of red wine that Morley Safer gave you for your birthday and you put it in the closet where you keep the things you don't like enough to keep yourself but bring to unsuspecting hostesses whom you expect to fall down on the floor and thank you for them. Nonetheless, I apologize.

When you are having a party and a guest brings you a gift, you really ought to make a fuss over it. Next time you have me over I plan to bring you some really ugly salt and pepper shakers that someone gave me for Christmas in 1992 and which have been sitting in my closet ever since. And let's just see how much attention you pay to them.

Liz:

It is always heartening to enter a house or apartment where there is the faint aroma of toast in the air, for then one can hope against hope for caviar. Sure enough, there it was in an encouragingly large tin, surrounded not only by thin crisp anorexic toast but also by slivers of browned potato crisps. The crème fraîche was also there and we fell to it like starving Armenians. (History put "starving Armenians" into the language after World War I and I see no reason for abandoning the expression now. It was one of my mother's favorites.)

Nora:

It was my birthday. You left this out, Liz. The caviar was a birthday present. I mention this because the piece sounds as if we're the kind of people who serve caviar all the time. The truth is I almost never serve hors d'oeuvres at all, except for an occasional nut.

Here is the reason for you to abandon the Armenian expression now. It originated at the time the Armenians were starved almost into extinction by the Turks. Ten million of them died.

Liz:

Of course, Nora and Nick have a lovely apartment with fireplaces on the Upper East Side and somehow they have managed to be on the fifteenth floor while still arranging that no tall buildings should block their view downtown of the inimitable Chrysler Building. This is in the Manhattan dream category, but what else do we expect from the woman who gave us Cher as a lesbian in *Silkwood* . . . Meg Ryan having an orgasm in public in *When Harry Met Sally* . . . John Travolta as a dirty-winged angel in *Michael* . . . the Empire State Building as a hero in *Sleepless in Seattle* . . .

or Nicole Kidman as a witch in *Bewitched*. (If there is one thing Nora does better than food, it's writing and directing movies.)

Another thing Nora did with her new apartment—and you might not think to do—is manage a terrace, large or small (in her case it's small). There she has put a tree covered with twinkle lights that shine brightly and can be seen through the French windows right from the living room. I thought this was absolutely the living end, but then I found another tree in the kitchen, a kind of artful skeleton hung with more lights and glass artifacts. Absolutely charming. Nothing like encountering gala trees when it isn't Christmas and you don't have to bring a present or do anything but gawk with your mouth full of crushed beluga.

WE CAN'T ALL ATTRACT the kind of people Nora gets to come to dinner. Often she has movie stars like Tom Hanks and Rita Wilson or Steve Martin or Meryl Streep or Mike Nichols and Diane Sawyer who might as well be movie stars they are so VIPish. But on this particular night, Nora produced—instead of high-voltage "stars" who sometimes misshape the evening with their importance—real talkers and doers and people who know what's what. There was one Oscar-winning screenwriter, his wife who is up to her hips in education, a famous literary agent, the head fund-raiser of a major political party, a writer for *The New Yorker*, a guy about to go to work for a seemingly hopeless but idealistic candidate, a distinguished, witty former ambassador and his wife who is herself one of New York's best hostesses, and frankly, a lot of people are afraid to compare their own entertaining with hers.

We can't all get this kind of guest list but we can try. You might be surprised at how willing important and semi-important people are to come to a free dinner. As a friend of mine says, "Just risk it. Put a Ritz cracker with Wispride on the windowsill and they will come." Risking it reminds me of my favorite limerick:

> There once was a man from St. Paul
> Who went to a fancy dress ball
> He said, "Yes, I'll risk it.
> I'll go as a biscuit"
> And a dog ate him up in the hall.

Liz:

So, okay, the pre-dinner conversation was of a high quality, mixing Champagne with quips, gossip with history, current events with contempt, and all the usual suspects in public life came in for a skinning.

Then, Nora did something unusual. She brought in a large book and sat on the arm of a sofa, quieted us down, and said she needed to read something to us. It wasn't short, but it was pertinent to the evening. The book was *New American Classics*, by Jeremiah Tower.

And here is what she read aloud, describing a Russian Easter dinner with formerly rich Russians who were so grand that they looked down on the Romanovs:

Mr. Tower's book:
. . . the conversation soon turned to which wine was superior, Burgundy or bordeaux, and then, white or red? My aunt would drink only Scotch, Cognac, and the very old first growths in prime condition. The rest of us drank anything good. My uncle had saved a dozen or so bottles of various esoteric things from before the revolution. He had been saving them for years, to teach me the immense difference between excellence and the very best possible. Talk of excellence divided the diners on the question of whether it is achieved through austerity or indulgence, purity or excess. Inevitably, the subject of decadence arose, with everyone invited to define it . . . Cheremetev said the best definition came from his boyhood friend Prince Youssoupof. The story involved Youssoupof and a French count. When the question of what is decadence came up, the French count said something lyrical about beautiful women. Youssoupof said, "Nonsense, my dear fellow, the epitome of decadence is to drink Château d'Yquem with roast beef." . . . There was a silence as we all tried to conjure up, unsuccessfully, the dangers of that combination . . . Years later . . . I decided to hold a summer test of the Youssoupof theory. I invited only my closest friends, those who would not seek vengeance if they became sick or pushed over the edge . . . The taste of Château d'Yquem with the rich, aged, perfectly cooked roast beef was indescribable. And "taste" does not adequately convey the sensation, because what happens . . . is like something out of recent space films—travel at warp speed through the stars. Only, with the wine and beef there is very little noise, unless it is the sound of someone going over backward in his chair and hitting the floor . . . The rest of the menu is not important, because when the beef was served, and the

wine was poured, when I demonstrated the necessary ritual of chewing the beef and taking a draft of wine, chewing twice and swallowing, there followed the familiar silence, the almost agonized sighs and rapturous smiles.

Nora closed the Tower book and commented: "This is the experience we hope to duplicate tonight, only instead of Château d'Yquem, we're having a similar, less expensive wine — Suduiraut."

We, her guests, were all excited and some people clapped. There was much discussion of the extraordinary thing she had read. Another person asked if Prince Youssoupof wasn't the man who helped murder Rasputin? (Yes! Felix.) We trooped expectantly into a perfect white dining room. Nora sent us to the kitchen where we helped ourselves and came back to the round dining table.

Nora's menu included whole roasted carrots and parsnips to add to the perfect roast beef, which had been divided into rare and well-done parts. There were also beautiful green peas and those often-hoped-for-but-seldom-received English popovers. We slathered on the horseradish dressing.

I know I took more than just two sips of wine with every mouthful of roast beef. But then I never know how to hang back. It was simply great, a real new taste thrill. We then had a dreamy salad with some cheese and Nora proceeded to bring to table herself a white frosted cake with a crackling of amber curls on top. She cut it and told of its origin.

Looking back, I recall that even the women ate every crumb of this cake because, after all, as the marine captain said to his men urging them over the top in World War I, "Who wants to live forever?" None of us had ever seen such a cake before.

Now, you can doubtless successfully replicate this interesting and well-researched and guided evening of perfectly thought-out surprise and charm. But probably no one except Nora can duplicate it.

The idea is to find a perfect occasion, like a birthday. Or no occasion. Research if possible. Try the Internet. Tell your guests what to expect and whet their appetites during cocktails. Carry it all off with panache as if you believe in it with all your heart. Did Nora's evening constitute "decadence"? I don't think so, it was more like having been granted a degree from Oxford in a single evening, a true culinary education, a look into the vast beyond, a glimpse of paradise.

And then, of course, life is always simpler and easier if you have rented two people to help for the night. But you *knew* that!

Nora:

Lizzie, you are quoted in this book. On page 175, Tower writes, "I think that the columnist Liz Smith's farewell to Rock Hudson—'So long, big boy, have a good rest'—is what I would like on my tombstone, but it will probably be 'He invented the black bean cake.'"

You should explain what Château d'Yquem is to the poor pathetic uninitiated reader who has no idea. Let's face it, you and I only learned about it a few years ago by which time we were already ancient relics. It is a sweet wine, the crème de la crème of Sauternes, made in France, and it costs an arm and a leg. I would never buy it—ever—but someone gave us a bottle. Well, not exactly, they gave us a Sauternes, Suduiraut, which is just as good. And we've been saving it up for years. For what? That was the question. A Sauternes normally accompanies a foie gras appetizer or a fabulous dessert like soufflé. It never crossed my mind it could be served with a main course. So when I read Mr. Tower I thought, finally, an excuse to serve the Suduiraut. Since you serve a thimbleful at a time, one bottle does serve about ten people.

THE CAKE IS COFFEE CRUNCH, just like one I grew up eating in L.A. A white cake covered with whipped cream, showered with a delectable crunchy candy. Blum's, where we used to buy it, vanished along with the cake sometime in the late sixties.

A few years ago my sister, Delia, and I were sitting around talking about food instead of working. We were feeling sad about the vanished cake; think Proust and his madeleines. I suddenly realized, thanks to the Internet, I could probably find the recipe. I went to a food area on AOL—Recipes Wanted. I posted a query. One day later a woman from Oklahoma sent the recipe, from an old *L.A. Times* cookbook.

You don't have to really make the cake. You can use a good store-bought angel cake and serve it with whipped cream and coffee crunch. You can buy undecorated layers of génoise cake from a good bakery and assemble it yourself, fooling people into thinking you made it.

A few years ago I sent the recipe to Nancy Silverton and she now serves it at Campanile, the L.A. restaurant she owns with her husband, Mark Peel. They omit the coffee, however. Go figure.

Here's how to make two layers of cake:

Preheat the oven to 375°F. Heavily butter two 8-inch round springform cake pans and line with buttered wax paper, butter side up. Sprinkle with flour. Cream 12 tablespoons sweet butter and 1 cup sugar until fluffy. Beat in 3 eggs, one at a time. Add 1 teaspoon vanilla. Sift 1 cup cake flour with 1½ teaspoons baking powder and a pinch of salt and add to the batter, beating until smooth. Pour the batter into the cake pans. Bake for 35 to 40 minutes. Cool on a rack and unmold it after about 20 minutes.

Coffee Crunch Candy Topping

Sift 1 tablespoon baking soda and set aside.

Combine 1½ cups sugar, ¼ cup brewed decaf coffee, and ¼ cup light corn syrup in a saucepan at least 5 inches deep

Bring the mixture to a boil. Cook to just below 310°F on a candy thermometer, to the hard-crack stage, where a small amount of mixture dropped into ice water breaks with a brittle snap. Remove from the heat.

Immediately add the baking soda and whisk vigorously until the mixture thickens and pulls away from the sides of the pan. The mixture will foam rapidly when the baking soda is added. Don't destroy the foam by excessive beating, but do your best to blend in the baking soda. Pour the foamy mass into two greased metal pans, 9 inches square, or one large greased metal pan or cookie sheet. It will look a bit disgusting, but be patient. Let it stand without moving until it is cool.

Then knock the hardened mixture out of the pan and crush it between sheets of wax paper with a rolling pin. Store in a closed plastic container until ready to use. Lasts about a week.

Assembly: Whip up 3 cups heavy cream, adding about ½ cup sugar when it is almost whipped. Frost the bottom layer of the cake, add some coffee crunch. Put on the top cake layer. Frost the top and sides of the cake. Put into the fridge. Before serving, top this with a mountain of coffee crunch and serve additional whipped cream and more crunch on the side.

Liz Ends:

I will close this chapter by simply saying that I considered Nora's researched dinner to have been the best dinner party I ever attended, anywhere! So it wasn't decadent. No—just good old American–Nora know-how! And also there was that feeling you always get at Nora's—that you have come home.

Ultimate Nora Quote

"What I love about cooking is that after a hard day, there is something comforting about the fact that if you melt butter and add flour, then hot stock, it will get thick! It's a sure thing. It's a sure thing in a world where nothing is sure!"

CHAPTER 15

O OYSTERS,

COME AND WALK

WITH US ...*

(BRING YOUR FRIENDS!)

I LOVE IT when my friends order oysters in wonderful restaurants like Ocean Grill or at the upscale Compass on the Upper West Side of Manhattan. These floppy sea items, the nurturers of pearls, are so unusual and they smell compellingly of the ocean as they arrive on their chipped ice with sea salt, in their handsome shells with the accoutrements. But I don't try to eat them. I've already "failed oysters" in a long lifetime of trying. I'm like the little boy whose father talks him into six on the half shell. Dad notes in a while that five are left and he says to his son, indicating the plate, "Don't you like your oysters?" The boy looks up at him, with his mouth obviously full and speaks without moving his lips . . . "No, I don't even like this one!"

* "O Oysters, come and walk with us,"
    The Walrus did beseech.
    "A pleasant walk, a pleasant talk,
    Along the briny beach: . . ."
From Lewis Carroll's poem "The Walrus and the Carpenter."

The food hallmark for the famous Washington hostess Evangeline Bruce was the oyster. During the Kennedy administration, in her George-town sunken living room, it wasn't unusual to find fifty or sixty guests milling about eating oysters. Sometimes the oysters were raw, sometimes they were grilled and wrapped in bacon. Then Mrs. Bruce called them Angels on Horseback.

Gourmets and gourmands must always at least consider the oyster. After all, oysters are a self-contained "health" food and you can eat a lot of them without worrying about gaining weight. Now and then I eat a fried oyster. The way avant-garde restaurateur Drew Nieporent served them when he began the Icon restaurant at the W Hotel—The Court in Murray Hill—was pretty near irresistible.* You didn't order them; they just arrived as a free appetizer, one or two with a dash of guacamole on the side. Then I throw in my lot with that good old country boy Roy Blount, Jr. He is the one who did a couplet on oysters. "I prefer my oysters fried/That way I know my oysters died."

But I couldn't possibly eat more than one or two. So I won't delve too much here into the oyster phenomenon even though I find them so fascinating and I secretly get crushes on people who can gulp them down. Their bisexual nature is a mystery and a come-on. I will just tell you to rustle up a copy of M. F. K. Fisher's *Consider the Oyster*, of which the critic Clifton Fadiman said: "Since Lewis Carroll no one had written charm-ingly about that indecisively sexed bivalve until Mrs. Fisher. . . . Surely this will stand for some time as the most judicious treatment in English of a mollusk whose life career is matched in improbability only by our rash decision in the distant past to use it as a food." (No doubt primitive man ob-served gulls dropping oysters and clams on rocks to break them open and decided if they were good enough for the gulls, perhaps they would suit man as well.)

Mrs. Fisher has some great suggestions for what to do with oysters, including baked oysters, fried oysters, oyster gumbo, oyster stuffing, dried oysters with vegetables, oyster ketchup, grilled oysters, oyster loaf, oyster bisque, cream of oyster soup, oysters and onions, oysters Rockefeller, and something called Hangtown fry (oysters and eggs mixed). She even gives two elaborate recipes for making oysters with ingredients that are difficult,

---

* The creative Drew still scores with his Nobu, Tribeca Gill, Montrachet, Layla, and even more in the Myriad empire spanning New York and California.

if not flat-out outrageous, to obtain. These recipes are titled "Oysters à la Foch" and "Oysters à la Bazeine or *Honi Soit Qui Mal Y Pense.*"

But boy, oh boy, even if you don't eat oysters, they are so much fun to read about. Mrs. Fisher evidently gave quite a lot of thought to the lowly oyster. She offers a knowing tip to raw oyster lovers as well. She believed it should be compulsory to eat them with a thin-sliced nicely buttered good dark bread of a fine-grained type and a few quarters of lemon for juicing up the oysters. And she recommends a nice Chablis with same.

Someone named Strange de Jim said, "I don't like to eat snails, I prefer fast food." Okay, that's funny and Mrs. Fisher not only does oysters but in another book, *Serve It Forth*, has a section on snails. Now, the French eat fifty million snails a year and many Americans like them as well. While the French would look down on an American eating fried rattlesnake meat, they adore snails. I too have eaten them in their beautiful little shells covered in hot green butter, but actually, I'd rather not. However, this doesn't save me from wanting to read Mrs. Fisher on the care and feeding and death of snails, for the details of how one raises them to eat, and the care that must be taken with cleaning and preparing them is quite something. Even Mrs. Fisher decided finally that "perhaps it is better to buy store snails after all," not try to raise them.

Mrs. Fisher offers us a snail story about the French that is just unforgettable. It describes peasants harvesting grapes for wine in the blistering noonday heat of summer. For lunch they would burn a stretch of grass at the edge of the vineyard and then sort through the ashes in search of snails. Those that had been roasted in the flames were picked out of their shells and eaten on the spot, washed down by the juice of half-rotted grapes that the peasants had also collected. Observers noticed that these people crossed themselves before eating. They seemed enormously grateful.

Oysters Postscript

Perhaps it would be a service if I tried to fill you in here as an adjunct of this section by discussing that dubious western cousin of the sea oyster. I mean the so-called Rocky Mountain oyster. This item of food has many other names and nicknames. Oh, let's call a testicle a testicle. We're speaking of Montana Tendergroins (any kind of animal testicle) . . . butterflied turkey nuts (pretty much what it says) . . . barnyard family jewels (calf, bull, sheep, and turkey) . . . ranch fries (any type testicle thrown on a hot iron stove until it explodes) . . . battered balls (any animal testicle, marinated, battered, fried) . . . crabby bull balls (bull or buffalo testicles battered and fried) . . . fried animelles (sheep offerings, peeled, drained, and fried) . . . *donbalaan* (sheep testicles in bread crumbs and beaten egg, fried) . . . Then there is goat testicle stew, made with natural saltwater, chili peppers, and celery, invariably served with mashed potatoes . . . *kokorec* (we'll talk of this later but it's sheep liver, lung, hearts, spleens, testicles, intestines, salt, pepper, oregano, and oil—the Greeks and Turks adore it) . . . Most recipes for testicles say they should be peeled before eating, but I never saw a Texas cowhand wait to do that. And finally, among recipes to end all ends, there is penis stew. Rams' or bulls' organs stewed, then fried. Oh for heaven's sake, let's fuggedaboutit.

There is historical evidence that since man discovered fire he has been eating genitalia because he feels it is an aphrodisiac and a road to sexual power. But there's an argument to be made that they are truly delicious, to hear the guys I know talk. At any rate there are testicle festivals all over the West every spring and fall, especially in Montana. (These are not to be confused with ongoing other types of "testicle festivals" having nothing to do with food!)

None of the above should confuse you with something that major drinkers also call the "Prairie Oyster." It is served in bars as a hangover pick-me-up. The P.O. is just a raw egg served with a little milk or sherry or Worcestershire sauce, a dash of Tabasco, and a slug of tomato juice or alcohol.

But please! About the Rocky Mountain variety. If you'd ever "run the dope bucket" as many times as I had to when growing up while ranchers were branding and castrating little calves, turning them into steers, you might want to avoid the subject, too.

I was often given this chore on a ranch way out near Midland and Odessa, Texas. (You remember hearing of Midland; it's the garden spot that George W. Bush always describes as "home," the place where he grew up and to hear the forty-third president tell it, Midland is the garden spot of the universe. Well, I'm here to tell you it's not. It's just a dusty place in the middle of the flat West Texas plains and there's nothing between Midland and the North Pole but a barbed wire fence running north.)

Anyway, the "dope bucket" is a paint can filled with black gunk that looks like tar but is actually medicine, and some poor soul (usually me) always got to carry it with a paintbrush in it to paint the medicine onto the burned brands on calves' rears as well as on their genitals where they had just been castrated. This isn't easy, as by that point, of course, they are crying their little eyes out looking for the mama they were separated from as they were herded into the castrating and branding gate. My college roommate, Miss Nita Mae Boyd, a Western beauty who had married the world-famous champion cowboy Louis Brooks (she is now in Fort Worth's Cowgirl Hall of Fame), thought I was hell on wheels with the dope bucket. She'd swear at me, "Goddamnit, Liz, you are painting everything in sight with that stuff; there's now more on my boots than on the calves." I never did graduate to the big time—that is, the branding iron or the cutting pliers. (Not that I could have!)

The cowboys doing this chore were careful to preserve the calf testicles, which they tossed into another clean bucket. Later, they'd be fried up around a campfire or in the cook's chuckwagon. They were considered great delicacies. Many a tenderfoot ate one of these "oysters" without knowing what he or she was eating.

But I had been "present at the creation" of this delicacy too many times. Like Clarice Starling in *The Silence of the Lambs*, I could hear those calves bawling for days after and I wasn't up to eating their private parts. I knew pragmatically that calves had to be rendered into steers or the world would be unmanageable from having too many bulls. And I liked my steak as well as the next person who doesn't want to get into the gory details. I even knew that the calves' pain was momentary and would be forgotten. But down deep I'm a sissy, so I never did try the infamous Rocky Mountain oyster.

I notice that honcho of cuisine Mrs. Fisher barely addresses eating such a thing, though she is heavy into brains, tripe, liver, lights, gizzards, and so forth. She has had her share, however, of the other kind of bar remedy hangover "oyster" and gives it two separate mentions in her famous book. I think Mrs. Fisher enjoyed a nip or two.

Postscript II

As long as we're on "unusual" things to eat, let me tell you about something else you might enjoy—or not. It's *escamoles*, ant eggs, known as "Mexican caviar."

New York *Daily News* writer Julie Benson says this is an old Aztec favorite served in soup, fried, or cooked in a rich tomato broth. The eggs and larvae exist in the earth, sometimes two feet down. Men are hired to dig them out, spreading pork fat over their naked bodies so they won't be bitten. Because finding these eggs is labor intensive, *escamoles* cost about sixteen dollars a serving. The eggs look like small kernels of corn and steeped in a sizzling sauce of butter and mescal are said to be terrific.

Fried bees, wasps, grasshoppers, and crispy maguey worms from the agave plant are also popular dishes all over Mexico, and Ms. Benson recommends La Catarina restaurant in Monterrey.

CHAPTER 16

BOOZE! OR MAKE

ME A LITTLE

OLD-FASHIONED, PLEASE!*

T HERE I WAS on the Papagayo Peninsula of Costa Rica as I
wound up writing and accumulating this book, or, some might say,
regurgitating it. And because of the daring of a little boy of six—my godson—I found myself flying on a wire hooked up to a harness, hurtling
twenty stories above the rain forest below.

I was traveling through thin air at breakneck speed from one plat-
form in the trees to the next, doing the infamous Canopy Ride, which simply can't be very safe because I notice they don't have it at Disney World yet.

A hard hand in a heavy glove on the wire acted as the only brake and
there were about nine separate platforms to land on after soaring along
past howler monkeys, screeching tropical birds, and over rivers and jungle

---

* The song, by Cole Porter, is, of course, "Make It Another Old-Fashioned, Please." I don't
think many people drink old-fashioneds these days. The combo of bourbon, bitters, sugar, crushed orange slice, and a maraschino cherry seems hopelessly old-fashioned. I do remember them from watching seniors in the now-defunct Schrafft's ordering them around 5:00 P.M. in the sixties. Or was that
Manhattans they were drinking? Even more old-fashioned. The recipe? Rye whiskey, a touch of sweet
vermouth and bitters, shake over ice, and garnish with a maraschino cherry.

below. At one of the launching spots we climbed down to the ground on a wobbly ladder and then walked, struggling up sliding rocky hills and crumbling steps, to the next station. At this site we stepped lively over a baby rattlesnake that had been dozing on a rock. My godson, the reptile expert, was quick to explain that baby rattlers' venom is more poisonous than even that of an adult snake.

The "flyers" running the Canopy Ride said I was, at eighty-one, the second oldest person ever to fly. I felt as ridiculous as George Bush jumping with a parachute at A&M College.

When I got back to the new Four Seasons Hotel, which has the bays of Virador and Culebra on two sides and the Pacific Ocean on the other, I remember my deathless words: "I need a drink!"

Being familiar for family reasons with the twelve steps of A.A., I know full well one is never supposed to "need" a drink. But that day, I did. (Not to worry; I'll never become a drunk. My hangovers are too classic. After one of those it's always a long time between drinks even if I know the governors of both North and South Carolina. Besides, I believe with Samuel Johnson that melancholy should be diverted by any means before drinking.)

The resort bartender was up to my need after the Canopy Ride. He set on the bar one of the most beautiful glasses I'd ever seen holding a Mojito with sugar on the rim and a short stalk of—what was it, celery? A piece of wood? No, the stirrer was a sliver of fresh sugarcane, which turned out to be very sweet and fun to chew on. I loved this drink innovation and though I'd had Mojitos before—because ever since Jennifer Lopez took over popular culture, they've been "hot"—well, I never had one as good as this one. Here's how they make it:

Mojito Papagayo

1½ ounces Cuban rum, Havana Club, or your preference
½ ounce sugar syrup or 3 teaspoons brown sugar
1 ounce fresh lime juice
8 sprigs fresh mint with stems

Add the rum, sugar, lime juice, and mint to a rock glass that has had its rim dipped in sugar. Muddle the ingredients to get the juicy flavors of the mint. Add

1½ tablespoons crushed ice. Stir a little bit with a cocktail spoon. Garnish with more mint; add a sugarcane stick.

WE WON'T BELABOR BOOZE too much. It's a book in itself. I'm not much for hard stuff without a good mixer, but I do like amusing cocktails and I love all kinds of wine, especially with meals. Now here are two of the best drinks I personally make, and if I pay attention, they never miss. My guests always come back for more. Maybe too much more!

The Bloody Clam

Even people who don't like clams like this drink. You'll never hear the end of how good this eye-opener is.

Pour two fingers, or two shot glasses (or even one) of vodka into a glass. Cover the top of the vodka completely with a liberal amount of Worcestershire sauce. Squeeze a good quarter of a lime or lemon into the drink. Add a dash or two of Tabasco.

Shake your bottle of Clamato juice hard to mix it before you pour, filling the glass with ice and Clamato.

The Lizzie
A Margarita with Heart!

First a word: There are many versions and varieties of margaritas. The drink's problem is that it's both delicious and lethal. So I'd suggest a really small, wonderful-looking little glass. Those big commercial wide-lipped stemmed glasses may look glamorous but they always spill. Margaritas served in fruit jars and big iced tea glasses are simply gross and sure to end the fun since everyone gets too smashed too soon. A perfect glass is the kind they serve martinis in at the Ritz Hotel in Paris. Even a good white wine glass is okay. Or you can find a rocks glass that is a little smaller and easy to handle.

Rub a lime on the rim and push the glass into a saucer of coarse kosher or sea salt.

Elsewhere you'll have mixed equal parts of freshly squeezed lime juice, tequila, and Cointreau (or Triple Sec) in a pitcher. The beaker of a blender is perfect. You can give the mixture a twirl; then put it in the fridge. Freeze it and serve it slushy or just make it very cold.

YES, I KNOW, I KNOW —most margarita makers do not suggest "equal parts." But I find it works fine. If you think it's too sweet, add a little more tequila. Every good tequila has its own margarita recipe on the bottle, so experiment. Though I'm a purist and will stick to tequila, Cointreau, and lime juice, here's a slightly unusual margarita from the Lonesome Dove Western Bistro in Fort Worth, Texas:

Tim Love's Sweeter Margarita

12 ounces Espolon tequila
12 ounces Cointreau
4 ounces fresh lime juice
16 ounces sweet-and-sour mix
12 ounces orange juice
1 can Sprite
4 limes

Mix all the ingredients together, except the limes—slice those. Pour over ice in tall salt-rimmed glasses and serve with a slice. This is obviously a thirty-five-people party mix, and Tim says his "white margarita" has just the right sweetness. "Sprite livens it up without being too sweet."

SERVE SOMETHING to eat along with the margaritas. It's the better part of reason and a way to avoid an aftermath that is sometimes referred to as "margarita poisoning." Remember, the margarita is a lethal weapon. Also a word of warning: avoid margarita mixes and Rose's Lime Juice like the plague if you want to be authentic.

Texas Monthly magazine gave the final word on limes and margaritas in its recipe for the Kentucky Club Margarita of Juarez, Mexico.

The single most important ingredient in a top-notch margarita is the Mexican lime juice. You will, of course, be tempted to go the easy route and substitute ordinary big, green, egg-shaped limes, called Persian or Tahiti limes, for small, round, greenish-yellow Mexican limes, which are also known as Key limes. Don't do it. Mexican limes are highly acidic and full of flavor nuances, whereas common limes are mainly sour.

I hate to be so impure but, honestly, if you have to even substitute lemons for limes, not many will twig onto the difference. Having said that, I confess that for large parties with lots of margaritas to be made — Santa Cruz 100% Organic Lime Juice from a bottle is excellent. As for brands of liquor, everything of quality is better than the cheap stuff.

Of course, true tequila addicts, like the grand actress Christine Baranski, would argue that only the best will do. They can tell the difference. This lady, awash in acting honors, can never be forgotten as the hard-drinking partner of Cybill Shepherd in the television sitcom *Cybill*. She sends me incredible tequilas with the worm in the bottle, or a tequila with a blown glass cactus inside, or she is quick to send flowers in a bouquet of airplane-size miniature tequilas. I do love this much attention from an acting phenomenon. Christine is a dedicated wife and mother and a pro actor who drinks only socially, but she has certainly improved my taste.

Speaking of the Ritz in Paris: They do make a perfect martini, elegant, crystal, sparkling, and tiny, offered in their famous Hemingway Bar. And I love those Ritz potato chips, homemade and incredible. This is the one perfect thing to spend thirty or forty dollars on. You don't have to stay at the Ritz: Just go there and have one perfect martini, believed to have been named for the Swiss inventor of the Martini-Henry Rifle back in 1869.*

* The Hemingway Bar is one of the most important in the universe according to the Forbes Internet magazine, which called it "the world's greatest." And if you want to give the drinkers you know something special, offer them the handsome little book *The Cocktails of the Ritz Paris*, by Colin Peter Field from Simon & Schuster. It tells how the first tomato juice cocktail came into being in Chicago, circa 1928, and how Hemingway perfected the Bloody Mary, named for his nagging wife, to make her think he wasn't really drinking — just having a juice. It also boasts unusual cocktails — the Sidecar, the Batonnet, the Dirty Earl Grey Martini, the Brandy Crusta, the Millionaire, the Brandy Sangaree, Midnight Moon, Miss Blonde, the Highland Cream, La Crevasse, the Georges Cocktail, the Benderitter, the Ritzini, the Serendipiti, the Kashenka, the Violaine, Le Loup fera nid, the Zelda, the Apple Pilar, the Platinum Bullet, Nicky's Fizz, the Green Hat, and many more, including Ernest Hemingway's famous Death in the Gulf Stream (juice and crushed peel of one lime with splashes of Angostura over gin on ice — no sugar; it's meant to be tart and bitter).

How to Make a Fine Martini

The only American invention as perfect as a sonnet.

—H. L. MENCKEN

Again, find a small, beautiful, thin glass. Find a good brand of gin or vodka. Pour some vermouth into the glass, then pour it all out; just throw it away. Now add your gin or vodka to the unrinsed glass. Then pour the gin or vodka and the hint of vermouth that clings to it into a cocktail shaker with some ice. Shake it. Then strain it out back into the glass. Add olives or pearl onions or even a bit of pickled okra.

THERE ARE PLENTY of people to quarrel with the above. Recipes vary grandly. Ernest Hemingway favored the recipe from the British general Bernard Montgomery—15 to 1. (Expert Ben Schott says these are the odds Monty gave on the battlefield.)

Richard Nixon suggested a ratio of 7 to 1. But as Schott says, "Luis Buñuel considered it enough to hold up a glass of gin next to a bottle of vermouth and let a beam of sunlight pass through." I do have to separate myself from the old master Somerset Maugham, who said martinis must always be stirred. I opt for the Ian Fleming credo of James Bond: "shaken, not stirred."

Honestly, it hardly matters, but vermouth is crucial. You must have a touch of it; otherwise, just ask for gin or vodka on the rocks and forget it.

Here's my recipe for how to combat boredom at any party. Early on, have one—count 'em—one perfect martini. This will be enough if your martini is a gin martini. You'll be surprised at how it soothes you through the event.

MAYBE I'M FIXATED on one perfect martini at the Ritz because the United States didn't end Prohibition until 1933, when the nation passed the Twenty-first Amendment. Texans didn't pay this much mind and I grew up under something called "local option," where every county had its own rules. Growing up, I never saw a mixed drink sold in a bar.

Some counties allowed the sale of wine and beer and some had liquor stores. If you could buy booze, then you had to carry the bottle around in a brown paper bag. (People from Dallas carried theirs in little suede or leather totes from Neiman Marcus.) When you arrived at the restaurant or nightspot, you'd buy what they called "a setup." This meant ice, lemons, glasses, mixers of ginger ale or Coke. My brother James, trapped for eighteen months during World War II as a weatherman in Greenland, was furious when he returned to Texas to find he couldn't buy a mixed drink at a bar. He'd say sarcastically to the setup waitress: "And do bring us another bowl of your delicious, expensive, fast-melting ice!"

The result of local option was the habit of people going to parties with "roadies." This made driving dangerous and people would get so fed up hauling their brown bags around, they'd stop on street corners and chug-a-lug the bottle to get rid of it. It was a great relief when the big cities of Texas joined civilization and voted in mixed drinks, but as of 1997, the state still had fifty-three dry counties. Believe it or not!

Restrictions always make people act out more than they need to. A lot of Texans continue the "roadie" and "brown bag" routine. Habits die hard. The very funny Helen Bryant in her book *Fixin' to be Texan* describes such behavior in this way: "In Texas they call the word 'drink' by this—drank.

"Present tense: Drank.

"Past tense: Drank.

"What you become after you drank: Drunk."

I once took my sophisticated world-traveler friend Diane Judge from the "no mixed drinks" Gonzales county over to another small town for dinner. My mother refused to have alcohol in the house, so Diane said as we left Gonzales, "I just can't wait to have a dry martini!" I laughed and said, "Oh, yes, you can." We settled for a dusty bottle of red Gallo wine that the local restaurant had been keeping for centuries.

When I got to New York in 1949 I didn't drink. But the racy crowd I fell in with did. And eventually I came to drink a bit in self-defense. One of my favorite memories is of eating and drinking fun in Bridgehampton, Long Island, during the days I cooked, hosted, and told jokes in the house of Lee Bailey.

We spent a lot of time shopping for every long weekend orgy of food preparation and sloppy sipping. We had to have enough of everything on hand because on Saturday night there could be no more rushing back to the grocery or liquor store. Every meal at Lee's ended in "another vodka stinger," so when Stephen Sondheim wrote that lyric for a song in the Broadway musical *Company*, using those exact words, we just knew he'd been listening in on us. Stingers came in two "colors"—vodka or brandy. We didn't much care which. You threw the booze in the blender with some ice; you added the all-essential touch of crème de menthe. You fell down in front of the fireplace with your drink and hoped you'd fall near or on someone you liked.

One night the gifted Elaine Stritch was in charge of the stingers. But she was depending on us as usual to provide all the ingredients. Buying them herself would have been uncharacteristic. It was late. No stores were open. Tragedy! No crème de menthe. How could we live? What could we possibly drink after dinner? Our routine had broken down.

Elaine had the vodka or brandy already in the blender. She had the requisite ice. She had her hand on the trigger of the blender. She started wailing. We were aghast as well. We milled about helplessly. Suddenly on the coffee table Elaine spied a bunch of hard peppermint candies that El Morocco press agent Jimmy Mitchell had given us along with some silver-covered almonds. No one had ever touched this stuff; Lee left them there, he said, "for decoration." But Elaine scooped up a handful of hard peppermints and tossed them into the blender. It whirred. She poured. We couldn't tell the difference. Someone accidentally flopped their shoe into the fireplace and set their sneaker laces on fire. We discussed the problem of melted sneakers. We were back to "normal."

A Final Touch

There are many recipes for intoxicating punches and bowls full of mixed ingredients, so let's just step right up and give the most famous one in history. It was kept a secret for nearly two hundred years. It is from the country's oldest club, Philadelphia's Fish House, founded in 1732. Indeed, originally the Fish House was a separate state, recognized by colonial governors.

The Fish House was a cooking club, in time known for its beefsteak, and its limited four hundred members gathered twice a month for dinner, cooked by its own "citizens" and served by the "apprentices" who aspired to full citizenship.

The Famous Fish House Punch

2 bottles of potent rum
1 old and potent bottle of brandy
¾ pound sugar to each bottle
1 wineglass peach brandy to each bottle
¾ quart lemon juice

The sugar goes in the bowl first. Water is poured in to make a syrup. After that comes the lemon juice. Then the liquors are added. Warning? It's dynamite!*

I HAVE BEEN SAVING the *New York Times* growing collection of brand-new, popular, and forgotten mixed drinks for several years. If I add my pet ones here, I'll have to expand this book into a booze encyclopedia. Go to the *New York Times* website.

A Slightly Tipsy Postscript

One of the best things I ever saw on film was a western movie to which the French had added subtitles. A cowboy goes into a bar, bangs down his fist, and says, "Bring me a shot of red-eye."

The French subtitle read, *"Un Dubonnet, s'il vous plaît!"*

---

* GQ magazine, in December 2004, offered an updated version of Fish House Punch, which you might like better. It includes Southern Comfort, black tea, and honey.

CHAPTER 17

IN THE

LEA OF

LEE

In my memoir, *Natural Blonde,* I offered up a historical and emotional version of my requited and unrequited love affair with the cooking-design maven Lloyd Lee Bailey, now unfortunately gone to heaven after a series of strokes incapacitated a great career. He and I were intimate friends almost from the moment we met in 1960. We should have married, but he didn't want to—and that was that. He loved me, but he didn't want to be an adjunct to my highly visible and irritating public career. He was nobody's "walker." He was his own man.

We made an accommodation. He mixed masterful food and created wonderful exteriors and interiors. I mixed masterful cocktails. I was "easy come, easy go"—he was more of a minimalist martinet, both giving and demanding. We had in common a childhood adoration of movies and an appreciation for the vagaries of growing up Southern.

When we met, Lee hadn't decided on a career. He was designing sets for advertising and later tried his hand at representing photographers. But soon he fixed on his destiny. Long-held family ideas of down-home cooking, his years studying at Parsons School of Design, a friendship with the famed Brennan restaurant family of New Orleans, plus his own approach to simplicity of living and design set Lee on his course. And the house he built that we shared in Bridgehampton, Long Island, became a mecca for our crowd. We lived there happily for almost twenty summers.

Before building our house we had visited for several summers with the acting and literary agent Gloria Safier in her tiny Quogue beachfront three-room cottage, the Mouse House. (So named because a mouse had been incinerated in the toaster.) The house and Gloria herself had a modicum of fame. Related to the Hollywood Selznicks, she knew everyone who was anyone, and as for the Mouse House, it had been famously visited by Marlon Brando and Wally Cox. It had been slept in by the great beauty Vivien Leigh, who, we discovered to our dismay, snored. Our next-door neighbor was the volatile, talented writer-director Arthur Laurents. And we had set tables for Nora Kaye, Jerome Robbins, Gloria Vanderbilt, Lena Horne, Rex Harrison, Arlene Francis, Ethel Merman, Anne Sheridan, Mary Astor. When famous people were present Lee and I sometimes had to sleep in our car, but even when only we three were in residence, don't ask where we all laid down our heads.

I recall that youthful era as a time of struggle, hours in the supermarkets, carrying huge bags of groceries up out of the car and over the sand dunes from Westhampton Beach Road. In spite of the small house and the informal beach life, Gloria was a maniacal cook and hostess, literally saying "Eat! Eat!" during every meal. If we suggested something simple like hot dogs or going out to one of the local cafés, she'd go wild. No! Food was important, food was all and its preparation was next to godliness. There were virtual orgies of menu planning, exhaustive shopping, peeling, slicing, cooking, serving, cork popping, ice cracking, clearing, washing, and left-over storing, punctuated by frantic departures back to New York City in a blur of Baggies. This all ended in the eventual throwing out of lots of Jewish family-style cooking with visions of stuffed cabbage dancing in our dreams.

Those were not the days of wine and roses, but of pot roast, kugel, versions of pasta with pesto, chopped liver, potato pancakes. We had courses and courses of food. We had all escaped our family orbits and were now busy as young "professionals" playing house on our own weekend terms. Or were we?

Lee and I had fled north toward home (to borrow the Willie Morris line) to find ourselves still bowing to a loving but harsh brand of domestic, motherly tyranny. We were so pleased to find ourselves under the thumb of this dynamic woman who had made a name for herself in the movie and theater world that we meekly assumed our chores. But Lee had his own ideas; underneath his kind, gentle exterior he was willful and stubborn. He wasn't much interested in accommodation. He would sometimes say to me, as we slaved away to please Gloria: "When we get our own house, we'll be relaxed. There'll be only the bare necessities . . . just enough in the kitchen for dinner that same night . . . never any leftovers . . . nothing taking hours to prepare! You'll see!"

When Lee inherited a small sum of money after his father's death, he plopped it down on a Sagg Pond property in Bridgehampton near the edge of the ocean. Owning the land, he managed a mortgage and built an open-air boxcar of a house, as simple as can be. He filled the yard with flowers and left the house open to the sea breezes and bought some simple white furniture. He said to me, "We have the view. We have an informal, easy house. We have white sheets and linens. We have good beds, no clutter, a marvelous fireplace and an excellent kitchen. Now all we need are happy guests!"

No clutter was his life rule. He didn't want refrigerator magnets, tchotchkes, artifacts, or collections. In his closet he kept about three shirts and pairs of chinos plus sneakers and loafers. He said of his wardrobe, "If I have anything more, Elaine Stritch will just borrow it when she comes to visit."

Lee and I did most of the work in this house and for a while we were touched by splashes of white paint. Finally all was done but one baseboard in the living room. I kept nagging him to finish it off. He said, "Honey, a man only has so much painting in him for a year and I am done for this year!" In this Tom Sawyer manner, of course, I had to finish it.

"Have a fried oyster as a reward!" said Lee, emerging from the kitchen to see my handiwork. In time, Lee's philosophies had a profound effect on me. I didn't want clutter either and I still spend all my spare time getting rid of things I accumulate with such energy.

We fried a lot of chicken in our kitchen; it was expected of us. But we stuck to Lee's rules of simplicity. Only enough groceries for the next meal, good-quality booze and mixers, no hors d'oeuvres beyond an occasional peanut. Homemade mayonnaise because Lee insisted it was "just like making homemade ice cream . . . it's not supposed to last; that's the beauty of it!" Lee was so implacable about extras coming into the house that I recall he always made me keep my inevitable package of potato chips in the trunk of my car.

Lee's good friend Lee Klein, a food and restaurant whiz from California, used to visit and comment on the "ageless good taste" in this house. He finally said, "Lee, we all need to know how to do this—what you do. Write it down." Lee's good friend Amy Gross also begged Lee over and over to do a book. And he had Nora suggesting the same thing. Thus, Lee's first book, *Country Weekends*, was born, published by Clarkson Potter and selling over one hundred thousand copies right off the bat. Lee went on to write eighteen more books about effortless living, good design, simple food, fabulous flowers, and how to entertain without breaking a sweat.

We began to collect a group of the talented, the aspiring, and some who had already "arrived." We fed them, we poured libations, and Nora Ephron claimed people loved the sexual frisson. "No one could figure out who was sleeping with whom!" It was true; if a strange person turned up in your bed, one merely shrugged and moved elsewhere. Or not. There were lots of beds, chaises, sofas, deck mats overlooking a jeweled body of water alive with swans and ospreys, sunfish, and no motorboats. The shore was marked by beautiful waving reedlike fragmities.

We entertained the blond bombshell Barbara Howar, then dating the super-silent Herb Sargent (premier writer at *Saturday Night Live*). As she entered our gangplank walk, she threw a glance back at Herb, saying, "And you know Mount Rushmore!" We had Mary Ann Madden, from *New York* magazine, the girl who knew everyone and everything. Carl Bernstein fresh from his Watergate scoop. Nora Ephron, of course, well on her way to becoming his ex and her own big success story. Marie Brenner, who said she moved back from L.A. just because of us. Helen Gurley Brown did her exercises, shaking the house to its stilts. Hubby David Brown roamed our beach, wondering if *Jaws* would be a hit. We had director-writer Frank Perry, who came with wife number one, Eleanor, and then wife number two, Barbara Goldsmith. We received Elaine Stritch between her SROs, and the Beatles guy, Peter Brown, plus Patsy Hemingway, the nightclub toughie who ruled the Bullshead Inn. We had playwright Arthur Laurents and his friend Tom Hatcher, as well as the enigmatic choreographer Jerry Robbins, the set designer Peter Larkin, and Jimmy Kirkwood, who would one day win a Pulitzer for *A Chorus Line*. Craig Claiborne graced us with his charming presence. Truman Capote liked our chili. We discovered Mississippi's shy Tom Harris, still to write *The Silence of the Lambs*. We welcomed lit agent Binky Urban and writer Ken Auletta. We sat at the feet of Elaine Steinbeck and lauded our duPont neighbor Francis Carpenter, a sort of "Auntie Mame" beauty who brought to us Jerome Zipkin, Ruby Schinazi, Louisa Carpenter, and Oscar de la Renta, plus steering her houseguests Greta Garbo and Gaylord Hauser across our lawn to the ocean. (We lay on the roof watching them with binoculars!) We had *Vogue*'s Carrie Donovan, fashion's Gillis McGill, Gerry Stutz, and Diane von Furstenberg, ABC's Roone Arledge, Lucie Arnaz, and Gary Pudney, a man who held the hands of stars like Diana Ross and would sometimes pose standing on his head for us so we could observe what he called his "heart-shaped balls." We had Rex Reed, Chauncey Howell, Amy Gross (one day to edit Oprah's *O*), Barry Diller, Kelly and Calvin Klein, Ralph and Ricky Lauren, and at least three Tony winners—Peg Murray, Ruth Mitchell, Florence Klotz. We discovered the actress Holland Taylor and she discovered us. One day the aspiring movie director Joel Schumacher came by for a drink and then moved in with us. I'm sure I've neglected numbers of wonderful friends.

The only clutter Lee would allow in the living room was photo albums. They still exist with their titled premonitions. One year we were "The Jet Nothings" and another year we titled ourselves "In Happier Days." We thought these albums would never end.

LEE'S GOOD FRIEND Nora Ephron has summed up Lee better than anyone else. Here's what the writer-director said about him not too many years ago in *The New York Times*:

I think I learned almost everything I know about having people to dinner from Lee Bailey. This was long before he began writing cookbooks, and, through them, influencing thousands of readers and a generation of cookbook writers. When I first met him, in the late sixties, he was a designer and he lived in the East 40s in a duplex that was one of those places you walked into and wanted to live in;

everyone felt this way. Every single object in it was simple and beautiful. The wood-handled knives and forks were beautiful. The seersucker napkins were beautiful, and what's more, they didn't have to be ironed. Everything was white, or beige, or sometimes gray, and fantastically easy on the eyes. In fact, right around the time I met Lee, Geraldine Stutz walked into Lee's apartment and wanted to live in it so badly that she hired him to open a small shop at Henri Bendel, the department store she was running at the time; as a result, I was able to buy the very glasses and knives and forks and seersucker napkins I had seen at Lee's, and before long almost everything I too owned was white, or beige, or sometimes gray.

Anyway, here's the thing about dinner at Lee Bailey's: First of all, there was the sense, at Lee's, that having people to dinner wasn't that big a deal. When you arrived, the table was set, it's true, but otherwise nothing much seemed to be going on. There was never a bartender. No one could afford a bartender in those days, but in any case, there wouldn't have been one. There was never anyone hired to serve the dinner or do the dishes. There were no hors d'oeuvres, although sometimes—especially at Lee's house in Bridgehampton—there was a bowl of unshelled raw peas, if they were in season, which they usually weren't. At a certain point in the cocktail hour, Lee would start to cook. If something like biscuits was on the menu, Lee's great friend Liz Smith would cook along with him. Anyone with a desire to chop onions or mince garlic was also welcome in the kitchen. And later, considerably later, after quite a lot had been drunk, dinner would appear. Platters of food were put on a table and guests would help themselves and sit down at the table to eat . . .

Why not just say that things at Lee's were relaxed? But you have to understand that back in those days, when I was learning to cook, people were nervous wrecks about having dinner parties. My generation had studied Julia Child and Michael Field and Craig Claiborne with something approaching religious fervor, and I had spent several years going to dinner parties where hostesses had slaved for hours over dishes that had capital letters in them, like veal Orloff and beef Wellington. When you arrived for dinner, their faces were red from kitchen heat, exhaustion, and sometimes tears. When you sat down to eat, they looked nervously around the table in the hope you would spend the entire meal discussing the food. There were cheese courses. There were elaborate desserts. There was the year of things wrapped in phyllo, and the year of the Brazilian national dish. There was, I swear to God, a week in the early seventies when every neurotic woman in the city of New York rolled strips of chicken breast in water-chestnut flour and made the lemon chicken recipe from Pearl's Chinese restaurant. We were looking for applause; we were constantly overreaching; we were desperate to be all things to all people; we were trying to astonish men and outdo other women; we were, in short, out of our minds. Lee, on the other hand, was not.

Which brings me to the second point about Lee; the food. Lee is from Bunkie, Louisiana, and whatever he served for dinner had a Southern feel to it. It was honest food, cooked simply, easy as pie, but every taste on the plate was delightfully tuned to every other taste on the plate. In Lee's childhood home, a number of dishes were served with his Aunt Freddie's famous pepper jelly (you could buy that at Bendel's, too), and he brought a version of Aunt Freddie into every menu and changed my ideas about what dinner-party food should be. I finally came up with a formula for Lee's menus, which I called the Rule of Four. Most people serve three things for dinner—some sort of meat, some sort of starch, and some sort of vegetable—but Lee always served four. And the fourth thing was always something playful and unexpected. A shallow dish filled with tiny baked apples. A casserole of lima beans and pears cooked for hours in brown sugar and molasses. Peaches with cayenne pepper. Sliced tomatoes with honey. Grits. Savory bread pudding. Spoon bread . . . Whatever it was, that fourth thing seemed to have an almost magical effect on the eating process. You never got tired of the food because there was always something else on the plate that seemed simultaneously to match it and contradict it. . . .

At Lee Bailey's, you could eat forever. This is important. This is crucial. There is nothing worse than having people to a dinner that they all just polish off and before you know it, they're done eating and dinner is over and it's only ten o'clock and then everyone leaves and it's just you and the dishes. And that was another thing about dinner at Lee's: On top of everything else, he had fewer dishes to wash, because he never ever served a first course or a cheese course; and if he served salad, it just went onto the plate along with everything else.

(And by the way, Lee never served fish, and, as a result, neither do I. Fish is way too easy to eat. Bim bam boom, you're done with a piece of fish, and you're right out the door. When people come to dinner, it should be fun and part of the fun should be the food. Fish—and I'm sorry to say this but it's true—is no fun. People like to play with their food, and it is virtually impossible to play with fish. If you must have fish, order it at a restaurant.)

Meanwhile, of course, there was the company. And somehow, the greatest conversation, the hugest laughs, and the most hilarious stories were at Lee's. The party never left the table, and lasted well beyond the time anyone intended to stay. Why? Simple: There was a round table. This was the third lesson I learned from

Lee . . . If you have people to dinner and make good food and then put your guests at a long rectangular table where people at one end can't hear what's going on at the other end and are pretty much trapped talking to the person on either side of themselves—well, what is the point? But put them at a round table, and at some point in the evening you can have one conversation. With any luck at all, the funniest person in the room will tell a great story and everyone will fall on the floor laughing and go home believing they've gone to one of the best dinners of their lives. I'm afraid I believe it's impossible to have a good dinner party at anything but a round table . . . The perfect round table is a sixty-inch round table which seats ten comfortably, but a fifty-two-inch round, which seats eight, is also nice, and you can cram eight people around a forty-two-inch table using very small chairs and they'll have a wonderful time because they're so excited to be so close to one another. Any round table is nicer than a table with corners. If you have a table with corners, turn it into a desk. That's my opinion.

Sometimes, I have to admit, I stray from Lee's lessons. I overreach from time to time. I am prone to serving not just four things but five. I have a weakness for salad. And on the design front, I long ago left behind white, beige, and gray, and, as a result, I have gone on to make all the decorating mistakes that are possible once you do. But every time I make dinner, I think about Lee.

Amy Gross once said that eating at Lee's was like going home. I hope someday someone who doesn't actually live in my house will say that about me.

At Lee's 2003 memorial in Le Cirque's biggest room, many spoke about his influence over them. Again, Nora reached the heights evoking him.

He was the closest thing to a Zen master I've ever known and we were slaves to the Zen koans he dropped into our brains. He taught by example and he loved you even if you were never going to be able to do things as simply and perfectly as he did. I've never understood why it isn't commonly known that he had a huge influence on life as we know it. It's easy to see the graphic influence—*Martha Stewart Living* and *Real Simple,* half the food and shelter magazines currently on the market and at least half the cookbooks look the way they do because of Lee's books. But beyond that he was in large measure responsible for a kind of laid-back informality that stemmed straight from his unflappable disposition and his deep gift for hospitality; that informality, it seems to me, is now the dominant style in this culture. If you learned anything from Lee, you learned to relax and to have fun and to love your guests and to try to make your house feel like their home and your dinner party feel like a family event. He was my friend and my guru. I'm not exaggerating when I say I worshipped him and made a religion out of everything he taught me. There are Christians who ask themselves what would Jesus do, but "what would Lee do" is my motto. It has been for more than thirty years and will be for as long as I can put a plate on the table.

THAT DAY, with four hundred people saying farewell to Lee, I remembered how only twice would he make for me the Wesson oil advertisement recipe I loved of chicken and peaches. "It's too commercial, Lizzie; I can't!"

He died, true to himself. I ate it twice and have never had it again.

Lee's Baked Lima Beans and Pears

Three 10-ounce packages frozen lima beans (6 cups)
2 large ripe pears, cored, peeled, and sliced crosswise
1 cup chicken broth
¼ cup brown sugar
¼ cup chopped onion
¼ cup light molasses
1 teaspoon salt
¼ teaspoon pepper

Preheat the oven to 200°F. In a heavy 2-quart casserole, combine the ingredients. Bake, covered tightly, about 8 hours.

YIELD: 6 SERVINGS

Lee's Heat-Resistant Biscuits

1 cup sifted all-purpose flour
1 tablespoon baking powder
½ teaspoon salt
6 tablespoons cold unsalted butter, cut into 6 pieces
⅔ cup milk, plus extra

1. Preheat the oven to 450°F. Sift the flour with the baking powder and salt into a medium bowl. Cut in the butter with two knives or a pastry blender until the butter is the size of small peas. Add the milk and mix quickly.

2. Turn out the dough onto a floured surface and knead lightly a few turns. Roll out with a floured rolling pin or flatten with the heel of your hand to ⅜-inch thickness. Cut out with a 2-inch biscuit cutter or a water glass, rerolling the scraps.

3. Arrange the biscuits about 1 inch apart on a heavy baking sheet and brush the tops with milk, using your finger. Bake about 10 minutes, or until golden.

YIELD: 12 TO 15 BISCUITS

CHAPTER 18

EATING WITH

FAMOUS MEN IN THE

SOUTH OF FRANCE

WORKING AS *Cosmopolitan*'s entertainment editor, I used to spend part of each May in France at the Cannes Film Festival. Certain people would pooh-pooh. They'd say Cannes was no longer chic and had been passé ever since the days of Federico Fellini and Anita Ekberg. No more bare-breasted actresses embracing big stars like Robert Mitchum in the surf. No glamour, no real stars. But it felt pretty glamorous to me when I sat down at the Eden Roc Hotel in Cap d'Antibes and ordered their special chocolate soufflé, or strolled down the Croisette toward Sam Spiegel's yacht in the harbor, or ate at night in what had been Picasso's favorite, the still-famous Moulin des Mougins, or walked through the open flower, vegetable, and fruit market in nearby Antibes. I would tool around in my rented car up to St. Paul de Vence to the hilltop restaurant, La Colombe d'Or, partly owned by Yves Montand and his French actress wife, Simone Signoret. She was usually found playing Scrabble in the empty dining room between meals. In the car I had a tape of Mabel Mercer singing Cole Porter's famous 1920s hit, "The Riviera." At those times, I didn't care that Cannes and environs weren't what they used to be. It was still rich for my blood.

The actual events of the film festival never much interested me. And, as Helen Gurley Brown let me write any impression I liked, I wasn't obliged to "cover" everything. I went to films that took my fancy and in between, there'd be an interview with some star who had flown in for twenty-four hours of hotbox promotion, usually for a movie having nothing to do with the festival. Cannes was a great place to catch the attention of the international movie crowd. And France was still the be-all and end-all of world food and drink.

Two of my famous "French" friends died just before the turn of the twenty-first century. Neither was from France but both were talented, creative artists. Their deaths took me back to the seventies and Cannes.

Cannes always gave me the chance to visit the British actor Dirk Bogarde, living in a rocky hilltop house in Châteauneuf de Grasse, right in the middle of the French perfume industry.

Dirk had total contempt for all things Hollywood and he was a demanding if studiedly informal host. He did not suffer American fools gladly. I'd show him my elaborate invitations for this or that festival happening, begging him to attend with me. "Are you insane, Sardine?" he'd snap. "I wouldn't be caught dead with those vultures from MGM" (or whatever studio was pouring).

He was equally contemptuous of filmmaking in general and carefully reserved his praise for the rare European directors like Alan Renais or Luchino Visconti or Joseph Losey. He seemed sometimes to be repudiating the business that had made him so famous. He had indeed run the gamut from being a popular movie matinee idol in the fifties to becoming what some called "the outstanding British cinema actor of his generation."

In the fifties, Dirk was a kind of Rock Hudson idol in a series of popular movies about a doctor. So crazed were his fans that he had to have the flies of his pants sewn shut for safety. Dirk himself said, "Actually, I had to wear a basket we called a 'cricket cage' when I went out to protect the family jewels." But at age forty he removed himself overnight from his detested early celebrity. He went against his leading-man image by playing a homosexual barrister in a controversial film called *Victim*. It was a watershed of frankness, daring for 1961.

Playing a homosexual on film was one thing—and he would do it a second time, for Visconti in Thomas Mann's *Death in Venice*. But *being* a homosexual was something else. Dirk and his life companion, Tony Forward, who was also his manager, behaved like two macho men of World War II—men who had thrown their lives together as dedicated bachelors. Dirk said for print, "Ours was a totally platonic relationship. Tony was rather a puritanical figure who also happened to hate the idea of homosexuality." For many years they lived together in Provence among olive trees overlooking a rocky, scrubby slope to the faraway hazy sea. Here they entertained the likes of Rex Harrison and his various wives, Sir John Gielgud, and other royalty of international entertainment.

And Dirk always went endlessly down memory lane, recollecting his days with Judy Garland, Capucine, Julie Christie, Kay Kendall, Vivien Leigh, and other actresses for whom he would express wistful romantic feelings.

Mr. Forward was a British military type—more English than the English—as they say. Early on he'd been married to the actress Glynis Johns and they had a son. Tony's family visited often. Dirk enjoyed showing off Tony's heterosexual past. Someone observed that everyone thought Tony and Dirk were gay, except Tony and Dirk. Striking blows for gays on film or off didn't make living such a life acceptable at the time.

I'd first interviewed Dirk for *The New York Times*, where he turned on his considerable charm. Learning that my name was really Mary Elizabeth, he equated me with a prized brand-name sardine, telling me how in the North African desert during the war, he had drooled over the memory of the Marie Elizabeth brand, vowing if he outwitted General Rommel's Afrika Korps and remained alive, he would eat his fill of the oily little fishes when he got back to civilization.

Later, I discovered he had misremembered. The sardines were actually called Elizabeth Marie, but who cared? My nickname stuck. In time, unsolicited, Dirk sent me a glamorous portrait of himself in riding boots, posing carelessly on a verdant lawn. It is inscribed "Dear Sardine . . ."

What I had done to impress the difficult Mr. Bogarde I never knew. But at our first meeting, I had been fan worshipful, and I suppose I asked good questions about his career, because we remained friends until his death. Some years before cancer claimed Tony, the couple had given up the charming French house and returned to England. There, Dirk became known for a second career, as a memoirist and writer of novels. Literary critics treated him respectfully and in 1992 he was knighted. He suffered a stroke in 1996. Although this disabled him, he continued to write by dictating, and insisted to the end that he not be described as a "recluse" or "depressed." This perfectionist and demanding friend taught me to curb my native-American exuberance because, obviously, he didn't like it. He wanted me to dress in a more fussy fashion and urged me to imitate his idol Kay Kendall. He was an autocratic host, an escapee from British food, saying it was perfectly acceptable to select one wine and keep serving it to your guests. In Dirk's case, this was Provence's L'Estandon — rouge, blanc, et rosé. I favored the rosé. It went well with one of Dirk's Provençal obsessions, the fragrant *brandade de morue*, made of codfish, garlic, and sometimes mashed potatoes.

Dirk was a gent, but an exacting one. I told him that I was a friend of the Countess Marina Cicogna, whose mother was the social arbiter of Venice. Marina had provided the money Visconti needed to finish making *The Damned*. I asked what Dirk thought of the countess, surely he approved of her Medici gesture? Dirk just snorted and said, "Sam Spiegel — in bobby sox!"

WHEN ANOTHER FRIEND, the American novelist Mario Puzo, died in the summer of 1999, I was sad, for I had loved and admired the creator of *The Godfather* and was amazed by his real-life creations, the Corleones of Sicily. They had translated to the screen in one of the great cinema triumphs of our time.

I remembered an epic moment then at Cannes with Puzo in the seventies, a moment when I did a rare thing and spoke up in defense of womanhood.

Puzo and I were sitting at lunch at the Carleton Hotel beach club. The salade niçoise was finished, the wine drunk, and Mario and I still sat talking about writing. Mario, the son of illiterate Italian immigrants, said he never felt he had done enough. (He would write eight novels and have at least eleven films made from his work.) But even though *The Godfather* was a success in print and on the screen, he was beating himself up for not working harder. "I need to do much more," he said. "Relax," I urged. "You have already given us a great classic book, and *The Godfather* is a film classic as well."

Near us sat a woman, no longer young, middle-aged, more than plump, casually dressed, wearing no makeup. She was smoking a cigarette, talking to a man at a deserted lunch table. Puzo glanced at her and started. "My God! That's Simone Signoret. Isn't that Simone Signoret?"

I observed that indeed it was. Puzo said, "I was madly in love with her after *Room at the Top*. She was my idol for years, my fantasy. But look at her now. She looks just awful, terrible!"

He shook his head.

I looked at Mario. He was fat and slovenly. His short hairy legs hung out of crumpled shorts. He was wearing a red Lacoste polo shirt that emphasized his rather pendulous breasts. Not becoming. He had a stubble of beard with a cigar stuck in it and resembled an old bulldog.

I said, "Mario, look who's talking. No doubt back in 1959 when *Room at the Top* was released, you looked a lot better yourself than you do today. Take into account the years. Grant Simone Signoret the right to grow old along with you. She doesn't have to keep looking like the movie image of your dreams. You can be kinder than Rex Reed was recently; he wrote that her skin now resembles an orange rind. It's not fair."

Puzo stared at me, silent and shocked. He knew I was his rabid admirer. This outburst was unexpected coming from me. He breathed deeply, exhaled, and burst into laughter.

"Liz, girl, you are a hundred percent right. I'm a fat slob looking at a queen. I should go apologize to her." I said, "Well, don't do that. Just grant women the right to be as unattractive as men sometimes are. Although you might stop by her table and say who you are and express your admiration."

Puzo stood, hitched up his shorts, bent down and kissed me good-bye, and headed for Signoret's table. I had never met the fabled French star though I'd seen her often. I didn't want to intrude on idols in communion. I simply left the beach in a self-righteous haze. My pal Gloria Steinem had always said that I wasn't good at women's liberation: "You, Liz, want to be the only Jew in the club." Well, she'd have been proud of me that day.

Bogarde's *Brandade de Morue*

A Triumph of Provençal Cooking
with special thanks to Elizabeth David

You will have to search for the dried cod. I suggest markets in ethnic neighborhoods, where you might have to substitute smoked cod. Treat it the same.

Take your fish, 2 pounds for 6 guests, and soak in cold water for 12 hours. Clean it, and put in a pan of cold water, cover, and remove from the pot as soon as it boils. Carefully remove the bones and any skin. Crush a clove of garlic, maybe two, in the bottom of a large pot and place over a low flame. In two other saucepans have some milk and some olive oil, keeping both warm but not hot. Now add the oil and milk to the fish, spoon by spoon, alternately, stirring hard all the time with a wooden spoon, crushing the cod against the side of the pot as you go with great energy. (In Provençal, *brandar* means "to stir or break," hence the name *brandade*.) When the mixture begins to look like a thick cream, you are finished. It is important that none of the ingredients get hot, or the whole operation is ruined. Some folk like to pound the fish in a mortar before adding it to the oil and milk.

Brandade can be served warm or cold, especially with great little pastries garnished with truffles, or fried bread. One of the most delicious *brandades* I tasted was served at Le Moulin de Châteauneuf-du-Pape and was made with smoked salmon. If you don't feel up to beating a cod, try this substitution.

CHAPTER 19

HOSPITALITY

AND

MANNERS

I HAVE ALWAYS LOVED books about how to behave. I read them, I aspire, I usually fail. Recently the designer Kate Spade put out three little works in blue, red, and green. They are really gems, titled *Manners, Occasions, Style.* Even if you don't read them, they'll dress up your room. Adding to Kate, I have already quoted Miss Manners in this book and I feel the need to remark that if you want to have more fun, read Charlotte Ford's book on etiquette.

This all set me to thinking about behavior in relationship to feeding, fueling, hosting, or interacting with those you like and love. It's much more than just the good table manners that I have tried to cover elsewhere.

It's about heart and feeling. It's what I remember my darling mother saying over and over: "The best-mannered person in the room is the one who never makes anyone else feel uncomfortable." (Such a thought in these contentious times.)

I had not been living in New York very long before I made the acquaintance of the Broadway costume designer Irene Sharaff, a formidable dragon lady who scared the hell out of everyone, including me. Shot to fame when she combined orange and fuchsia and pink for the authentic Thai costumes in *The King and I*, Irene won many kudos in the theater. She was also given to high pronouncements, such as that Michelangelo was a simply horrible artist and his sculpture vulgar in the extreme. I had only just discovered Michelangelo, but after that I stopped having opinions around Irene and simply listened, which pleased her no end.

I think the total Texas cultural vacuum of my life appealed to her teaching instincts, and for her, I was a blank canvas. Soon I was invited to meet her life companion, the equally formidable Mai Mai Sze, who had written a book everyone said was incredible, titled *The Tao of Chinese Art*. These ladies were such a talented duo that they brooked no competition or opposition. Perhaps they were lovers; they were certainly some kind of force unto themselves. But as Tina Turner always says, "What's love got to do with it?"

One evening I was in their East 50s apartment manfully (or womanfully) trying to eat celestial tree fungus and other unknown Chinese delicacies, and I was overcome to find myself sharing sea cucumbers with two of my idols face-to-face. They were Mary Petty, the great cover artist of *The New Yorker* magazine, and her husband, *New Yorker* cartoonist Alan Dunn, who almost always used the White House in his satiric drawings. They told me right off the bat that they seldom went out and were rather reclusive. "But we always accept invitations to come to Irene and Mai Mai's because their apartment is on a very low floor of this building. And," said the genial Mr. Dunn, "I have a phobia about being trapped in a high-rise fire, so I try never to go above the second floor in any building."

I asked if this didn't make his work at *The New Yorker* difficult. "Oh," he smiled. "I don't go in. I work at home on the ground floor." I liked Mr. Dunn's rather Caspar Milquetoast look and his obvious adoration of his wife. She had long been the paragon of class consciousness to me as I had been collecting her divine magazine covers for years. They were usually of starched Victorian maids leaning out of upper windows looking down on their betters. Mary Petty had made upstairs/downstairs famous long before the BBC thought of a television series.

She was plump and lovable and as eccentric as her husband. But I'm sure my adoration exhausted her and after dinner, Ms. Petty left me and slumped her ample body into a nearby chair. Irene's living room was full of people and we all watched, incredulous, as the chair under Mary Petty slowly collapsed into a cracking heap of antique splinters and Louis Quinze armrests.

I rushed to rescue her and ask if she was hurt. "No, nothing but my pride," said Mary Petty as she tried to rise. Before she could do so, Irene arrived, eyes blazing. She was an avenging virago, shouting insults, denouncing Mary Petty's weight, her villainous intent in sitting down, her deliberate destruction of a priceless artifact that "could never be replaced," as if Ms. Petty had done it on purpose.

This sort of embarrassing social behavior among the high and mighty was definitely a new experience for me as I helped Mary Petty rise from her wooden spears with caning stuck to her backside. She and Mr. Dunn then ruefully departed, murmuring their regrets. Irene continued to rage in the background.

I was too cowardly to make a comment, but I couldn't get over it. It had never occurred to me that a host or hostess was allowed to be so rude and insulting. When I described this later, on the phone to my mother, she asked if I was making it up. Then she said, "Maybe you better come home away from people like Miss Sharaff."

I did indeed never go to Irene's apartment again though she often invited me. I watched in awe as she slaughtered other Broadway costumers, winning a Tony and six nominations and even collecting five Oscars and nine Academy Award nominations. In later years she did me a tremendous favor in smoothing my way with Elizabeth Taylor. But I remained awestruck and insecure around her as if she were a tiger on a leash.

I always envisioned my mother as Mary Petty's host. She'd have helped her up with apologies for having a rotten old chair in the house and she'd have tossed the priceless splinters into the fireplace without giving them a second look.

I think I am very lucky to have had a mother like that to remember.

CHAPTER 20

1. NEVER QUIT.

2. BE YOURSELF.

3. DON'T PUT TOO MUCH FLOUR IN YOUR BROWNIES.

I SUPPOSE YOU REALIZE already those rules to live by were handed down by Katharine Hepburn. She made them for a girl named Heather Henderson whose father lived in Kate's Turtle Bay neighborhood. One day he asked Kate if she'd intervene in his daughter's decision to quit college. So Miss Hepburn did. She telephoned Heather at 7:30 one morning and asked if she was speaking to the person who wanted to quit Bryn Mawr. "What a damn stupid thing to do!" growled Kate. Then the star invited Heather and her father to tea. They came and she told Heather that although she had been miserable at Bryn Mawr and still had nightmares about going there, she was glad she'd gone. Later, Kate admonished Heather's father that the brownies he'd delivered to her had too much flour. "Don't overbake them. They should be moist, not cakey."

And so we shall retell again the famous Hepburn recipe, which first appeared in *Ladies' Home Journal* in 1975. Kate herself called these "the best brownies ever!"

I had many occasions to sample Miss Hepburn's ideas of perfection.

I met her in 1997 and she fed me often before her death in 2003. When her book, *Me*, came out in 1999, I did a Q & A with her for *Vogue* that I still think ranks right up there with the best of any answers she ever gave.

Dinner with Kate was highly regulated. One had to ring the bell at the Turtle Bay house promptly at six. Kate would bound down the stairs herself to bring you into her town house, saying "Do you drink?"—then pouring a whopper for you and keeping your glass refilled. Sometimes when I left promptly at 8:30 so she could go to bed early, I was looking for a potted plant to empty my glass.

Kate was more like a director than the greatest star that the American Film Institute said she was. (During the time I knew her, the AFI named her number one along with Humphrey Bogart as the male number one. She was disgusted that her great love, Spencer Tracy, came in at number eight!) Kate was definitely in charge in her living room; one could not bring in any object—a coat, an umbrella, a briefcase. Everything had to be left in the hall. She told you where to sit. She rearranged pillows, urged you to eat and drink more, and poked the crackling fire. If the fire failed to crackle, Kate convinced it to do so.

Her longtime cook, Nora Moore, served us fabulous meals on trays in the living room where we talked as we ate. Typical Hepburn dinner: large cup of beet soup with dill, or zucchini with shallots. Thin Portuguese bread buttered and toasted, or bagel chips. Steak, curried lamb, fish, roast chicken, roast beef with Yorkshire pudding; potatoes au gratin, baked potatoes (one of Kate's favorites, and the very item to which she compared Spencer Tracy, saying that's what he was like—a perfect baked potato, skin on, ready to eat).

Kate also loved caviar, chocolate from Mondel Chocolates on Broadway and 114th Street, deviled eggs heavy on the cayenne, and little sandwiches of ham and chicken with the crusts off. She made a mean fried egg, punching a hole in a slice of bread with a glass, cracking the egg into the center as it lay in the frying pan. Miss Hepburn drank Famous Grouse or King William IV scotch. Once when I jokingly brought her two bottles of vodka and gin produced in Vermont, she wouldn't accept them. "Why," said she, "they're only sixty proof. It's not real liquor!" Carrots and celery were standard at most meals. Dessert was inevitably coffee or vanilla ice cream with hot fudge or thick butterscotch sauce. Nora always offered guests her lace cookies.

One of the best things about dining with Kate in Turtle Bay was her manner of calling down for service. Like Sylvester Stallone in *Rocky*, she'd simply give a great holler, "Yo!" Nora would dash up.

Her favorite comments in the brief years I knew her were usually, "Thank God, I'm so glad I don't have to go" in describing some event . . . "Never heard of them!" in reference to other famous persons being talked about . . . "I could never do that!" referring to some feat, some chore, some trip or other. When we went to the theater Kate masterminded everything from tickets to timing to the car. It had to be white so she could find it after and make her getaway. But first we had to go backstage to congratulate the cast. That was a law.

You could never approach a seedless grape unthinkingly again after encountering Kate, who insisted that grapes for chicken salad be sliced "Vertically! Vertically! They don't taste the same cut across."

Let me recommend, if you want more Kate Hepburn foodlore, that you buy *Guess Who Came to Dinner . . . ?*, compiled by Nora Moore's daughter, Eileen Considine-Meara. You can reach her on email at Tmara2@aol.com, or write her at 2971 Hyatt Street, Yorktown Heights, NY 10598.

Kate's Famous Brownies

1. Preheat the oven to 325°F.

2. Melt 2 squares unsweetened chocolate and ¼ pound butter over very low heat in a heavy saucepan.

3. Remove from the heat and stir in 1 cup granulated sugar.

4. Beat in 2 eggs and ½ teaspoon vanilla.

5. Quickly stir in 1 cup chopped walnuts, ¼ cup all-purpose flour, and ¼ teaspoon salt.

6. Spread the batter in a well-greased 8 x 8-inch baking pan. Bake for 45 to 50 minutes. Remove the pan to a rack to cool.

YIELD: 12 BROWNIES

Nora's Incredible Lace Cookies

⅛ pound (4 tablespoons) butter
½ teaspoon vanilla
1 cup chopped walnuts

⅓ cup raw sugar
1 egg
⅔ cup light brown sugar
1 heaping tablespoon flour

1. Preheat the oven to 350°F.

2. Mix all the ingredients in a bowl and drop by the spoonful on a greased cookie sheet.

3. Bake for 7 to 8 minutes.

4. Let them cool before sliding them off the sheet.

RECIPE YIELDS ABOUT 40 THIN, CRISPY COOKIES.

CHAPTER 21

BABY,

WHEN IT'S COLD

OUTSIDE!

H AVE YOU EVER WINTERED in Vermont, New Hampshire, or Maine? There, one spends an inordinate amount of time in the winter just staying alive, struggling through icebound roads to the nearest supermarket, struggling to bring in firewood, struggling to keep warm and make the kind of food that keeps body and soul together.

The greatest thing about Vermont is its slogan, "The Way America Used to Be." I think that is still true. Likewise, I loved the roads with no advertising to speak of. But some of my less endearing memories are of standing next to a frozen car door with a long extension cord attached to a hair dryer, trying to get locomotion started. Once upon a time I was in Vermont with the down-to-earth *Vogue* editor Billy Norwich. We took blue photographs of each other because it was minus ten degrees and the Polaroid film didn't like that.

But I have two excellent food memories that could be quite effective when it's cold outside anywhere. The first is adapted from James Beard's *American Cookery*. This is a really unusual winner!

Jessie Duncan's Steak Three Inches Thick

Preheat the oven to 450°F. Place a prime cut (sirloin or shell) 3- to 4-inch steak on a rack in a roasting pan and top it with 2 thinly sliced onions, 3 thinly sliced seeded green bell peppers, and 1 peeled and thinly sliced lemon. (Yes, a thinly sliced peeled lemon!)

Salt and pepper to taste or after cooking. Cover the steak with 1½ cups of ketchup. After the first 5 minutes in the oven, add 1 cup beef bouillon to it. Keep basting from time to time with the ketchup and beef broth until the meat is done. Roast for 20 to 30 minutes for rare to medium rare.

Here's a good twist for this recipe. You can sear the steak on the stove or on a barbecue grill before adding the other ingredients. Then put it in the pan and start roasting. This seems to give it a head start.

Diane Judge's Food Mill Masterpiece

Don't bother with this one unless you are willing to buy a food mill. You know, one of those red plastic affairs you put together and take apart to wash. But believe me, if you get one, you can make a tomato sauce work of art.

The only work is in the beginning. Miss Judge insists that she has tried every which way to make this sauce less labor intensive, but the result is never as good as if you follow her lead.

Take two 28-ounce cans of whole peeled tomatoes, Italian style. (Progresso is fine.) Put them through the food mill. It seems silly not to just buy cans of already squooshed-up tomatoes, but it does make a difference, so do it Diane's way.

Put the tomatoes, after having "milled" them, in a large skillet and place it on low heat. Then peel a large sweet onion, like a Vidalia. Cut that in half and stud each half with whole cloves. Put the onion in the pan with the tomatoes. Add ¼ pound of sweet (unsalted) butter. Cook slowly until the butter has melted and the onion is soft but still whole.

Remove the onion and discard. Add salt and pepper to taste. Serve this over perciatelli pasta, which seems to like the sauce best!

Don't forget to wash the food mill. It's really quite easy to deal with once you face the fact and buy one.

YIELD: ENOUGH FOR 6 FOR DINNER

CHAPTER 22

A BITE

OF

HISTORY

People are always eating, have you noticed? If they are not eating, they are planning to eat, shopping, experimenting, talking of the next meal or the last one. They eat in novels, in plays, in opera, in art, and in musical comedy.

Food features in many works of nonfiction. For instance, in *Moscow 1812*, by Adam Zamoyski, much of the story is about people desperate to eat, dying of starvation as Napoleon's army did in its retreat out of Russia. A million people died because of Napoleon's hubris and many perished not from battle, but from lack of sustenance.

In the movies, eating on film is a serious problem for actors who want to be realistic but not gross and don't want to ruin their dialogue with a mouthful. Uma Thurman is described by *The New York Times* as saying that an actor can cook her goose chewing on-screen. "I do anything I can to avoid eating in a scene. The self-conscious chew of the actor is very tough," she adds with a hearty laugh. "Some people love to eat. I call them food actors. They love to eat, eat, eat. And the food on the plates? It usually is so revolting. Canteen slop. That is why, when I made *The Golden Bowl* in England with James Ivory and Ismail Merchant, I felt really cheated because Ismail, who is famous for cooking on his sets, cooked his delicious Indian food only once."

In the film *Ocean's 11*, Brad Pitt distinguishes his character from the other ten guys by almost always eating through all his scenes. Onstage in *Hello, Dolly!* Carol Channing and other Dollys had to consume a great meal before a live audience. Someone devised a kind of frothy disappearing rice cake that looked like mashed potatoes.

IT'S INTERESTING TO THINK that at the time Jean-François Millet was painting pictures of agricultural nineteenth-century France, the peasant subjects of *The Gleaners* and other famous works did not even have furniture in their houses. These hardworking souls sat down on whatever was handy, a stool or on a dirt floor, they slept on rags in a corner of a hut, and the preparation of food was probably minimal. But kings and potentates, emperors, pharaohs, dictators, and despots already had refined kitchens, cooks, and some—like the court of the Bourbon kings—had silver furniture. Excess had been going on for quite some time for those at the top throughout the history of man.

LUCULLUS SAID that when men dine alone, at such times they try to forget they are dining with only themselves. They want to ignore this frightening truth. He evidently enjoyed eating alone, saying, "This evening Lucullus sups with Lucullus!"

And speaking of dining alone, one of the grandest kings who ever reigned, Louis XIV, took his lunch every noon all by himself. He was served by court nobles at a square table, where he might have four plates of soup—pheasant, partridge, stewed mutton with garlic, cauliflower in stock. Then he'd have ham and salad, some roast, pastries, fruit, and hard-boiled eggs. Although the fork had been in use since 1648, the king preferred to eat with his fingers. He liked to dip sweet biscuits in Burgundy and he enjoyed Champagne and the turkeys he bred at Versailles. He had many greenhouses for exotic fruits, like the pineapple. He loved ices and drinks, which he often requested to be served in goblets carved out of ice.*

Why did the Sun King dine alone? Perhaps it was a sign that he had no peer. Most people feel eating alone is a bad sign, a signifier of loneliness, desperation. But at the height of his popularity, Robert Redford told me he couldn't think of anything he'd rather do than sit down to a meal and not be bothered by another human being. And perhaps Louis XIV, who had to rise, retire, and perform ablutions in public, simply liked a few moments to himself.

Two years into the Revolution, the French royal family fled to the sixteenth-century convent of the Feuillants. They'd lost most of their clothes, but still, King Louis XVI managed to have himself served two soups, eight entrees, four roasts, and eight desserts. He ate heartily, as if he were at Versailles, and drank Bordeaux, Champagne, and liqueur.

When the family was imprisoned in the Tower of the Old Templar Order, food was served liberally. The servants, knowing no other way of attending to their masters, produced soups, entrees, roasts, fowl, and desserts with which the court was familiar.

In fact, for all those of a high order who were imprisoned, food soon took on enormous importance. Its acquisition necessitated trips to the outside world and was a way to send and receive messages. Some in prison paid exorbitant sums for meals, especially last ones.

During his trial, the king never lost his appetite. At one point he was distracted by a plate of rolls and, in tears, unable to concentrate on questions put to him, blurted out, "Please, might I have one of those?" For his last meal, Citizen "Louis Capet" ate sixteen pork chops before going to the guillotine.

THE LADY WHO KNEW IT ALL, M. F. K. Fisher, says that the nineteenth century will never be forgotten for its great contribution to gastronomy—the restaurants. But as the Terror in the eighteenth century ebbed, a few chefs from the houses of aristocrats emerged from hiding. They gathered up pastry cooks, roasters, sommeliers, and the like and

* I am grateful to Lisa Hilton's *Athenais: The Life of Louis XIV's Mistress, the Real Queen of France* for insights on the apex of seventeenth-century French culture. Her Little, Brown book on Madame de Montespan is just great.

began opening furtive eating places and cafés. As time went on and having an aristocratic trade didn't mean a death sentence, places became more glittery and grand. People began to eat as lustily and enormously as had the dead king and vanquished court.

Fisher says an obsession for fine eating swept over Europe. Dining, once again, became an art. Cooking and food and great chefs became food for thought for French writers like Dumas and de Maupassant. Meats, fruits, vegetables, and wines were combined and cooked and served in a thousand new ways.

Flavors and aromas never dreamed of rose from exciting new dishes. The French, ever imaginative, had invented the *pièce montée*. Contests were held. Some food was five feet high with Doric columns, full-blown flowers, and castles. Birds and people once again escaped from huge pies just as in the lusty days of Roman excess.

In America in the more recent seventies the first "painted plates" of food came into being. Writer Tom Wolfe later had one of his characters expire with his face fallen into the plating. We thought all this was grand and new in *The Bonfire of the Vanities*.

Actually it was 1919, the aftermath of World War I, when the U.S. society arbiter Maury Paul, the first Cholly Knickerbocker, was dining at the Ritz that his eye fell on a group about to have dinner—Mrs. Allen Gouverneur Wellman, Joe Widener, Laura Corrigan, Whitney Warren, Jr., and assorted Goelets, leading social names all.

Mr. Paul said to himself, "Society isn't staying home and entertaining anymore. Society is going out to dinner, out to nightlife, and letting down the barriers. Heavens—that I should see a Widener, a Goelet, a Corrigan, and a Warren all together. It's like a seafood cocktail with everything from eels to striped bass!"

According to the late Cleveland Amory, the very next morning, Mr. Paul batted out, in his two-fingered typing, the phrase "café society." He put this in his newspaper column and the handwriting was also on the wall. America had begun to dine out, especially on Thursdays, which was the cook's night off. And much later, in 1950, Emily Post herself described café society as an "unclassifiably mixed group of restaurant and night club habitues."

So there was no "revolution"—no reign of terror—no guillotine to punish the upper classes in the U.S. when they began to eat out. Restaurants had been trying to flourish from the days of Delmonico's on. And food grew more important for both rich and poor, as we imported increasing numbers of immigrant cuisines of both the upper and lower social orders and as we grew more sophisticated and experimental.

Today restaurant chains have been somewhat supplanted by fast-food chains,* and we are all discussing calories and cholesterol and carbohydrates and FAT. Great restaurants and famous chefs rise and fall on fads and foibles. Once we needed lots of fat to keep us warm and alive, but now we run from it. Food has gotten itself inextricably mixed up with medicine, science, and health.

---

* There are a few chains such as Seattle's Bonefish Grill and the Cheesecake Factory, Oceanaire in Minneapolis, plus the Houston's chain that draw high marks from Zagat and others for quality.

CHAPTER 23

SWEET

STUFF

URING THE KENNEDY ERA, Evangeline Bruce was a renowned Washington hostess. Her husband, David K. E. Bruce, had been ambassador to France, to West Germany, to Great Britain, and to NATO, as well as our envoy to China. But Mrs. Bruce did not want to be described as a "hostess." She said that word "presumably means you have people in for food and drink. I am an ambassador's wife. I run the social wing of the embassy. I entertain. I organize."

Mrs. Bruce claimed the notable element in entertaining was "the cast of characters." She insisted, "You never have a dinner of nothing but people you 'owe.' That is fatal. You must mix and match. Different types love to gape at one another. Mix ages, professions, and nationalities. Perhaps you might have a guest of honor who is willing to speak about his field of expertise."

According to C. David Hegmann's *The Georgetown Ladies Social Club,* Mrs. Bruce's true secret weapon, however, was this advice: "Always invite several beautiful young women and some wealthy older men!"

• • •

WHO GIVES EXCELLENT DINNER PARTIES in New York, in the Hamptons of Long Island, in social Connecticut, or on Martha's Vineyard—places I seem to go these days? Well, lots of well-heeled people do. And the invitation I never turn down always comes from Barbara Walters. I have never had a bad time at Barbara's and I've never had a bad dinner either.

This is because she has generosity, good taste, the wherewithal, and also a great sense of fun. (To say nothing of a world-class staff.)

Usually, Barbara has someone special she is honoring, which provides a focus for toasts, roasts, and pointed conversation. Her guests can be titans of media, government, the arts, or one of her big "get" names from television. So her dinners are illuminating and often spellbinding. But Barbara allows lots of leeway for informality.

She will always call her round dinner table or tables to order at midpoint so that a general conversation can take place. And if that isn't forthcoming, she will mount the good questions to get things started. Everyone is allowed to have his say. If you don't have fun and learn something at Barbara's, then you're not trying.

It has been said that Barbara could easily assume the mantle of social leader of New York now that Brooke Astor has retired from the scene. In fact, this was suggested in *The New York Times* a few years back by reporter Judy Miller. But Barbara doesn't want that social role; she is too busy still with her ABC news specials, her leading entrepreneurial position on her daytime hit, *The View,* and what will probably be a new book project. She isn't about to "retire." Whether or not she has the position of society's grande dame, Barbara certainly knows how to host New York's most interesting dinner parties.

Barbara doesn't hesitate to ask her guests to participate, to make a speech, sing a song, give a toast, write a poem. At a party honoring Sir Howard Stringer, of Sony, and his Japanese bosses, she asked me to do the honors. I wrote a little speech, had it translated into Japanese, then hired a teacher to help me memorize the sounds and give it phonetically. This was not a huge success; that is, my Japanese wasn't. But it was a great try and it delighted Howard's boss, the handsome CEO Nobuyuki Idei of Tokyo. And this delighted Howard and also Barbara.

I could tell of some high and mighty dinners I've had at Barbara's Fifth Avenue apartment. I could ask for her most highfalutin' menus. But my pick is one Barbara dreamed up on her own. It begins with large offerings of excellent caviar, toast, the works. What a warm-up! "That part is easy," says Barbara. "All you have to do is get your hands on increasingly rare, hard-to-come-by caviar. It's the rest of the dinner that seems to drive caterers crazy, but nowadays I think the people who work for me have it down pat."

For guests, sated with rare beluga, next comes "The Children's Menu," perfected for the delight of kids of all ages. Small, delicious hamburgers, tiny baby hot dogs on delicate buns are scarfed up by people who say to themselves, "Take two, or three, they're small!" With this comes a miniature ramekin of macaroni and cheese, french fried potatoes, incredible little dishes of coleslaw, and large servings after of ice cream and sauces. All accompanied by incredible wines. And when the coffee is offered, there are also big glasses of the one important thing many hostesses forget—ice water! I have watched grown men like Henry Kissinger, Alan Greenspan, George Steinbrenner, Jim Garner, Elton John, Benjamin Netanyahu, Kofi Annan, Jack Welch, all but cry when they realize they are getting Barbara's "kid's meal." Everyone is so relieved to be offered something they really like instead of poached salmon or whatever is currently floating society's boat.

And, throughout dinner, the inimitable Forrest Perrin is softly playing the piano in the living room, waiting for us to storm him and make our requests and start trying to remember the lyrics to everything Jerome Kern, Irving Berlin, Cole Porter, and Jerry Herman ever wrote. Barbara likes her guests to sing. If you go to a Christmas party at Barbara's, she always has the Salvation Army in to sing carols. They are religiously nonexclusive, so you can sing too, and it's not unusual to find a major Jewish mogul warbling "Chriii-sss-t the Saviour is born . . ." right along with the Christians and their lions.

Barbara's only concession to posh at her parties is to ask everyone to sign her handsome guest book. So it's fun to put your John Henry down on pages featuring kings and queens, dethroned empresses, people who've walked on the moon, divas of stage/screen/television, mighty anchormen and -women, politicians, tycoons, and stars, stars, stars, as well as Barbara's longtime childhood pals and her college chums.

• • •

I HAD A SLEW of fabulous hostesses who gave me an eightieth-birthday party at Le Cirque not long ago. This world-class event came off without my even knowing the names of my various hostesses. I knew I was having a party but that's all I knew. In time I found their names on the evening's printed invite lying in my plate. They were Barbara Walters, Louise Grunwald, Joan Ganz Cooney, Ellen Levine, Marie Brenner, Joni Evans, Cynthia McFadden, and Ann Richards.

They had talked Mike Nichols, Vernon Jordan, Joel Schumacher, and Pete Peterson into saying a few words. Governor Richards was the irreverent emcee, and that was all before Bette Midler, Tommy Tune, Michael Bublé, and Liza Minnelli entertained. What a party!

Not only was I surprised, but in such a beautiful way. My ladies had won the help of New York's well-known Gayfryd Steinberg. She designed the yellow tables, linens, and flowers. The upstairs room at Le Cirque fairly sparkled. And my pal Suzanne Goodson oversaw most of the problematic seating with an overlook from Joan Ganz Cooney. (It is said that by the time the great night of February 2 rolled around, Joan had "lost the will to live" over seating logistics.) This party included my very own wax statue on loan from Madame Tussauds New York at the suggestion of my agent, Joni Evans. In spite of a waxy Liz, the evening was incandescent.

The Sweetest Teeth

I mustn't belabor the glory of candy just because I am a junkie and an addict in need of candy's instant gratification. But I would say, offhand, that the cheaper, the better. While that's not always true, I honestly believe Godiva and those fancy chocolates can't hold a candle to your Snickers or your Hershey bar or Butterfinger or O. Henry or Baby Ruth.

Now, I know that fancy upscale folks pretend they don't eat or don't like candy, but three of America's best hostesses prove this is a myth at almost every one of their classic dinners. Tita Cahn, the merry widow of Oscar songwriter Sammy Cahn, gives some of L.A.'s best at her house in Beverly Hills. Her guest mix is breathtaking; it could include Jack Nicholson, Tina Sinatra, Sean Connery, Tony Danza, Warren Beatty, Annette Bening, Oliver Stone, Jeannie Martin, Patricia Newcomb, Gareth Wigan,

Dominick Dunne, Larry King, James Woods, Shakira and Michael Caine, and the hottest agents and producers galore. I've seen them all there, including Frank and Barbara Sinatra.

So, after Tita has loaded these worthies down with southern Italian cooking, what else does she offer? Why, Raisinets! The men all seem to go mad for these; it's as if they can get a Raisinet only at Tita's. God forbid they'd ever go buy any personally.

A NEW YORK/SOUTHAMPTON/MARTHA'S Vineyard party giver, Louise Grunwald is someone I've written about throughout these pages. I've known her since she was debutante age and I knew her best-dressed mother before her. Louise cut a swath during and since her career working for *Vogue*, wed a smashing tennis player, after that a charming investment banker, and now is married to the retired, last great managing editor of *Time*, the aforesaid Henry Grunwald. (Asked to name the quality all of her various husbands shared, Louise thought and said, "Well, they're all Caucasian!")

This delightful friend puts together evenings where you rub elbows with the top television names, curators from the Metropolitan, controversial tycoons like Conrad Black or Alfred Taubman, a great British actor such as Simon Russell Beale, the *Times* critic Ben Brantley, top designers, decorators, diplomats, the nation's most interesting governors, mayors, socialites, intellectuals, and even Nancy Reagan. Louise's dinners are open discussions, arguments, political and cultural harangues accompanied by the most delicious real food imaginable.

As Henry's wife, Louise was a valuable secret weapon when they were in Austria. As his better half on the Vineyard, she is rapidly filling the shoes left vacant when publisher Katharine Graham and former First Lady Jackie Onassis died, leaving the Massachusetts island bereft.

Louise is famous for her ability to make any room look super-elegant. "Well, my amazing mother left me some of her things, and I've been married three times, so I have a lot of stuff." She shrugs. But whether it's a common beach shell with your name on it gracing your placemat, or fabulous silver, china, porcelain, and flowers, she gives her guests sumptuous settings. It was at Louise's dinner table that I first encountered a special silver implement with which to bring the marrow out of bones. Heavenly days! I think she put this on the table just for the hell of it and to make conversation.

Louise serves food you can get your teeth into—fried chicken, ham, hamburgers, steaks, chops, crisp vegetables, corn on the cob, roasted potatoes, Caesar salad, pasta with wonderful sauces, and all manner of delicious cocktail tidbits and desserts. And then—Louise puts candy on her tables: wonderful bite-size jellied and sugared slices of orange, lemon, and lime, tiny chocolate caramels, nonpareils. I am always going to take only one, but. . . .

AND I CAN'T FORGET another of my favorite hostesses—Joan Ganz Cooney, who was the driving force behind the creation of *Sesame Street* and the Children's Television Workshop, now the Sesame Workshop. She has the Presidential Medal of Freedom to prove her worth. Wed to the Blackstone investment titan Pete Peterson, who she is determined to keep alive and healthy, Joan does the impossible. Her staff creates meals that are both good and good for you. You can be sure the carrot soup does not have cream just because it tastes perfect. Her tables are laden with beautiful flowers, often from her own garden. The conversation is so good at Joan's table that it would, in the words of Scarpia to Tosca, "make you forget God."

Again, a news-making mix of young, old, family, outlaws, in-laws, friends, enemies, and movers and shakers come to the Petersons' tables in Watermill, Vero Beach, and Manhattan.

Joan's secret for a happy guest? She leaves you to your own devices, only expecting you to show up on time for meals and "come to the party."

And then when all is eaten and done, she offers an array of the most wonderful, moist cookies made by her longtime housekeeper and major domo, Angela. Pete is sent away from the table when these are served.

Candy?

Well, the candy is hidden in Joan's bedroom. You have to go to her door after dinner and knock three times.

I KNOW YOU'RE SAYING "Oh, well, I could entertain well too, like Barbara, Tita, Louise, and Joan, if I had endless money and staff."

Yes, but even I now entertain better for having observed their energy and tricks. You can easily imitate many of these women's hosting attributes.

The Angela Matos Supercookie

3 cups unsifted flour
2 cups sugar
1 cup butter or margarine, softened
½ teaspoon salt
1½ cups dark corn syrup
6 ounces sweet chocolate
4 eggs, slightly beaten
1½ teaspoons vanilla
2½ cups chopped pecans

Preheat the oven to 350°F. Grease the bottom and sides of a 15 x 10 x 1-inch baking pan.

In a large bowl with a mixer at medium speed, beat the flour, ½ cup sugar, butter, and salt until the mixture resembles coarse crumbs; press firmly and evenly into the pan. Bake for 20 minutes.

Meanwhile, in a 3-quart saucepan, stir the corn syrup and chocolate over low heat just until the chocolate melts. Remove from the heat. Stir in the remaining sugar, then the eggs and vanilla until blended. Stir in the pecans.

Pour the filling over the hot crust; spread evenly. Bake for 30 minutes, or until the filling is firm around the edges but slightly soft in the center. Cool in the pan on a wire rack.

YIELD: AT LEAST A DOZEN COOKIES

CHAPTER 24

HOW TO GIVE A TOAST

WITHOUT BURNING IT!

Plus Good-bye Dear and Farewell
Plus "and now one who needs no introduction"
which is why I'm giving one!

SINCE GEORGIE JESSEL DIED, I seem always to be called on to emcee, to preside over the dear departed or salute the living. It's all one and the same when you get right down to it.

1. First, don't just assume you can make this kind of important public appearance off the top of your head. That's what some stars do at the Oscars, and they invariably leave the stage having forgotten to thank the director or producer or their mother. You also have to prepare to "run" an occasion or to rise to one. So I say, *write it out*. Pare your extra words. When you don't prepare because you believe you know or knew the person so well, when you think you have a handle on it—that's when you ramble, mess up, forget the main thing you need to say.

    If you have a bad memory, take your notes on hard stiff cards to the podium. Try not to use the notes. Carry a pen to the event in case you need to make a last-minute change or have an inspiration. Don't drop your head the way Teresa Heinz Kerry always did when speaking. Lift your head; look directly at the audience. *Project.* My theory is, forget being ladylike when speaking in public. You can't command the audience's attention if they don't clearly hear you.

If the exercise doesn't seem all that important to you—well, it is important to the poor devil being buried, to his loved ones, or to someone who is about to follow you and speak. Or it's important to whoever is being honored. Impress upon yourself the importance of having been given the responsibility.

A public toast or eulogy or whatever is like a precious mosaic. Every little bit of mica or glitter counts. You want to be precise. And making these public appearances is, incidentally, quite good for your self-esteem, providing you work at it.

2. Research. Arm yourself from the Internet, talk to friends, get a curriculum vitae if such a thing exists, or find a press release when applicable. Discover the details of the person you are talking about. Talk to his/her friends. You'll be surprised. From this usually dry-as-dust research come real gems. Almost every important piece of historical background will yield unsuspected little things you can dress up. These background papers are the basis of toasts, of roasts, of sweet good-byes, and introductions. We need to first read the background, then adorn the armature.

3. I think it is best to be wry, witty, funny, and charming in public appearances. But then, it almost always is, save for highly emotional funeral and memorial speeches. But "highly emotional" is the lit firecracker of horrid eulogies, so be careful. If you are going to break down, you'd better be a very good actor. And I'd say that while being trenchant and pointed about the dear departed, it is also usually okay to be wry, witty, funny, and charming at some point. It is good to tell one story that will elicit a smile or a laugh. And it is very good if eulogies can end on a poetic or beautifully sensitive note. Diane Sawyer is excellent at this sort of thing—evaluating the late Lucille Ball, Diane said she could remember little of her own childhood but could tell listeners everything about Ricky and Lucy Ricardo. She closed

by saying, "Let the wondering end; there *is* laughter in heaven!" This was just the right touch!

One is always lucky to have a Diane Sawyer or a Peggy Noonan, who wrote the great Reagan tribute to the *Challenger* astronauts, remembering a poem about souls who had "slipped the surly bonds of earth to touch the face of God."

In roasts and toasts, anecdotes are good if not too long. And humor is essential. It is boring just to recite a list of accomplishments. Introductions should be brief and to the point; again, a little humor helps. So lighten up. I guess I think humor is always better; I am like one of those decorators who always wants a beige or white room.

When Joan Ganz Cooney was to receive the Presidential Medal of Freedom from President Clinton, she was in a unique position. She was a rare thing for that award: a woman, an educator, an innovator who had helped television address the needs of children all over the world. This honor itself is the civilian equivalent of the Congressional Medal of Honor.

On the occasion I was to toast Joan, I realized that she would not be given the medal until the next day. So I was talking about something we would never likely see. I had read her curriculum vitae and realized that her accomplishments were too grand to be reiterated and would also bore us senseless. I saw that she had gone to college in Arizona, so I waved aside her grand reputation and made a few jokes about gila monsters, desert cacti, and The Order of the Iguana. Then I said that not having her presidential medal in hand, I would give her instead one of my own medals, a rather garish medallion the size of a saucer that I had received—the Medal of the City of Beverly Hills. This caused great glee and it helped, for she was too distinguished for me to run down the memory lane of her accomplishments. Joan put on the big medal and wore it all evening. Sometimes it's better to just "glitter and be gay," as Richard Wilbur wrote.

4. You are performing as much for yourself as for the person who is being honored. But don't make the entire of your remarks about you and go on and on about when you met and so forth. Many speakers tell you much more than you need to hear about them-

selves. Madonna got big mileage from opening her eulogy to Gianni Versace by saying, "I slept in Gianni Versace's bed!" This was definitely about Madonna, who was a bigger star than Versace. Still, it turned out to have its own charm when she finished her story. It was offbeat, daring, and got the audience's full attention.

5. Be brief. Remember how boring sermons often are in church; they usually run about twenty minutes. I think in public speaking even three minutes can be an eternity. Time yourself and pare down and pull back. Try to end with a bang, not a whimper. I know it's corny to say, but using the words "In closing," when you mean it, will actually give the audience a lift and an incentive to applaud if applause is called for.

6. If you stand behind the speaker you have introduced, stay still until the speaker is finished. Don't fidget, and never never never ever look at your watch. Appear to be attentive.

7. If you are the one to speak after having been introduced, unless you are giving a true lecture or a policy speech, affect a genuine modesty. It will help the proceedings a lot. At my eightieth birthday I received some important and brilliant accolades. What could I say? I said I had never planned to be eighty years old and didn't deserve so much credit for it. Then I quoted Shakespeare's Cleopatra. The Egyptian queen had said, "It is my birthday. I had thought to have held it poor. But since my lord is Anthony again, I will be Cleopatra." And I added that I equated the audience as being my lords and so I would "be Cleopatra just for tonight." Then I sat down.

CHAPTER 25

BE

ITALIAN

(As They Sang in the Musical *Nine*)

Y<small>OU MAY WONDER</small> why I am not dealing with Italy in this book—but briefly, I am. Let me just say, it is because the boot is just about my all-time favorite place, I have ever only had one bad meal in that country. My first experiences were back in the late fifties when I was introduced to Hosteria dell'Orso by the producer David O. Selznick, his wife Jennifer Jones, her co-star Rock Hudson, and various other players such as Elaine Stritch and Kurt Kazner.

Hosteria was then Rome's finest restaurant and greatest nightspot. But all I remember is a glaze of glamour and asking myself the question— what am I doing here? (Actually, Miss Stritch had taken me along as her secretary and aide-de-camp. I fear there was plenty of camping, eating, and dating fabulous Italian men, but not much aid was offered. She was always at Cinecittà working and I was always in the museums and tourist spots of note. I certainly had the best of it.)

I was so utterly ignorant of Italy and its great food connection that my memories are silly, sputtering things—being served the tiny strawberries, *fragole di bosco*, which I had never seen before. They came covered with orange juice . . . eating buffalo mozzarella and fresh tomatoes at stands on the side of the road to Naples—with the very buffalo in the fields behind . . .

Gazing into Rock Hudson's eyes on the Via Appia in a café named for a donkey. In my naïveté it seems I was actually the donkey, but those were more innocent times . . . Finding the restaurant Otello in Rome just off the Spanish Steps, a wonderful inexpensive café that still exists and has wonderful everything, including spaghetti with basil in fresh tomato sauce . . . and as the years passed, becoming spoiled in Venice's Cipriani Hotel with its outsize swimming pool, rooms with cabanas, and the most wonderful food and service . . . learning about the Amalfi Coast with all its traffic, crowding, monumental views, and charms, including, of course, visits to Capri and moments in both the Blue and the Emerald grottos . . . eating *fritto misto* in the open-air tourist restaurants on the Bay of Naples . . . watching fishermen beat and tenderize octopi on the rocks before they head for the nearest frypan . . . scarfing pizza in the open-air opera *Mefistofele* at Verona under a full moon that only added to the drama . . . eating pasta in an Orvieto restaurant where the owner was called "Angel" after having risen to the top of the ladder to see the restorations of Luca Santorille's frescoes in the local cathedral . . . Now, that can give you an appetite—and on and on.

And the single bad meal in Italy? As a matter of fact, I've had two bad ones—both in Pompeii, where tourism is rampant and visitors, perhaps oversexed after doing the ruins, just can't get enough special treatment.

CHAPTER 26

WHEN SHALL

WE LIVE IF

NOT NOW?

— SENECA

I ASK MYSELF THIS EVERY DAY, in the original Latin of course. And what follows are some odds and ends that defy category. I hope they entertain you.

Gourmet Gottis

People do love to try to go where they're not wanted or there is no room. This holds true for the so-called Mafia restaurant in Harlem — Rao's. Talk about underground undercurrents of gossip and scandal making a place famous! Rao's, with its unassuming southern Italian menu, is one of the most cherished and desired reservations in New York. The tables are farmed out carefully by the owner, Frankie Pellegrini, to his personal favorites. Some people keep franchises on their seats and booths. In other words, the table is held for them on certain nights. Other famous persons, such as television star–gossip columnist Victoria Gotti, the daughter of the late mob king John Gotti, seem able to get a table anytime it's needed. The joint is always filled with politicians, lawyers, judges, movie stars, writers, and just plain folks. Although a man was murdered in Rao's not long ago, that was very unusual. For the most part Rao's is like any "family" café.

For one of my birthdays I was taken to Rao's by Victoria Gotti and here's what they laid on us—baked clams, roasted peppers, ziti, fried mozzarella, big steaks, lemon chicken, ice cream, sherbet, a salad, plus those famous tennis ball–sized meatballs. Happy heartburn, Liz! That night because I behaved myself and I was with my friend Victoria, Frankie sang along for me with his Sinatra records as backup.

Frankie is talented. He has his own CD and my favorite thing about it is what it says right on the package: "Buy this record because it's a cinch you're never going to get a reservation at Rao's!" Now, that's telling it like it is.

Waiter, There's a Fly in My Soup

When Louis XIV had four soups for lunch, did he have any idea that two famous women of the nineteenth and twentieth centuries were going to come along and slam soup?

The very first was Mrs. Astor, Mrs. William Backhouse Astor, whose tyranny caused the famous "400" list to be established. This was the number of people Ward McAllister said could be accommodated in her ballroom. Well, that Mrs. Astor decreed no soup could be served in her house as a first course. "Who wants to build a meal on top of a lake?" she asked.

Later, in Washington in the forties, prominent hostess Agnes Meyer, the mother of publisher Katharine Graham, echoed Mrs. Astor, saying, "No soup. Never start your meal in a swamp. It's bad for the digestive tract."

And to make matters worse, Lord Curzon declared that "no gentleman ever has soup for lunch." (I guess the Sun King would blanch, though the word *gentleman* was doubtless beneath him. And what would he have made of Lord Curzon anyway?)

Well, I'm happy to stand with Louis XIV. Personally, I love soup! To me it's the ultimate comfort food, but then if I have soup with toast or croutons or potato chips or something else crunchy that I probably shouldn't eat, then that's it for me—an entire meal. I could live for moons on Camp-bell's tomato soup put together with a full can of whole milk and bedaz-.zlingly beaten together over heat with a whisk. Yes, add a dollop of butter just to remind your arteries who is boss.

Now, if you like bouillabaisse, I'm going to offer the poor-man's ver-sion of something a little like it. But before I give this amazing recipe, you must decide for yourself whether or not you like canned red sockeye salmon. If you don't, then rush past what follows as if the hounds of heaven or hell—whichever you fear most—are at your heels. Don't even read it. This is for canned salmon appreciators, the kind of people who like salmon croquettes.

Salmon Soup

Drop a can of red sockeye salmon in a saucepan and remove as much as you can of the dark band surrounding it, with a fork. Leave the little bones and all of the juice.

Mash the salmon, adding some small amount of flour (maybe 2 table-spoons worth) to make a kind of roux. Add a lot of pepper and salt to this mix.

Over medium heat on the stove, slowly add whole milk. I'd say 3 cups at least. You can tell as you mash it all around over heat if this begins to look like soup or not. So add a little more milk if you like it soupy.

Begin tasting using a lot of pepper and salt.* Eat this soup with Lay's po-tato chips and then don't eat for several days after. I have to admit most of my friends think this dish is disgusting, but if you like fish soup—it's so easy.

As long as we're speaking of easy, I have never had much patience with people who try to make baked beans from scratch. Just go buy a can of B&M baked beans, which are pretty good as they are.† But they can be made into a mir-acle by simply heating them and stirring in 2 tablespoons of good maple syrup and a teaspoon of dry mustard. Don't overheat or the beans get mushy.

---

* Could I say another word here, in defense of the culprit *salt*?—a victim of our age and doc-tors. Incidentally, there are five tastes—salt, sweet, sour, bitter—and the newly discovered umami, which detects savory or meaty sensations.

† In the Lone Star State, a famous Aggie joke tells of the Texas A&M guy who wouldn't serve barbecued beans because he was afraid they'd fall through the holes of the grill.

The Real Fishy Thing: Jim Sterba's Bouillabaisse
Made with Periwinkles for Sound Effects

30 show mussels
2 cups of mussel meat
2 small lobsters, steamed
1 pound sea scallops
1½ pounds of halibut, hake, or haddock.
Onions
Tomatoes
Garlic
Potatoes
Cilantro
Parsley
Thyme
Basil
Oregano
Tarragon
Olive oil
Chile pepper flakes
Clam juice
Periwinkles (in the shell)
Butter
Lemon juice
Pepper

Pour half a cup of olive oil into a wide (at least 12 inches) and deep pot. Add 2 medium, roughly chopped onions. After they sizzle for a few minutes, add 6 cloves of chopped garlic (always remember Calvin Trillin's line: with enough garlic, you can eat *The New York Times*). Then add ½ cup of chopped parsley, and ⅔ cup of a combination of chopped fresh thyme, tarragon, oregano, basil, and cilantro and a couple of shakes of chili pepper flakes. Once the onions wilt, add a large can of Italian peeled whole tomatoes (or 2 or 3 fresh ones cut in eighths, skins, seeds, and all) and a bottle of clam juice.

(If you see you don't have enough stew for eight people, add another bottle of clam juice, a can of chicken broth, and an 8-ounce can of tomato sauce.)

Cook the sauce for 10 minutes, add half a dozen quartered new potatoes, simmer for 10 minutes, then turn it off. (Don't fill the pot with liquid because it's amazing how fast it fills up once you start adding the seafood. You can always top it up later with more chicken broth, clam juice, or tomato juice, which I recommend in that order.)

Meanwhile, steam 2 small 1-pound lobsters and let them cool. Cut their tails in three parts, pull off the front claws and arms, and crack their hard shells with a hammer; otherwise leave them intact.

About half an hour before serving, bring the stew to a slow boil, then add the shelled mussels. Then, in succession every 3 to 4 minutes, add the show mussels in shells, the periwinkles (which fall like sinkers to the bottom), the whole lobster claws and arms, and the scallops, cut in half. Then, in the last 5 minutes, add the halibut (or whatever) cut into ice cube–sized pieces (add this last so it won't flake into tiny bits). Finally, add ½ stick of butter. (As far as butter is concerned, see the garlic rule.)

Also 5 minutes out, add the juice of 1 lemon, lots of fresh ground pepper, and almost a cup of the chopped herb combo (thyme, tarragon, oregano, basil, and cilantro). And a few more sprigs of chopped parsley. Last-minute fresh herbs do wonders. Indeed, lots of last-minute tasting and adjusting with more lemon juice or lemon pepper or various herbs is the secret to making this dish taste alive.

Boil some ziti al dente to serve as a base and offer fresh croutons as topping or toasted French bread on the side. When you serve, the periwinkles will sound like marbles. Always serve hot crunchy bread, red wine, salad, cheese, and blueberry pie.

WELL, THAT RECIPE is from former *Times* correspondent Sterba's incredible little book, *Frankie's Place*, written several years ago as his paeon to summer life with his love, the Pulitzer Prize–winning Frankie Fitzgerald, and published to acclaim by Grove Press. It tells of their rustic togetherness on Maine's Mount Desert Island in a tiny cottage overlooking a fjord called Somes Sound.

You'll never read another food love story quite like this one and I know you'll love it.

Amid Jim and Frankie's adventures, there are wonderful self-created recipes for how to roast corn in the oven, make crab cakes, find your own mussels for *moules marinières*, steam lobsters, and create soups from sorrel to coral mushroom to cold cucumber.

The very best thing about this work of art is the presentation of the Frankie Fitzgerald Protestant work ethic idea that lobsters are only for special occasions, a reward for good works and achievements big and small. In Frankie's distinguished Peabody family, there were rules about how to eat lobsters, with the restriction on going overboard even if they are easily available.

Rereading this, I am reminded of a New York socialite who recently complained to me about having been entertained in New England at a dinner outdoors in almost total darkness where whole lobsters were served. "It is impossible to eat a lobster in the dark or to handle one at dinner. It's such a messy business. Nutcrackers and picks and sometimes hammers are needed. Plenty of towels are necessary and you are still a fishy mess after!"

After you read *Frankie's Place*, you'll know exactly how to start with the lobster's legs, use the secret crevices for choice morsels, plumb the green tomalley inside, save the claws and tails for last. And you'll be guilty when you indulge in lobster out of place and out of season as if you were a glutton like Diamond Jim Brady.

Ask Governor Ann

I asked my pal, the brilliant former governor of Texas, Ann Richards, for some food ideas. She responded that I should not neglect the church supper. (Neglect one? Why, I hadn't been to one in years.) But here's Ann:

"The worst thing to happen to church suppers was the invention of the 'casserole'—green beans with mushroom soup and canned fried onions or slivered onions on top.

"Second worst—all forms of Jell-O salad. Orange with shredded carrots, lime with cottage cheese and canned pineapple, etc.

"The best thing to happen at church suppers, picnics, family reunions, or anything else is the deviled egg! There is no such thing as a bad one. Deviled eggs are the first plate to empty at any buffet.

"Excellent food is anything you grew yourself like okra, cucumbers, pickled peaches, beets—home canning!

"Pie is everyone's favorite dessert. Chocolate and lemon meringue toppings are the favorites. People may think they want cherry or apple, but that's only because they think fruit is good for them. My daughter,

Ellen, had pies instead of a wedding cake when she got married. This was a big hit!

"Don't forget corn bread and cornmeal recipes. People forget how much they love this. Muffins, sticks, squares, cooked with pig cracklings or with cheese and jalapeños, or eaten plain crumbled into buttermilk!"

I SUPPOSE YOU THINK I just embraced Ann's suggestions without question. No.

First, I think casseroles have saved many a busy woman's life over and over. But maybe the Campbell's soup folks do have something to answer for in having invented mushroom soup as a cover-up for everything ever cooked.

Second, I gasped at Ann's anti-Jell-O stance. I used to smack my lips when Mother put her version of a "salad" on the table—a ring of canned pineapple atop lemon or lime Jell-O on an iceberg lettuce leaf, with half a banana standing erect and a cherry on top. It was so much prettier and tasted better than most of her cooking.

I do totally chime in and agree with Ann on deviled eggs. I literally gasp when I see one and quickly look around to be sure no one is about to beat me to it. I like these in all manifestations, especially with a little mustard and curry powder added. This is the one food that has its own special plate (a platter with egg indentations) that you don't resent taking up space in your cupboard. That is because every time you see it, hope springs eternal that someone will soon fill it.

I am a sucker, too, for home canning, things like bread-and-butter pickles made by my former aide Saint Clair Pugh. Lots of people have died from botulism from home canning, so one needs to be careful. But as I would never can or jar anything myself, I love those who do.

Pies!? I love pie, as you may have read elsewhere. My admiration for Ellen Richards has increased over its already elevated state as she is a social worker and humanist to the max. So naturally she understands PIE in the scheme of things.

Corn bread? Well, here's a recipe for my personal favorite. It's the one thing my mother excelled at. I could eat it hot, dripping with the bacon fat it was fried in, or I could wait until it congealed and eat it cold. Cornmeal is one mighty fine invention and any kind of corn bread dresses up a meal. It makes it look as if the cook cared enough to really try, even if that be only opening a box of Jiffy mix.

But if you make Hot-Water Corn Bread you'll be special, as many people never heard of it.

Hot-Water Corn Bread

2 cups of cornmeal, either white or yellow
2 eggs
Salt and pepper
½ teaspoon baking soda

Put a layer of bacon drippings, lard, or vegetable oil in a cast-iron skillet. Mix together these simple ingredients.

Pour boiling water over your cornmeal mixture, adding a touch of grease to form patties. When you can handle this hot mixture, roll it into balls and flatten to "hamburger" size.

Get your skillet hot and fry the patties, turning them over once or twice with a spatula, until browned. Drain on a brown paper bag or paper towels.

This can be eaten hot, cold, or reheated in the microwave.

THIS SERVES 2 LUCKY PEOPLE

THIS CHAPTER may have disgusted some (canned salmon soup, indeed!) or daunted amateurs (Sterba's real bouillabaisse) or appealed to your nostalgia (church suppers) or caused the health-conscious to gasp (hot-water corn bread!)

But as long as we're on salmon, here's a treat. I don't like salmon and have given away many slabs of smoked salmon that seem invariably to come my way as thank-you's. But live and learn! Never again will smoked salmon escape my grasp.

I went to a New York Public Library dinner where I sat down at a high-toned table and glanced suspiciously at the menu card. "Smoked Salmon Napoleon" it read for the appetizer. I winced. But I'd never seen a napoleon that wasn't a dessert before, so when the Glorious Food waiter put it down before me, I was entranced. It was so attractive. I decided to give it a try; then I ate every crumb because it was one of the most delicious things I'd ever put in my mouth.

So I asked Sean Driscoll, who owns Glorious Food, if there was a trick to it. He wrote back with candor: "I can only give you a rough interpretation for this 'napoleon.' The dish is a creation of Jean-Claude Nedelec and his pastry chef; we have no published recipe for it. It hasn't been tested so we don't feel comfortable about its appearing in a cookbook. But this gives you an idea how to make it. Remember, cooking is not an exact science. On any given day Jean-Claude could stick his finger in the mousseline, taste it and decide we need to add something else. Who knows, maybe it needs chili powder!"

I do love my friend Sean, a man I once went to the top of the Parthenon with—we stood there on a rickety scaffold surveying a view seen by very few other than workmen and the architects who built this Greek masterpiece. So naturally, as we have a history, I loved Sean's very frank and entertaining letter. And here's how I *think* you make the

Smoked Salmon Napoleon

Buy some flat puff pastry. It's everywhere. Bake it.
Have someone give you some expensive sliced smoked salmon.
Using your common sense, make a mixture of

1 tablespoon thinly sliced fresh chives (reserve some chives for garnish)
4 tablespoons fresh lemon juice
2½ tablespoons crème fraîche
2½ tablespoons mayonnaise

Whip together a lemon mousseline sauce:

½ cup of heavy whipping cream
Lemon zest and a couple of tablespoons of juice

Set this sauce aside.
Slather on several layers of the crème fraîche mixture with alternate slices

of smoked salmon and puff pastry. Finish off the top with a layer of puff pastry. Sprinkle that with chives.

Add a touch of the mousseline sauce across the top of the napoleon and pool some on the side.

Go crazy! Enjoy.

CHAPTER 27

DO VEGGIES

LACK A SENSE

OF PURPOSE?

I FEAR I'm a meat-and-potatoes kind of person with some sweets thrown in. But of course there is much to be said about the healthy eating of vegetables, fruits, and whole grains.

Joining me, however, in my idiosyncratic blind spot when it comes to doing what's good for one, are the following famous people:

I just hate health food. . . . When they talk about healthy food, they usually mean it doesn't taste very good.

—Julia Child

George Bernard Shaw would not have hurried off at the absurd age of 94 had he not progressively weakened himself with his lethal vegetarian messes.

—Clifton Fadiman

Old people shouldn't eat health foods. They need all the preservatives they can get!

—Robert Orben

If a man prepares dinner for you and the salad contains three or more types of lettuce, he is serious.

—Rita Rudner

An onion can make people cry, but there has never been a vegetable to make them laugh.

—Will Rogers

A cucumber should be well-sliced, dressed with pepper and vinegar and then thrown out.

—Samuel Johnson

Vegetables are interesting but lack a sense of purpose when unaccompanied by a good cut of meat.

—Fran Lebowitz

The very first off-color joke I ever heard was told to me in the E. M. Daggett first grade, Forth Worth, Texas. "Why did Miss Tomato blush when she looked over the garden fence?"
Answer: "She saw Mr. English Pea."
Oh my. And the veritable craze for green peas didn't begin until 1660 when a M. Ordiger returned to France from Italy with a hamperful. These were ceremoniously shelled by the Comte de Soissons because the French court of Louis XIV was wild for new dishes and, as author Lisa Hilton tells us in her book *Athenais*, "appetites among the privileged class were positively scandalous." One of the pet dishes served the king by Sieur Baudoin was cauliflower, steamed in stock and served with butter and nutmeg. It was considered fashionable to eat this. Just as Louis XIV dreamed up wearing shoes with red heels, his court rushed to get their heels painted red and to tell their wives how the servants must now serve the cauliflower.

A little later, the great Durand made a name for himself at the court of Louis XVI. He invented *petits pois aux noisettes grillés* and once corrected Marie Antoinette for adding mustard to a salad dressing before she put in the salt. (Everyone is a critic, it's true.)

One thing the French did well was to roast beets instead of boiling them. They are very good however you make them, having the flavor of the earth no matter how they are cooked. But these days I put a sheet of aluminum over the root. Cut off the upper leaves but not too close to the root. Leave a little stem so they do not "bleed." Roast at 350°F for 45 minutes. The peels just slip off under running water.

Or you can just clip them as above and boil them in water for about half an hour. They taste better roasted. Add a dash of butter, salt, and pepper, of course.

In trying to be fair and open-minded, I crammed on vegetables and fruits. I actually learned a thing or two—for instance, the archive of *Internal Medicine* does say that fruits and grain fibers help prevent heart disease. (They claim you can drop the risk of a heart attack by 14 percent for every 10 grams of grain or fruit fiber you eat daily. And they think these fibers are better than vegetable fiber.) They urge you not to just drink juice, but to eat green leafy veggies and fresh fruit itself because juice doesn't begin to have the fiber that the real stuff has. And an apple a day might actually keep the doctor away, truly.

I DO HAVE TWO RECOMMENDATIONS if you're into this stuff. Buy *Super Foods Rx*, published by William Morrow, which claims that the fourteen foods named can rescue your health. Some people think that the author, California's Steven Pratt, is overreaching in his claims, but spinach, tomatoes, blueberries, broccoli, oats, wild salmon, turkey, soy, and walnuts must be good for you.

My favorite reading in order to alarm myself and dish up a veggie or whole grain or pick up a piece of fruit is *The Doctors Book of Food Remedies*. This claims to be the latest in "power food" discoveries. You have to order this one from 1-800-848-4735. This thing is very specific and actually kind of fun to read because as you go along, you'll feel the very reading of it is clearing up your arteries.

•   •   •

I WAS THRILLED in researching this chapter, if you can call it that, to learn that undercooked, frozen, and even canned vegetables have lots and lots of vitamins in them. I am assuming you probably won't use too many canned veggies unless you end up at the North or South Pole and find a cache left over from some doomed expedition. (Though I think canned LeSueur green peas are totally delicious.) But you needn't shy away from the frozen food case either. And I'd rather eat a raw carrot than a cooked one any day.

My darling housekeeper Rachel Clark puts out raw carrots, peppers, cucumbers, onions, celery, plum tomatoes, and radishes for me every day. I am even inveigled to eat some of this stuff with a dash of ranch dressing during the workday. You might try the same approach if you aren't crazy for the five big helpings of the real thing that you are supposed to actually eat every day to stay alive.

One of the best things about writing on this subject is discovering that iceberg lettuce, long denigrated, "too common" for salad purists, out of fashion, and as Julia Reed writes, "flat-out maligned in some quarters," is making a comeback! Hallelujah!

One reason I like to go to the Irish café and bar Donohue's on New York City's Lexington Avenue near 64th Street is because the owner, Maureen, still serves a chunk of iceberg with Thousand Island or French or blue cheese dressing hiding in its crevices and giving a satisfying crunchy result. Poet Gerald Locklin has even written an ode to same titled "The Iceberg Theory."

Just to be perverse and to try to hold on to the franchise, I will recommend how to cook only one vegetable. It's my absolute favorite, next to okra prepared in any of its myriad ways. I would eat okra and/or collard greens every day. And in the case of collards, I'd be wondering if the use of pork fat, ham hock, or bacon in the recipe is offset by the positive quality of the leafy green leaves.

Rachel's Collard Greens

1½ pounds ham hocks
4 pounds collard greens, rinsed, trimmed, and chopped
½ teaspoon crushed red pepper flakes
¼ cup vegetable oil
Salt and pepper to taste

Place the ham hocks in a big pot with 1½ quarts of water. Bring to a boil, then set the heat to very low and simmer, covered, for 30 minutes. Then add the collards and pepper flakes. Simmer, covered, for about 2 hours, stirring occasionally. Add the vegetable oil and simmer, covered, for 30 minutes. Add salt and pepper to taste.

SIX SERVINGS

CHAPTER 28

UNBIND

MY

ASPARAGUS

Asparagus inspires gentle thoughts.

—CHARLES LAMB

Dear Reader: This chapter appeared not only in my syndicated column, but also in my memoir, *Natural Blonde*. I can hardly believe it, but there was an actual request that it be reprinted.

I HAVE BEEN WRITING GOSSIP COLUMNS for almost thirty years. People always ask, "What was your biggest scoop?" I have to hang my head. "The Donald–Ivana Trump divorce." (But that wasn't really an important story; it didn't change history except *my* history.)

Or sometimes folks ask, "What is your favorite column you've ever written?" Then I don't blush. I don't stammer. I don't hesitate. I know my favorite. I wrote it in answer to critiques leveled at me by Jonathan Yardley and Maureen Dowd in *The Washington Post* and *New York Times*. They hadn't liked a report of mine on a book party for Colin Powell. This rejoinder column doesn't have movie stars in it. It didn't break new ground. It didn't make headlines. It was absolutely of no consequence, but it's still my pet. Here it is, circa September 1995.

"The sin of newspaper people is almost invariably the sin of envy," writes David Remnick.

Recently I had the "good fortune" to be the only print reporter covering a dinner in New York given for General Colin Powell by his Random House editor, Harold Evans. That isn't to say there weren't many other media-type guests, but after dinner, and after General Powell's dynamic speech kicking off his book, Harry Evans interrupted the fine time I was having with my dinner partners Barry Diller and Bob Woodward. They were discussing the joys of "vertical integration" in big business mergers when Harry whispered in my ear, "Go sit by the general, ask him questions. You're the only one invited here tonight to report on this party!"

Well, had I known that earlier, I would certainly have taken notes, been paying attention, and observing more carefully. So I did go sit by the general. He was very nice. I liked him. He said he'd decide about running for president after he got *My American Journey* out of his system. He told me he liked the press. I told him, "General, you'll get over it."

When Tom Brokaw joined us, I ceded my place next to the general and rushed out of the café knowing that now—dammit—I had to write a story, which I hadn't planned. And it was this story that got me in trouble with Maureen Dowd of *The New York Times* and Jonathan Yardley of *The Washington Post*. Both of them seemed mad as hell in print, a few days later. General Powell had dared to act as if he might run without their approval—or without their being present at his book party? Both of these highly placed, well-regarded columnists seemed to take scornful exception to my description of the dinner that had been served in the I Trulli restaurant, down in Manhattan's East Twenties.

We were offered bound asparagus and three kinds of pasta, plus a fruit tart. Wondering what the hell I had to write about, as I taxied to my office in panic, I remembered the great Professor DeWitt Reddick of Journalism 101, the University of Texas: "Details! Details!" he had cautioned.

"Good feature writing is in the details!" (Well, I thought, it certainly had worked for Tom Wolfe.)

So, in addition to writing that guests around me were placing bets as to whether or not the general would run, I added a few colorful garnishes about the dinner menu. Big mistake.

It was the bound asparagus that got Yardley and Dowd. Either they hate silly details, or they are genuine asparagus liberators. These columnists most likely belong to organizations like People for the Ethical Treatment of Animals, so they may be all for freeing asparagus as well. Instead of reporting on the party, I should have called Madeleine Albright at the U.N. over human and vegetable rights transgressions. And I wasn't even a good enough reporter to say what the I Trulli asparagus had been bound with? (Proscuitto, it turns out—not even good old U.S. bacon.)

And the three kinds of pasta: definitely un-American. I ask you, if it's against the law to bind asparagus, then why didn't NYC police chief William Bratton, a party guest, place the I Trulli chef under arrest right then and there?

But Yardley wasn't just offended by my food comments. He didn't approve of the guests themselves. He wrote: "The guest list as reported by Smith consisted of all the famous and beautiful people whom, if God is on your side, you will never have to meet, much less break bread and/or beautifully bound asparagus and three kinds of pasta with."

Hmm, I know I'm culpable in not having unbound my asparagus, but I thought the guest list was fine. What's wrong with guests such as Anne and Vernon Jordan, Sally Quinn, Ben Bradlee, Bob Woodward, Elsa Walsh, Norris and Norman Mailer, Len and Sally Garment, Carol and Joe Lelyveld, Don and Marilyn Hewitt, Tom Brokaw, Barbara Walters, Lynn Sheer, Leslie Stahl, Jessye Norman, Jennifer Patterson, Howard Stringer, and New Jersey's Bill Bradley?

Yardley also referred to "Hollywood saps" at the party, but I'd only mentioned Barry Diller. Does Yardley honestly think of Diller, of all people, as a sap? My, my.

Dowd wrote a satire on planning such a book party. "Liz Smith will rave about the bound asparagus. Wait until she sees the bound book!" (I did see the bound book: It was full of blank pages since the text hadn't then been released.) Well, I'm sorry I mentioned food at all. But as I rushed out of I Trulli, I'd seen the owner sitting alone at the door. He looked dejected and shell-shocked. He had given his all to what Yardley called "publishing twits" and they had laughed, talked loud, gossiped, carried on and paid little attention to his very nice dinner. I felt rather sorry for Nicholas. I could just imagine some PR person from Random House saying, "This party will *make* your restaurant." It had been so crowded and noisy as to almost unmake the place and poor Nick had turned away his neighborhood regulars.

So I decided to add food details to make him happy. Did I know this was a crime against nature? Next thing we know there'll be slogans, marching, picketing and people throwing things at Korean veggie stands. "Let our asparagus be unbound!" the righteous will yell. And, yes, I'll join them. Never again will I leave an asparagus bound on my plate, let alone eat one that can't defend itself, or invade asparagus privacy by writing about one in bondage. It's too S & M.

Probably Harry Evans made a mistake, too. He should have had the general's book party down in Washington at Kay Graham's house. That way those sensitive Beltway insiders would have been in control. They wouldn't have felt left out of General Powell's plans.

As it was, a gossip columnist had to lead them—right into the asparagus patch.

CHAPTER 29

KID

STUFF

As I've said, my mother hated to cook, but she didn't mind diverting us when we were bored or upset or "sickly." Her best idea was milk toast. Just toasted bread, buttered and sugared and served in a bowl of scalded milk. I don't know if anyone even makes anything so simplistic nowadays. I guess today children get a video game when what they need is milk toast.

We were also happy to have for breakfast—bread, toasted, buttered, sugared, and stuck under a broiler until it caramelized. This was a big treat.

The other nice thing Mother always did for us was make extra piecrust when she baked. This she would butter and sugar for us and we'd be happy. In my comments on pies, I forgot to mention their once very popular offshoot—the homemade fruit cobbler. We'd have big ones in large rectangular pans. The problem was that if one was left to cool, brother Bobby would eat the entire thing, six or eight servings.

Bobby was inventive. When not gourmandizing, he wanted to create a new dish. The one he claims was peanut butter on a *buttered* cracker. He called this "the Scotch Mantivery" in honor of the McCalls, the true Scots in our ancestry.

Another childhood constant was when Mrs. Smith did not want to cook. She'd whomp up some rice, butter and sugar it, and that would be dinner. No wonder we all grew up with such sweet tooths.

My favorite childhood treat was chocolate fudge made with Texas pecans, popcorn balls made with ribbon cane syrup, and molasses taffy. The latter had to be "pulled" while hot with buttered hands and this was a tiresome job. But it was delicious.

CHAPTER 30

ROTHSCHILD

RAGOUT

F ANTASTIC THINGS HAVE HAPPENED to me at dinner. Sitting next to the elegant and urbane Baron Guy de Rothschild at a charity dinner at Tavern on the Green, we had a talk about the difference between his French and my Americans—and this was long before the U.S. hit the Maginot Line of invading Iraq.

At this time in the late sixties, the baron was banker extraordinary and exemplar of the French branch of his renowned family. His wife, Marie-Hélène, was the premier hostess in Paris, and her private parties and galas recalled the glory days of Bourbon royalty. The baron expressed to me his amazement at the U.S. custom of paying money to dress up, wine, dine, and dance in order to raise money for charity.

I told him that it was our most booming "cottage industry"—the charity event—a happening to make up for the needs of others and to atone for the government's lack of interest. "You Americans are incredible. The French would never do anything like that!" I asked why not. The baron smiled. "We are too selfish."

Then Baron Guy moved on and asked me the kind of question I had grown used to: "Tell me, Mlle. Smith, what is Barbra Streisand really like?"

Later in life I sat with the baron's British cousin, Sir Evelyn Rothschild. He had married my friend, the U.S. dynamo Lynn Forester, and they were entertaining in a Central Park South restaurant. The honored guests were the friendly but divorced Prince Andrew and Sarah Ferguson, the Duchess of York, or "Fergie," as Americans call her.

Lady Lynn had placed the royal prince between herself and Barbara Walters, so I lucked out, sitting next to her husband at a separate table. Sir Evelyn is a handsome, tall, white-haired devil, and we talked about history and exchanged some slightly naughty jokes while drinking his family's famous wine, which goes for thousands of dollars a bottle. And many a bottle became a "dead soldier" as we shot off our punch lines.

On my eightieth birthday, Sir Evelyn and his Lady offered regrets about being out of New York and sent along a case of Château Lafite Rothschild as a gift. I told them later that considering the magnitude of the gift, I was happy they were unable to attend.

HERE IS A TYPICAL MENU from a dinner with the Rothschilds in their New York apartment overlooking the East River:

Hors d'oeuvres during cocktails:

Goat cheese baked in puff pastry with lemon and fresh thyme . . .
Garden crudités with basil sauce . . .
Mousse of foie gras on toasted brioche . . .
Green pea blinis with caviar and crème fraîche.

FIRST COURSE

Seared Scallops with Wilted Spinach, Lemon Zest, Beurre Blanc

MAIN COURSE

Roast Breast and Leg of Poussin Stuffed with Porcini Mushrooms, Jus de Rôtis, Herbed Fingerling Potatoes, Sugar Snap Peas

DESSERT

Tuscan Pear Tart with Vanilla Mascarpone,
Fig and Orange Salad

Coffee, Decaf, and Tea
Mignardises

The wines:

1999 Puligny-Montrachet, Les Chalumeaux
1978 Château Lafite Rothschild
2000 Château Rieussec

N O W ,   D O N ' T   T H I N K I haven't reciprocated in kind to Evelyn and Lynn de Rothschild. I invited them to the open porch of the West Chop Club, one of the most down-to-earth, shirtsleeves-to-shirtsleeves, unassuming little enclaves in all of Martha's Vineyard. There we lunched on clam chowder, hot dogs and hamburgers, coleslaw, and heaps of french fried potatoes. The "vegetable"—ketchup—was in great demand. There was even a chocolate fudge sundae for dessert.

As we enjoyed our al fresco meal with many glasses of homemade lemonade, I tried to tease Evelyn about his elevated position in such an informal atmosphere. He just laughed, "Liz, obviously you don't realize that as a boy in World War II, during the Battle of Britain, I was sent to the United States for my safety. I lived here a number of years and developed quite a taste for all-American food!"

Soon Evelyn gave me a heavyweight copy of the family history, *The World's Banker.* I am still in the early stages as it's quite a tome. But it reminded me of a story Iris Love told me about frequently visiting the home of other French Rothschilds, Alain and Mary. She shared with them a love of dachshunds. She says that wherever you ate with them, in Paris or in the country, there were always matzos on the table. They did not eat them, but they did not forget their heritage.

CHAPTER 31

THEY

STARVE TO

CONQUER

I ONCE INTERVIEWED Julia Roberts in her New York office. As we rolled along through the questions, I alluded to her Southern up-bringing and mentioned beaten biscuits and red-eye gravy made from ham. Julia stopped me: "What are you? Some kind of terrorist! Why did you bring up biscuits? You know everyone in the movies worries all the time about their weight. And now it's no use. I won't be able to think about anything until I get some biscuits."

I met Nicole Kidman for the first time to talk in the Pool Room of the famed Four Seasons restaurant in the Seagram Building. She came in alone at 6:30 and I spied her trim slim figure far across the room. I figured we'd have a drink or tea or bottled water and she'd soon rush off some-where. Nicole sat down. She had no PR person with her. She began talk-ing and eating the bread in the basket. She ate every single kind of bread and roll they offered. When that was gone, she said, "Should we have some of those lovely fried shrimp with mustard fruits?" We had them. We de-cided then we needed Dover sole cooked the Four Seasons way and in the meantime, she had a baked potato prepared with their special olive oil. By now we had gone way beyond her then husband, Tom Cruise, and her movie co-star George Clooney and her beloved Australian family, her children, her ambitions, her hopes, her dreams. We had drunk a fine white Chablis and we ended up with chocolate cake and vanilla ice cream. I asked Nicole what her favorite food really was. She opined that she adored Krispy Kreme doughnuts and ate them every day when she was in New York City. Nicole weighs about 100 pounds, maybe 119 soaking wet. I weigh about 156. Don't ask what this means, but evidently she can eat anything.

I met Renée Zellweger in a Central Park South hotel lobby one early morning. She was a tiny slip of a thing wearing gray sweatpants, a nondescript T-shirt, and running shoes. No makeup. We talked about Sugarland, Texas, where she'd grown up, and we drank lots of coffee and tea and bottled water during this sparse interview. I was resolved not to ask her about gaining weight to play in *Bridget Jones's Diary* because everyone always asked her that. We parted as if we were old pals. I chalked her up to a health fanatic who did not eat normally. Then it began. From Los Angeles came boxes of Renée-sent cookies created by Deluscious Cookies & Milk, 829 North Highland, L.A., CA 90038. My staff was thrilled. Okay, we'd eat until we finished them. But no, soon more cookies came and arrived regularly and on schedule. After Renée won her Oscar for *Cold Mountain* I heard she was again packing on weight to play the *Bridget* sequel. So obviously Renée likes her friends to join her as she yo-yos up and down. The trouble is, Renée is already thin again and the second *Bridget* is behind her. But the Deluscious cookies keep coming. Beware what you wish for — you may get it!

CHAPTER 32

GRAND

GESTURES

Miss Manners, the columnist, says the traditional order of food should be: oysters, terrapin, soup, fish, mushrooms or asparagus, roast, frozen punch, then game, then salad, then creamed dessert, then frozen dessert, cheese, fruit, candy and nuts. But she says, "No one insists on it anymore."

She adds, "People now start with salad because they have picked up the habit from restaurants . . . staving off hunger while the main course cooks. Others start with a salad for healthy reasons. Miss Manners does not object, provided she doesn't have to listen to a lecture about why."

Once upon a time, the heiress Gloria Vanderbilt lived at 10 Gracie Square in Manhattan in an apartment overlooking the East River. Her living room was all white, with her own paintings on the walls and a white vinyl floor dotted with fantastic real black bearskins as throw rugs. One hot summer day the director Burt Shevelove went to visit and as they sat down, Gloria said, "It's such a brutal day, wouldn't a banana split taste simply delicious?"

Burt agreed and thought where he might take her to get one, but Gloria waved her hand, rang for the butler, and said, "Please bring us the banana split tray."

Soon, in came a silver tray with proper dishes, three kinds of ice cream, sliced bananas, cherries, toppings, nuts, and whipped cream. Gloria set about making the splits, talking animatedly. She paused with a spoon of whipped cream in flight and a big portion fell plop! into the bearskin rug at her feet.

Gloria never looked down. She quietly said, "Oh, dear." And put down the empty spoon. Never looking away from Burt's face, she said, "Let's move into the library." They both rose and did so with Gloria still chatting. Sitting again, she rang for the butler and said, "Bring the tray in here." He did. They had their splits. Burt departed. He said to me later, "This was the single classiest thing I'd ever experienced."

Yes, but you need a butler and a black bearskin rug.

AND WHILE WE'RE ON grand gestures that don't necessarily have anything to do with food, let's not forget the Baron de Montesquieu who went all over Paris seeking gray flowers to place in a gray room as an homage to the great painter James Whistler. The baron was said to be the prototype for Marcel Proust's Baron de Charlus in *Remembrance of Things Past*. He was the ultimate snob who said that every party must be given "against" someone.

The Baron looked down on a certain woman he considered a social climber and though she wrote him many love letters, he never responded nor did he invite her. When he died, she was amazed to receive a rich-looking casket left to her in his will. It contained all her love letters to him, and none had ever been opened.

IN THE 1300S IN FLORENCE, the Ghibellines cut their fruit crosswise. The Guelfs cut theirs straight down. This, among other things, produced feuds and vendettas in the Middle Ages.

After Lorenzo di Medici introduced the lemon tree to Italy in the

1500s, everybody began to feel much better. Some say that started the Renaissance. But the ubiquitous tomato was not eaten in Italy until the sixteenth century and at first the superstitious shied away from it because when sliced, some folks thought there was a cross inside. Imagine southern Italy if they had never brought in the tomato! Imagine a world without ketchup! *

I DOUBT IF ANYONE has reached the heights—or do I mean the depths?—of decadence better than J.-K. Huysmans, who wrote *A Rebours* in 1884. In this controversial work, Huysmans describes an all-black dinner party that became the talk of Paris.

The dinner was organized as a funeral feast with the dining room hung in black, looking out on a strange garden where the walks had been strewn with charcoal; a little basin in the lawn was bordered with black basalt and filled with ink. The dining room tablecloth was black, bearing baskets of violets and scabiosae, and food came on black-bordered plates. Turtle soup, Russian black bread, ripe Turkish olives, caviar, mule steaks, Frankfurt smoked sausages, game in sauces colored to resemble liquorice water and boot blacking, truffles in jelly, chocolate-tinted creams, dark cherries. The wines came in dark-tinted glasses—Limagne, Roussillon, Tenedos, the Val de Penas and Oporto vintages. Coffee, kvass, porter, and stout followed.

The eccentric host claimed he was giving the dinner in pious memory of his lost virility. The invitations were like those sent for memorials. The most startling aspect of the evening? A concealed orchestra played funeral marches, and guests were waited upon by naked black women wearing only shoes and stockings of cloth of silver dotted with tear drops.

And Nora Ephron thinks *I* make her dinner party sound decadent!

AND JUST FOR FUN —during the coronation of Queen Elizabeth II, the tiny South Pacific nation of Tonga sent their three-hundred-pound queen to the festivities. At the coronation parade, swells were

---

* Credit for this exotic lore goes to Harriet Rubin, whose book *Dante in Love* is a twenty-first-century marvel.

gathered along the route in parties, crowded at windows, drinking Champagne. The queen of Tonga came along in her open carriage and she was impressive in red, covered with jewels. She drew great applause. Across from her sat a very small black man in frock coat and spats.

At one party everyone was enthusiastic about the ample ruler and someone asked, "Who is that with the queen?"

Noel Coward responded, "That's her lunch!"

CHAPTER 33

THOSE

PIGGYBACK

HOLIDAYS

I'M TALKING THANKSGIVING AND CHRISTMAS. The first one is wonderful because you aren't pestered to buy gifts that nobody needs or wants. But there is some cooking involved if you want to stay traditional. I have two suggestions to make things easier and yet different. Don't make a pumpkin pie. Try instead The Pink Tea Cup's recipe for sweet potato pie. I've been giving this recipe in my column annually for years and now here it is for eternity between hard covers. Believe me, once you try this, you'll never make a pumpkin pie again. Pumpkins are really only good for looks, decor and jack-o'-lanterns.

Tea Cup Sweet Potato-Patootie Pie

2 pounds yams
½ cup butter
1 teaspoon cinnamon
¼ teaspoon ginger

½ *teaspoon salt*
¼ *teaspoon nutmeg*
2 *tablespoons white sugar*
1 *cup brown sugar*
3 *large eggs, separated*
½ *cup orange juice*
1 *tablespoon grated orange rind*
½ *cup evaporated milk*
1 *unbaked pie shell*

Peel and boil the yams until mashable. Add the butter, spices, salt, and sugars to the hot yams. Beat until light and smooth. Beat the egg yolks until light and add to the mixture. Stir in the orange juice, orange rind, and milk. Preheat the oven to 350°F. Beat the egg whites until stiff and fold in. Pour the mixture into the unbaked pie shell. Bake 35 minutes, or until the pie puffs up and is firm in the middle. Cool on a rack.

Add whipped cream to servings. Dig in, Pilgrims!

1 PIE

Cranberry Smash

There isn't a real recipe for this. But here's the drill that you can improve on or change by simply tasting as you go along. Buy 1 package of cranberries and smash in a blender, a food processor, or one of those chopper things they sell on television. You can even cut and mash them by hand if you like trouble. But don't chop them too fine.

Add 1 cup sugar. Set aside 1 cup of fresh orange juice. Now put in with the cranberries some orange rind and rind of a lemon. Plus half a chopped orange. Take a package of white seedless raisins and add the orange juice to that. Now you have two containers—one of the cranberries, another of the raisins. Refrigerate. Keep another cup of sugar standing by to add to taste. Then, combine the cranberries and raisins.

This will be better if you make it a day or two ahead of the meal. You can still put sliced cranberry jelly out of a can on the table, but I guarantee you, they'll be using up your Cranberry Smash instead.

8 SERVINGS

•   •   •

AND WHEN YOU ROAST that turkey according to all the excellent
recipes that exist, be sure to cover his breast with clean white cheesecloth
for part of the process and wind bacon around the tips of his wings for flavor and to keep the tips from burning up.

Give thanks!

CHAPTER 34

MALCOLM

AND MY

MIDDLE

OH, I KNOW —these corny titles are getting you down. But I have already written reams about the late rich and famous Malcolm Forbes, so now I must concentrate upon the fact that knowing him caused me to gain weight. I seemed always to be sitting with Malcolm somewhere—eating—while we experienced a great publicity cycle. (He was very fond of these, for he had *Forbes*, his own magazine, to keep in the public mind.)

Malcolm died in 1990 but before that he is the one person I ate the most unusual meals with in the most unusual places. Malcolm had already run for governor of New Jersey and failed. He didn't fail, however, at the dynasty business. He had four sons, a daughter, numbers of grandchildren, and he clung to family and friends, remaining on good terms with the divorced Mrs. Forbes. His children, their spouses, their kids, his co-workers, his well-known friends (Elizabeth Taylor, the Walter Cronkites, the late Mrs. Douglas MacArthur), and certain of us in the press were taken all over the world by Malcolm. He didn't like to be alone.

My first meeting with Malcolm was at a private dinner given by Barbara Walters where Malcolm roared up on a motorcycle and came in wearing black tie, carrying his helmet. He offered me a ride home but I dislike flying through thin air at sixty miles an hour. Soon Malcolm added Elizabeth Taylor to his entourage and functions. He knew she liked me, so he'd invite me when we were both in New York. I served a purpose for Malcolm; he was incapable of not mixing business with pleasure. And I gave him excellent coverage—he was intelligent, courteous, generous, kind. I tried to be fair-minded in covering Malcolm and he never complained if I criticized him. Usually, he was doing quite colorful things, though he was personally quiet, gray, and understated.

I went on many trips with Malcolm on the Forbes yacht. The food was always first-rate, all-American cuisine. And then Malcolm gave a seventy-fifth anniversary party for his magazine at his New Jersey manse with marching bands, fireworks, bagpipers; this ended with his giving Miss Taylor a million-dollar check to fight AIDS. More great food! Then we took a trip on the *Highlander* up the Hudson River to the famed Rockefeller properties. I remember we had oysters Rockefeller in our buffet and Malcolm took a ribbing about that. Why not oysters Forbes, I asked? He said, "The Rockefellers still come first."

I went with Malcolm to Normandy on a ballooning week at the Forbes château, where I slept in a room named for Napoleon III. We were only a stone's throw from the World War II cemeteries, the famed Bayeux Tapestry, and the Eisenhower Military Museum. There was a Roosevelt, a MacArthur, and an Eisenhower on this trip, and I also remember the king of Romania, who wore a red Ralph Lauren Polo–polo shirt to dinner, sitting next to Regis Philbin of ABC-TV. The food was totally divine—well, we were in France!

But soon I found myself flying twenty-five thousand miles with Malcolm in his jet, *The Capitalist Tool*. We landed in Hawaii and had an enormous luau overnight before going on to his private island in Fiji. What did I learn about food in Fiji? That Malcolm's calm and friendly natives on his island, all worshipping placidly in their Methodist church, had once been cannibals. I remember that we were eating al fresco in front of an authentic straw-thatched South Pacific hut when someone served me a big, dripping hunk of barbecue. Malcolm jokingly said, "I hope you enjoy that. You know the natives here? Well, their ancestors' favorite thing was to roast a man's hand in the fire and make him eat it before they killed him!" That put me off my feed and I didn't include barbecue in this book because there's a barbecue argument every minute and I'm a pacifist.

Later in Morocco on Malcolm's seventieth-birthday blowout, to which the international set and many lesser lights had been invited—seven hundred in all—we ate from Le Cirque picnic baskets on private planes going over. That was posh! We went to one great yacht party after another—Gianni Agnelli's on his red-sailed, two-masted schooner and Rupert Murdoch's on his big power yacht, and press lord Robert Maxwell's bash on his even bigger boat. (Months later he fell, jumped, or was pushed from this same boat, and Mr. Murdoch took the press lord title for good and all.)

The actual Moroccan birthday party was a kind of crisis night. Dinner wasn't even served until 10:30. They ran out of liquor and wine. Some sober people departed in a huff. (Remember, seven hundred guests may be one too many.)

And then, before we left Morocco, the king of that country gave Malcolm's hundreds of guests an unforgettable picnic at the Tangier Country Club. (How's that for a place drop?) We ate in silken tents on big pillows, passing large silver platters of greasy lamb and couscous and drinking copious amounts of Coca-Cola and orange and coconut juice. (The king observed religious prohibitions on liquor.) Just as I was enjoying the bedizened Berbers on horseback riding at us, shooting rifles in the air, screaming, and waving swords, David Frost told me that at another recent party, sixty-one guests had been killed when there was an assassination attempt on the king. (Hmmm . . . was my last supper going to be in Morocco!?)

But the most memorable meal I ever had with Malcolm was one in January shortly before his death. He asked me to breakfast in his 60 Fifth Avenue office building where he had a museum of collectibles—first editions, famous autographs, the letter Einstein had written to FDR telling him there could be an atom bomb, letters from Lincoln and Kennedy, sailing trophies, artifacts. And not the least of this collection was Malcolm's priceless grouping of Fabergé eggs. Next to the Hermitage Museum in St. Petersburg, he had the best.

I had seen the Fabergé eggs, of course, but on this morning, Malcolm had removed them from their locked glassed shelves and placed them all around the china and silver on the table. They were strewn hither and yon. There was the Coronation Egg with its tiny jeweled coach standing outside of it and the Cuckoo Egg and the Lilies of the Valley Egg. I knew it was Elizabeth Taylor's favorite and Malcolm had once given her a cake shaped like it. It was all just too much.

These things took my breath away. I gasped, "Malcolm, what would your insurers think of this?" He shrugged, "I don't care. They're my eggs and I'll do as I like with them. But, look, don't mention this to any of my boys or to the curator, Margaret Kelly Trombly. I just wanted to bring them out and hold them in my hands and show them to you. After all, it will be Easter in three months and we'll be saying, "Christos Anesti—Christ has risen!" I murmured back the Episcopal response, "He is risen indeed!"

I said, "Malcolm, promise me you'll lock these back up as soon as we have had breakfast." He laughed. "Okay, just don't say I took them out." (I was shocked that on this day, he did not want me to write about anything.) It would be my last meeting with Malcolm, but neither of us knew that.

Recently the Forbes estate sold these famous eggs for $90 million. That's a lot of eggroll. But it certainly represented the most expensive breakfast I ever attended. And I don't remember what exactly Malcolm and I ate between wisecracks about eating eggs and being surrounded by some incredible ones. I think we had a very ordinary breakfast—bacon and scrambled eggs and toast. So I asked my pal Sean Driscoll of Glorious Food to dream up the breakfast Malcolm *should* have served with the Fabergé eggs. Here it is:

Poached Fabergé Eggs Deluxe

2 fresh artichokes
1 lemon, halved
6 ounce beluga caviar
2 poached eggs
Hollandaise sauce
Chopped chives, for garnish

1. Bring a large pot of water to a boil.
2. Cut the stems off the artichokes and rub with the halved lemon. Cut off

the top leaves just above the choke and discard. Rub the tops of the artichokes with lemon. Squeeze any remaining juice from the lemon halves into the boiling water.

3. Cook the artichokes in boiling water for about 25 minutes, or until the bottoms can be pierced easily with a sharp paring knife.

4. When the artichokes have cooked, cool them briefly under cold running water. Remove all the remaining leaves and chokes, and trim the bottoms to a nice round shape. Shave the bottoms flat so they will sit level on the plate.

5. Place each artichoke bottom on a warm plate. Fill each well with a spoonful (approximately 3 ounces) of the beluga caviar and place a poached egg on top of it. Pour the hollandaise sauce evenly over each egg. Sprinkle with chives to garnish.

SERVES 2

CHAPTER 35

EATING THE

FAINTING

PURPLE PRIEST

For a number of my many years I have often lived vicariously through the multiple adventures of a friend, Professor Iris Cornelia Love, who is one of the world's leading classical archaeologists—a genius at Greek, Etruscan, Roman, and Egyptian lore and findings. Briefly, she single-handedly mounted a major expedition on the Turkish coast of Asia Minor, there discovering on the same day that man first walked on the moon the long-lost Temple of Aphrodite at Knidos. That was just one of her discoveries. Later she found the head of the Praxiteles statue of Aphrodite under a dust cloth in the basement of the British Museum to great controversy. As a Smith College student, she had proven that her childhood favorites, the Etruscan warriors in the Metropolitan Museum of Art, were fakes. She discovered one of the lost Roman road milestones for the Via Cassia and therefore archaeologists were able to connect the ancient road that linked Rome to Florence going north. Iris is an adventurer and scholar with a vivid mixture of specific information and a still-collegiate love of hijinks and fun.

As she fluently speaks six languages, this makes traveling with Iris easy and convenient. (Though one does have to struggle with a lot of luggage and cameras. Iris never throws anything away, not even envelopes that read "Occupant.")

Schlepping with Iris through Greece and Turkey was like a super college education for me, but eating with her—well, that was another matter entirely. On a trip to Mycenae in the heat of an excruciating Greek summer, I discovered that heat meant nothing to Iris. As we approached the famous Lion Gate and Agamemnon's supposed funeral monument, the temperature was about 110°F. Iris was used to working under such conditions. I grew up in Texas so I thought I could take it. (But Texas is now air-conditioned. Greece mostly isn't.) We had brought a "picnic" of olives, figs, cheese, bread, and Coca-Cola, the last being, in my opinion, the most necessary liquid ingredient for staying alive and functioning in the Mediterranean. We also had Portuguese sardines packed in oil and very hot red peppers.

Like many famous discovered archaeological sites, at Mycenae there is nothing—no city, no town, no café. It's just where Perseus flung it and Heinrich Schliemann discovered and probably looted it back in the 1870s.

A merciless sun beat down on us. There were no trees, only the bulging Cyclopean walls of stone and an occasional shadow. After we had trudged through the site and Iris had told me more than I actually needed to know about Mycenae, adding all the Greek myths that she believes are invariably true, we came back out under the Lion Gate and she excitedly pointed at a small slender bush on the side of the road. I will never forget sitting down in the dust under that little scrap of vegetation, which was something like sitting under a tall sunflower. We scrounged for every bit of its "shade" and ate our lunch. It was quite a relief to get in our inadequate little rented car and travel back to Nauplion to see the boar's tusk helmets and other paraphernalia in the tiny museum and later to sit in the shadow of small charming cafés on the port. (I had already seen the so-called gold Mask of Agamemnon and Mycenae's other super treasures in the National Museum in Athens. It's a good idea when touring Greece to go to the National Museum first before visiting the sites of discovery and history. And if you do get to visit the places the museum's treasure comes from, it's a good idea to go back and see the finest again at the National Museum before leaving Greece. It boasts one of the greatest collections of ancient Greek art in the world. But that's just my tourist advice.)

It was in Nauplion that I was introduced by Iris to the whiskered *barbounia*, a little fish with a beard. Cooked crisp and crinkly, along with a lot of succulent watermelon, it saved my life in Greece, where frankly, there is not a lot of what I like to eat. Although Iris repeatedly tried to make me drink retsina, I finally drew the line. This Greek treasure—wine put into wooden barrels where the resin of pine gives it taste—was like turpentine to me.

One of the great dining experiences in all of Greece has nothing to do with food. In Athens go to the Plaka area to any one of the many tourist restaurants. It hardly matters what you eat; there is the Acropolis looming over you with the lighted Parthenon making its own statement. If you can manage this al fresco dinner with a full moon—well, then you are dining in the lap of the gods.

I remember one such dinner, not in one of the big commercial restaurants that look onto the Acropolis, but at a tiny sidewalk joint where we were seated in rickety chairs with our table slanting sideways down a concrete-paved hill. It didn't matter that the plates kept careening away and we had to catch them or that our wine bucket was tilted. We became "tilted" ourselves and we hardly cared what we ordered or ate. But, of course, we had eggplant.

And now we enter the Scylla and Charybdis of food in the Mediterranean. Greek or Turkish or both? Whatever—both cuisines almost always feature the ubiquitous eggplant. The novelist Erica Jong made her fame and fortune from her sexy book *Fear of Flying*, but anyone who knows this blond bombshell knows she is also a student of the classics. Erica has given permission to reprint here a poem from her book *Becoming Light*. She dedicated this poem to the aforesaid Iris Love and you'll see why:

The Eggplant Epithalamion

"Mostly you eat eggplant at least once a day," she explained. "A Turk won't marry a woman unless she can cook eggplant at least a hundred ways."

—archaeologist Iris Love, speaking of the cuisine on digs in Turkey,
The New York Times, February 4, 1971

1. There are more than a hundred Turkish poems about eggplant. I would like to give you all of them. If you scoop out every seed, you can read me backward like an Arabic book. Look.

2. (Lament in Aubergine)
Oh aubergine,
egg-shaped
& as shiny as if freshly laid —
you are a melancholy fruit.
Solanum Melongena.
Every animal is sad
after eggplant.

3. (Byzantine Eggplant Fable)
Once upon a time on the coast of Turkey
there lived a woman who could cook eggplant 99 ways.
She could slice eggplant thin as paper.
She could write poems on it & batter-fry it.
She could bake eggplant & broil it.
She could even roll the seeds in banana-
flavored cigarette papers
& get her husband high on eggplant.
But he was not pleased.
He went to her father & demanded his bride-price back.
He said he'd been cheated.

He wanted back two goats, twelve chickens
& a camel as reparation.
His wife wept & wept.
Her father raved.

The next day she gave birth to an eggplant.
It was premature & green
& she had to sit on it for days
before it hatched.

"This is my hundredth eggplant recipe," she screamed.
"I hope you're satisfied!"

(Thank Allah that the eggplant was a boy.)

4. (Love & the Eggplant)

On the warm coast of Turkey, Miss Love
eats eggplant
"at least once a day."

How fitting that love should eat eggplant,
that most aphrodisiac fruit.

Fruit of the womb
of Asia Minor,
reminiscent of eggs,
of Istanbul's deep purple nights
& the Byzantine eyes of Christ.

I remember the borders of egg & dart
fencing us off from the flowers & fruit
of antiquity.
I remember the egg & tongue
probing the lost scrolls of love.
I remember the ancient faces
Of Aphrodite
hidden by dust
in the labyrinth under
the British Museum
to be finally found by Miss Love
right there
near Great Russell Square.

I think of the hundreds of poems of the
eggplant
& my friends who have fallen in love
over an eggplant,
who have opened the eggplant together
& swum in its seeds,
who have clung in the egg of the eggplant
& have rocked to sleep
in love's dark purple boat.

I discovered Erica's eggplant poem many moons after I'd met Iris. When I asked the latter how she felt being so celebrated, Iris just nodded and went off on what I call her eggplant tangent.

I was always sorry I never had a chance to tell Miss Jong about my favorite dish—*imam bayeldi*. This is a wonderful dish that is served in both Greece and Turkey and it means "the priest who has fainted." *Imam* means "priest" and *bayeldi* means "fainted." This is because Muslim imams wear purplish cloaks that are the color of eggplant. *Imam bayeldi* is eggplant stuffed with fabulous spices— cinnamon, garlic, tomatoes, and onions that have been sautéed to the point where they are almost glacé. The idea is the imam has eaten so much of this delicious dish that he has fainted on your plate. And indeed it looks just like a big flat imam lying there. This dish is also served in Greece; sometimes the Greeks add tomatoes that have been cooked and mixed with onions and meat of the eggplant.

Perhaps Miss Jong will write another verse to her famous poem in which she includes details of the *imam bayeldi*. But let me make a few points about Mediterranean cooking. In my opinion, there are three great cuisines in the world. One is Chinese, from which so many other Eastern cuisines developed, like the Vietnamese, Korean, Thai, Japanese. Then there is Italian cooking; I know, I know—you thought I'd say French, but even Caesar and the Roman historians commented on the paucity of food in France, the poverty of Gaulish dishes. French cuisine did not really develop until Catherine de Médici married Henri II and she brought her chefs with her from Italy, along with her spices and her poisons. And so French cuisine derives from the arrival of a poisoner. And it is very derivative of the Italian cuisine of the Renaissance.

Finally, there is Turkish cuisine, which is simply wonderful and your present-day Greek cooking is totally Turkish in derivation. The Turks are simply incredible at spicing things up, working with what they have, using rosemary, garlic, oregano, and a mint that is so much stronger in taste and smell than anything we have. I guess it's the Mediterranean sun. They can perfume meat and vegetables in ways we can hardly imagine. They use a lot of pine nuts in their cooking. As for tasty hot peppers, the Turks put our Mexican cousins to shame.

Because the glory that was Greece was spread all over the Mediterranean and many of the greatest Dorian Greek and classical Greek sites and ruins lie in Turkey, which was part of the Dorian Hexopolis of Asia Minor, people forget how much alike the Turks and the Greeks have come to be. I know there is a fierce enmity between them. I had to stop excavating at Knidos because I spoke Greek and the Turks were so worried about a foreigner working on their border with a Greek island, Kos, only a few miles away. But actually I feel the Turks and Greeks are the same people and the Greeks took their entire cuisine from the Turks. But the Turks do it better.

After traveling through both Turkey and Greece with Iris, I came to understand, to some extent, her mania for any meat broiled, roasted, fried, or barbecued to a crisp. Rare is not a word known in the Mediterranean. And we were forever on the receiving end of servings of lamb and goat that had been done to a turn. Because she had spent many summers excavating at Knidos on the southern coast of Turkey, any meat at all had become a treat.

Knidos, once a center of early civilization where hordes came to worship the goddess of love, Aphrodite, had all but dried up and blown away. An earthquake had doubtless diverted its water supply at the same time it also threw down the Temple of Aphrodite, leaving it under a mass of dirt and stone. Here Iris and her volunteer archaeologists toiled every summer for ten years, bringing in even the water they drank. They bathed only in the sea with a special saltwater soap. They imported everything, every pen, paper clip, tool, and most of their food.

They brought in sardines, canned sausages, beans, and tuna fish. Nearby fishermen provided an occasional catch, but with no water for farming, vegetables were few and far between, and one season after everyone else left, Iris toiled on alone, living on the only food, a sack of onions. "I had onions raw, sautéed, stewed, fried, roasted—in every imaginable way. Now and then someone would catch a fish. I remember once they brought me a very gamey haunch of wild boar, but cooked long enough on an open fire, it was delicious! How I wish I *could* have had eggplant every day at Knidos, but that was fanciful thinking on the part of Erica Jong!"

SINCE TURKEY ostensibly offers one of the world's three great cuisines, I asked Iris to tell me about her first visit to Turkey. She had spent her student summers toiling on the Greek island of Samothrace under her German professors. It was there that she found and excavated the base of the statue of the great Nike that now stands at the top of the stairs in the Louvre Museum. During this apprenticeship, she decided in 1955 to go to Turkey.

IRIS SPEAKS: There was very little travel at that time between Greece and Turkey. In fact, there was very little travel in Turkey at all. There were still Bulgarian partisans in the hills behind Istanbul, or Constantinople. American Express in Athens did everything to discourage me. But I was enthralled at the thought of Byzantium and determined to go. I had to promise the head of AmEx that I would be in my hotel room by 8:00 each night. I arrived at the Istanbul airport, which is called Yesilkoy, which means green village, although it didn't look green at all and one could hardly see the airstrip.

In spite of not speaking Turkish at this point, I was lucky to find a porter, my luggage, and get a taxi, and I arrived at the Hilton alive and counting my blessings. But I couldn't just sit in a hotel room, so I went down and asked the concierge where were the restaurants visited by Turks? He kept giving me Greek places. Finally, I asked where I might see a beautiful church. And so I visited Hagia Sophia and began walking down the fascinating little streets that had grown up around this great church, which became a mosque in 1453.

There were many small restaurants along the streets; none seemed very clean but I was full of adventure. I had learned from my English governess that I would eat at least a half a peck of dirt in my lifetime, so what would a few extra spoonfuls mean? I decided to go stand in the middle of the street and watch to see where people who I believed to be Turks were going. I saw many waiting in line before one café. As there was a crowd, it had to be a big place and very popular, but I got in and came eventually into a big room. I was stunned by what I saw.

In the center of the room of the restaurant was a young boy in a bed with white sheets—a horseshoe-type bed. He was sitting up surrounded by gifts, being congratulated. I assumed it was a birthday party for a sick child. Before I knew what was happening, I was being seated nearby and they started presenting food. I protested that I had not yet ordered. Oh, never mind, you must try some of this and some of this. I was now speaking half in Greek, half in French, and with a lot of gestures. But everyone was friendly and they began bringing me wine to my great pleasure.

Someone spoke to me in French. "You know, it only happened an hour ago." I replied, "Yes, what happened? Now we are celebrating his birthday?—the gifts, the balloons and all?" The man protested, "No, it's not his birthday. He was circumcised just an hour ago. This is a circumcision party and you are most welcome."

"This is my first circumcision," I exclaimed, little knowing it would be only the beginning. (Later, as the director of the Knidos excavations, I would be invited to a chair of honor up front for every circumcision in the area, seated among the most important men and receiving the full blast of the ten- or eleven-year-old victim's cries and spatters of his blood. No women were allowed, so I was always called 'Mr. Director' to take the curse off my womanhood, for how, wondered the Turks, could any but a man be an important director? I learned to drink quite a bit of raki for these occasions, for I could not lose face or my Turkish workmen would never obey my orders.

The good thing about circumcisions was that a wild party and feast always followed. And on my first visit to Istanbul, quite a bit of raki was being drunk by the young boy in bed. "Raki dulls the pain," said my adviser.

The thing that was dulling *my* pain was the food. I had never eaten anything quite like it before. I remember my first plate was a mashed grain with honey. I'm sure the grain was symbolic that the boy would be fruitful and multiply. He had experienced a rite of passage and become a man. Then they began serving *mezedes,* or Turkish hors d'oeuvres. First you are served cold *dolma;* the verb *dolmek* means "to stuff." And any vegetable is stuffable—squash, tomatoes, eggplant—stuffed with a mixture of delicious rice, mint, pine nuts, and meat. You could say *"etli,"* which means with meat.

We had simply wonderful moussaka, which is definitely Turkish although it has become a big part of Greek cuisine. This is layered slices of eggplant that have been fried, placed between layers of ground meat seasoned with salt, pepper, a little sugar, cloves, and cinnamon, and topped by a sort of béchamel sauce that has all been put in an oven so that the sauce becomes like a hard soufflé topping.

We had many kinds of filling, like feta cheese put in filo dough and fried. Or spinach with feta and in a triangular filo dough, fried, called *borek.* Much better than anything like it that I had experienced in my beloved Greece.

With all of this we had *cacik,* which is just like the Greek *tzadziki*—yogurt mixed with chopped cucumbers, oregano, and lots of garlic. This is great to eat against hot peppers or firey food. It cools off the mouth. We also were served *kofti,* meatballs of all kinds. The Greeks call them *keftedes.*

By now everyone who could speak any English or French had joined my table. They didn't take me for an American. Because I am blond and spoke several languages, they thought I was Scandinavian, Austrian, or German. They could hardly believe an American was visiting Turkey. Remember, this was a long time ago.

I think the most amazing and interesting thing I ever ate in Turkey were peas which had been—get this—peeled. I have sat in private houses where green peas were being peeled. You know the saying, "Beulah, peel me a grape!" Well, these people sat for hours and peeled the skin off the green peas and they were exquisite. A true Turkish meal would last all day.

And I recall on that first night we ate and ate because we danced in between courses. We did the dances I had already learned in Greece. Or dances that
were very similar. The ring dances called the *kalamatiano*, the *hassapiko* which
comes from the Turkish word meaning butcher. So it's the butcher's dance. And
because there was so much dancing, toasting, celebrating, translating, and conversation, we also ate all the offered delicious desserts. In Turkey these are
strangely enough usually named after parts of women's bodies. Like the navel or
the angel's navel, or the angel's finger, or one called *kadaiife*, shredded wheat with
honey plus the famous *baklava* with chopped nuts, layers of honey and fig that has
been mashed into a paste.

The unfortunate thing for me about eating in Turkey was that I didn't care
for the national dish—*kokorec*, a greasy combination of toasted bread and fried
lamb intestines. This is the hamburger of Turkey, so we Americans must be respectful. At lunchtime the Turks pour into the streets to hit the *kokorec* stands
where rolls of cold intestine, wrapped around a spit, are sliced off and put on the
griddle. The sizzling meat is dusted with red pepper and cumin.

I understand that when mad cow disease caused Europeans to restrict
the sale of animal intestines, brains, livers, the Turks went wild with fear that
their *kokorec* might disappear. Songs were written defending it, T-shirts made,
and people went on television to complain. The *kokorec* is Turkey's favorite
fast food to the max and considered a link to the traditional past, according to *The
New York Times*. Someone even said the *kokorec* is a drug, like morphine, to the
Turks.

I reminded Iris that when we had been in Athens or any part of Greece, she
was just as fanatical about the *souvlaki*, served on the streets from carts with
wheels. She always insisted we should stay in the Grande Bretagne Hotel
because nearby on Thesion Street was "the best *souvlaki* in the world."
(*Souvlaki* is shish kebab, barbecued lamb or goat served on pita bread with
tzadziki, hot red peppers, and onions.) Or we would have *gyros*, shaved
sliced lamb with all the same trimmings. Another Greek delicacy was
sayanaki, strips of feta cheese fried in olive oil and served with squirts of
lemon juice. We would emerge to look for those low-brow items from our
expensive room overlooking the Presidential Palace. That is the only place
you can still see "the ladies from hell" * patrolling the front of the building
with their rifles, doing a kind of goose-step.

* Six-foot-tall soldiers in the traditional pleated white skirt and *evzone* red shoes with
pom-poms.

I always wanted to have lunch in the Grande Bretagne, where they made one of the best hamburgers in the world. But Iris always wanted to head for the *souvlaki* stand. On one occasion where I prevailed, we looked up to see two women entering the dining room. Iris said, "Oh, look, there's the Baroness Cecile de Rothschild. I know her well and have been on her boat."

I responded, "Cecile de Rothschild, hell! That's Greta Garbo!" Miss Garbo was still splendid, wearing a tailored beige shantung Chinese outfit. But when Iris went to say hello, I went back to the room. I figured that all the anonymous "Harriet Brown" needed was to be introduced to a gossip columnist. As it turned out, the baroness asked Iris to sit down and they had a charming chat, without the baroness ever introducing Iris to her famous friend, who didn't utter a word.

Later, when Iris visited the baroness in her Greek villa, the maid complained that Miss Garbo was not a generous guest.

"She left without even giving me a tip. She left me this!" She extended a hand holding a beat-up old straw hat. "And it has a hole in it!" So much for glamour.

POSTSCRIPT TO ALL THAT: Although I went to Crete with Iris I don't remember eating there. I was too bowled over by the drama of Knossos, the wonderful museum in Iráklion where you can see how vase painting began and progressed through the centuries. (The Minoan jewelry in this little museum is also fabulous. Barbra Streisand certainly thought so when Iris took her there!) And Crete overwhelms one with its music and the dancing of fierce-looking men in red uniforms.

But according to Diane Kochilas, a food writer from Athens, the large island of Crete is the culinary cradle of Greece. She wrote all about these treasures for *The New York Times* on May 23, 2004. Log on and read the whole thing, but briefly Ms. Kochilas mentions dishes I don't want to forget. I intend to go again to eat in Crete's tiny, family-owned restaurants in remote villages:

Crisp, fried zucchini blossoms with a creamy garlic sauce

Incredibly flavored runner beans lightly stewed with whole fresh plum tomatoes and mint

Rabbit casserole

Local cured pork cooked with eggs

Snails seared with vinegar and rosemary

A wild greens omelet called *swfouggato*

Thorny wild cardoons sampled as a boiled salad with olive oil and lemon juice

Raw sea urchin

Char-grilled sepia oozing with local cheeses

Grilled fresh bream and grouper

Potatoes baked whole in embers, smashed open by a fist and seasoned with sea salt and fresh olive oil

Sfakiani pita, a cheese pie of local fame, something between a crepe and a pancake. The cheese is *xynomyzithra*, panfried and served with a drizzling of thyme honey.

Organic pork braised in wine, chestnut, tomato, and potato stew

Boureki — zucchini and cheese pie

Rice pilaf fragrant with local clarified butter called *staka*

Hondros — cracked wheat cooked with snails

Kaltsounia — pastries filled with wild greens and cheese

Sunny-side-up eggs drizzled with lemon juice and served in chartreuse olive oil

Tiny cracked green olives flavored with bitter orange juice

Rabbit fried in olive oil, "extinguished" with red wine, as the Greeks say

Candied bergamot and quince, preserved fruit

If the above sounds like too much, remember the Greek saying: "What good is it to refrain from food but devour your brother?"

CHAPTER 36

THE

MARTHA

MATTER

No book about food and living delightfully well in this particular era would be complete without a mention of Martha Stewart. Every time I give a lecture these days, in the Q & A period that follows, I am asked what I think about Martha.

So Martha matters. Well, I always say that I know and like and admire Martha Stewart even though she is not warm and cuddly like some of the rest of us hypocrites. I honestly think that her magazine and the product catalog put out by Martha were/are the best quality of their kind and, as such, enormously entertaining and helpful. And even if you don't want to bother to emulate Martha's particular arts, it's fun to read and know about all of them. I hope by the time this is published, Martha's troubles will be behind her.

She can then go back to behaving pretty much as she did before, being efficient, driven, a perfectionist, an obsessor, a kind of kitchen decor genius manqué, ruthless, if you will, yelling at people from time to time when they irritate, annoy, or disappoint her. In other words, I want Martha to go back to being Martha. She doesn't have to be humble or contrite. She was always a big business person to the max and after she became successful, she was even more so. It always exhausted me to watch Martha on television as she piled on the details and went for the gold, creating recipes that would have balked Marie Antoinette.

Martha created a business out of nothing and then created a demand for more of the same. I hope she will go on doing that. She didn't rob widows and children and exhaust their pension funds. The FBI said she lied to them; that was all they needed to go after her. And they did.

I think Martha Stewart was made for America and vice versa. Long may she wave. But she doesn't have to be warm and cuddly, friendly and romantic. She only has to be herself. I will go on buying her stuff. I will go on admiring the hell out of her. Why, I'd even let her stencil my driveway.

DIRTY DISHES

This is not a cookbook. I really don't know what the hell one might call it—an arrogant extension of my previous memoir, perhaps. *Dishing* will appear some months after a stressful and arduous presidential election campaign that divided this nation as never before. We find ourselves the Red and the Blue, rather like the Blue and the Gray of the Civil War of 1861 to 1865. Perhaps we could call our situation, circa 2004–2008 The Uncivil War, because it seems the U.S. may well be divided and contentious and doing a lot of name-calling for some time to come.

While I don't think of *Dishing* as having any political or ideological point of view, I realize that many food purists and health nuts won't like the idea that in these low-carb, low-calorie times I seem to be advocating having fun with food, living it up at lunch and dinner, occasionally even frying something. I realize that I have committed heresy in today's more fastidious eating and diet-conscious world.

This book doesn't pretend to be comprehensive in any way, so there is even more to quibble with. I'd say if you are a food purist and want to stock your recipe shelf, you'd do better to buy *The Joy of Cooking* or *The New York Times Cookbook* or *The Fannie Farmer Cookbook* or any of the works of Julia Child, who effectively brought French cooking to the U.S.* or the relatively new Ruth Reichl work, *The Gourmet Cookbook.*

I do like the idea of *Dishing* creating a few controversies, however. Although I'm all for healthy eating and cutting calories, I still say you only live once and you need to have some fun during this go-around. As this work came to a grease-stained close, I did note that Crisco has invented a new zero grams fat-free shortening that combines sunflower oil, soybean oil, and fully hydrogenated cottonseed oil. It has only a trace of the trans fats that Crisco had formerly. The Smuckers folks say their new product maintains taste and "the integrity of the final product." Let us pray that it does! You can look for this in a new green can that literally shouts the word "healthy."

At the same time as discovering that encouraging aspect of frying, I note that another statistic has emerged. About a year ago, a British hotel chain introduced "fried chocolate sandwiches." In one month, they sold 1,256 of these things. So, you see, human nature and curiosity and the love of things that just have to be bad for you prevail!

And there is always Linda Stasi's famous dicta that we may need to refer to for common sense when it comes to fattening foods. The columnist notes that indeed many Americans are vastly overweight and this is medically dangerous, but she goes on to note that we now live longer than ever before in human history. So I suppose that we are overweight as we go to our graves, digging them with our own teeth, yet we do go later and later. Well, it's a thought and a slight defense.

I guess my point is that I take exception to the growing narcissism of Americans about diet, the refusal to eat and celebrate world classics. And I just happen to believe that enjoying yourself at table, in a great restaurant, at a street fair, or in a fast-food joint is one of the rare privileges of a true democracy.

So just as the U.S. is going to continue to be ideologically divided, maybe soon you'll see me on television under this kind of controversial promo: "Liz Smith will discuss the real threat to American patriotism — the careful American diet!"

Then, I guess, I'll be saying, "Eat, drink, and be merry. So, sue me."

---

*The divine Julia would never give up butter or any of her classic cuisine needs. She lived to the ripe old age of ninety-one.

A FULL PLATE OF THANKS

As stated, the initial inspiration for this book came from the editor-writer Billy Norwich. He became my protégé while he was still trying to pay off his college loans. Any favor I ever did for Billy has been amply repaid by his brilliance, perspicacity, and unique approach to life. He was a helmsman for this book.

I am eternally grateful to everyone I've written about in *Dishing*. If their name appears, I owe them. This is especially so for Nora Ephron, Iris Love, Erica Jong, and Ann Richards, who spoke in their own voices.

I also thank the many writers who allowed me to reprint their recipes and their publishers who duly charged me for that privilege.

A special thank-you goes to my aide Mary Jo McDonough of Ho-Ho-Kus, New Jersey. Where she once worked for Brentano's and Waldenbooks, she now gives her expertise to me. If ever I go to my "reward" or whatever else, I urge every busy executive in America to vie to hire this paragon of initiative, organization, and energy. I could not have written *Dishing* without her.

Likewise, I am always happy to have my sainted agent, Joni Evans of William Morris, in my corner. A former editor herself, she has gifted me with her giant talents for honesty and care. Let's add my gratitude for the loyalty and help of Denis Ferrara, and the cuisine expertise and re-membrances of Diane Judge. I thank my brother Robert Jerome Smith for his prodigious memory in the exercise of his own splash-and-dash cook-ing. I am beholden to writers Bud Shrake and Marie Brenner and to those two cuisine queens of the Redneck Riviera, Barbara Kaster and Carole Duncan.

Many writers inspired me to alleviate my ignorance when it comes to food, cooking, and the history of same. I am especially grateful to the late M. F. K. Fisher, whose collected work under the title *The Art of Eating* (John Wiley paperback) is so comprehensive and delightful. This book in-cludes *How to Cook a Wolf, Consider the Oyster, Serve It Forth, The Gas-tronomical Me,* and *An Alphabet for Gourmets.*

I was set on fire with enthusiasm from the get-go by the enlightened energy of a great editor, Michael Korda, himself a tremendous writer-producer and one to be envied and emulated.

I am a lucky well-fed dog.